Deliberative Environmental Politics

D1481647

Deliberative Environmental Politics
Democracy and Ecological Rationality

Walter F. Baber and Robert V. Bartlett

The MIT Press
Cambridge, Massachusetts
London, England

MIT Press books may be purchased at special quantity discounts for business or sales promotional use. For information, please email special_sales@mitpress.mit .edu or write to Special Sales Department, The MIT Press, 55 Hayward St., Cambridge, MA 02142.

This book was set in Sabon by Graphic Composition, Inc., and was printed and bound in the United States of America.

Library of Congress Cataloging-in-Publication Data

Baber, Walter F., 1953– .
  Deliberative environmental politics : democracy and ecological rationality / Walter F. Baber and Robert V. Bartlett.
    p.   cm.
  Includes bibliographical references and index.
  ISBN 0-262-02587-6 (hc : alk. paper)—ISBN 0-262-52444-9 (pbk. : alk. paper)
  1. Environmental policy. 2. Democracy and science. I. Bartlett, Robert V. II. Title.
GE170.B33   2005
333.72—dc22

2004065619

Printed on recycled paper.

10   9   8   7   6   5   4   3   2   1

To Katherine, Emily, Helen, and John

Contents

Acknowledgments

All of the chapters of this book except the first two and the last were originally presented at scholarly conferences over several years. We thank all of the copanelists, discussants, and audiences that have helped us sharpen our thinking and sometimes fill gaping holes in our arguments. In particular, we thank Eric MacGilvray and Lisa Ellis.

Different versions of four chapters of the book have been published as journal articles. We thank the editors of these four journals and we also thank a number of anonymous referees who read earlier drafts of chapters in the form of journal submissions. We don't know who any of these colleagues are, but by providing invaluable criticisms and suggestions for improvement, they deserve some of the credit for whatever quality is reflected in the current book. Likewise, the three anonymous reviewers of the manuscript for The MIT Press provided the kinds of reviews that authors dream of—declaring "Publish!" while providing numerous constructive suggestions for further improvement. The book is better for their efforts and expertise, and we thank them. Our thanks too to MIT Senior Acquisition Editor Clay Morgan, who made the review process run smoothly and expeditiously, and to Editor Judy Feldmann, who suggested many small improvements in the text.

A version of chapter 2 was published as Robert V. Bartlett and Walter F. Baber, "From Rationality to Reasonableness in Environmental Administration: Moving beyond Proverbs," *Journal of Management History* 5 (1999): 55–67. We acknowledge the author reuse policy of Emerald Group Publishing.

An earlier version of chapter 3 was published as Walter F. Baber and Robert V. Bartlett, "Toward Environmental Democracy: Rationality, Reason, and Deliberation," *Kansas Journal of Law and Public Policy* 11

(2001): 35–64. Reused with permission of the *Kansas Journal of Law and Public Policy.*

A slight variation of chapter 4 can be found as Robert V. Bartlett and Walter F. Baber, "Ethics and Environmental Policy in Democratic Governance: John Rawls, Public Reason, and Normative Precommitment." Adapted with permission of *Public Integrity,* vol. 7, no. 3 (summer 2005).

Most of chapter 6 is derived from Walter F. Baber, "Ecology and Democratic Governance: Toward a Deliberative Model of Environmental Politics," *Social Science Journal* 41 (2004): 331–346. We acknowledge the author reuse policy of Elsevier.

As with any project that has gestated as long as this one has, there are many people who deserve acknowledgment of appreciation. Bartlett would extend thanks to Priya Kurian for an ongoing dialogue; to Amy Zeitler, Nicholas Guehlstorf, Lars Hallstrom, and Manjusha Gupte, whose doctoral dissertations inspired further investigation of developments in democratic theory; to Leigh Raymond, Laurel Weldon, and Pat Boling, public policy colleagues at Purdue University who share a commitment to theoretical empirical scholarship; and to William Shaffer and the late Frank L. Wilson, who encouraged and supported this project in practical ways. Bartlett also is especially grateful to the Department of Public Policy, the Frank Church Institute, and the School of Social Sciences and Public Affairs at Boise State University for a rewarding 2003–2004 academic year spent as the Frank Church Distinguished Professor of Public Policy, an appointment that made timely completion of this book possible. Special thanks at Boise State University to Leslie Alm and Shelton Woods.

Finally but preeminently, our deepest gratitude is owed to Carolyn and Sally—who allow only reasonable deliberation, who keep us grounded by continuing to laugh with us and at us, and whose steadfast support makes all things possible.

1

Green Democracy, Ecological Rationality

Hargrove (2000, 3) laments that decades after Earth Day, the environmental movement is still plagued by a serious gap between theory and practice. This observation follows his earlier assertion (1989, 3–4) that, although environmental ethics had made significant advances, it was no closer to becoming fully integrated into environmental affairs at a practical level than it had been twenty years before, in the early 1970s. Hargrove (1994, 115–116) also suggests one reason why this might be so, observing that the language being taught to environmental professionals is so stunted and shallow that it is unable to deal adequately, or even understand accurately, questions of moral value. If this is even approximately true (and there is no reason to believe that it is not), environmental ethics faces a communication gap of truly daunting proportions. By Hargrove's account, current environmental professionals are incapable of recognizing philosophical issues when they encounter them, much less of learning from philosophers how to deal with them.

And, yet, the fault may lie less in the stars than in ourselves. A review of journals such as *Environmental Values, Ethics and the Environment,* and *Environmental Ethics* reveals a startling array of topics that reflect the genuinely diverse membership of this scholarly community and the evolution of its interests. The largest number of articles pursue the entirely justifiable goal of exploring a relatively narrow environmental issue from a single philosophical perspective, with an emphasis on clarifying the grounds upon which an individual might build his or her own view of the subject. On only rare occasions (perhaps 5 percent of all articles) have the authors directly examined what political philosophy or a particular political philosopher might contribute to a practical environmental ethics that would advance the cause of reconciling democratic politics and environmental protection. Little wonder that the field of environmental ethics remains distant from the arena in which environmental decisions are made.

At the same time, some argue that the scope and seriousness of the environmental problems confronting humankind have rendered liberal democratic government virtually obsolete (Heilbroner 1996; Ponting 1991; Stavrianos 1976). Among those holding this view, William Ophuls's analysis of the problem is one of the most wide-ranging and pessimistic. It is also likely that Ophuls has influenced the thinking of contemporary environmentalists more strongly than any other representative of this viewpoint. According to Ophuls (1977), humanity faces a future of lower living standards, population loss due to famine and disease, and a politics that is decidedly more authoritarian than any we would currently find acceptable. Ophuls (1997) claims that an individualistic and rights-based liberalism is fundamentally inadequate to meet the environmental challenge. Our real choice, he argues, is between an elite meritocracy, on the one hand, and an aristocratic oligopoly on the other.

There are, of course, those who would point to the indisputable achievements of industrial society, capitalism, and interest group democracy with respect to environmental policy over the four decades or so since the emergence of the environmental movmement. In the wealthier countries, levels of many pollutants in air and water have been lowered (sometimes dramatically), some species have been saved, dramatic landscapes have been set aside, and economies have become more energy efficient. This wave of reform environmentalism succeeded in creating institutions and enacting rules that reduced the severity of many of the most blatant symptoms of environmental degradation (although sometimes by shifting the problems elsewhere). Yet these same policy efforts have not succeeded at all with respect to any problems not easily understood, not fixable without fundamental social, economic, or political changes, or not readily dramatized by electronic media. They have encountered increasing resistance from political and economic interests deeply vested in the status quo. Even within the wealthier countries, much less globally, progress toward the goals of sustainability or ecological rationality is difficult to discern with respect to, say, the six critical environmental problems (atmosphere, water resources, oceans, soil, forests, living species) identified in the 1993 "World Scientists' Warning to Humanity," which was signed by 1,670 scientists from 71 countries including a majority of living Nobel Prize winners. The environmental protection achievements of four decades have given rise, as much as anything, to a widespread environmental complacency and to entrenched and even more sophisticated green oppostion from political and economic interests. The resulting policy stalemate within liberal interest-group democracies seems destined to persist as long as interest-group democracy prevails, or until some external shock forces a fundamental realignment of the political system.

With these perspectives as part of their shared intellectual background, it is little wonder that liberal environmentalists would jump at the chance to redeem democracy and protect the environment simultaneously. (We are, after all, no less fond of our political theories than were the socialists who so enhanced the ecology of Eastern Europe.) Just such an opportunity has been presented by the recent turn in political theory toward deliberative, or discursive, democracy. First used by Joseph Bessette (1980), the phrase "deliberative democracy" defies precise definition. It roughly refers to a school of political theory that assumes that genuinely thoughtful and discursive public participation in decision making has the potential to produce policy decisions that are more just and more rational than existing representative mechanisms. The conviction among environmental theorists is that such an approach to democracy will also be more environmentally friendly than interest-group liberalism has been.

Liberal democracy, as it stands, can be criticized as *inherently* unfriendly to the environment because it takes human interests as the measure of all values (Mathews 1991). Any suggestion that the ecological failings of democracy can be cured by the application of more democracy is, therefore, in need of supportive argument. As Robert Goodin has correctly pointed out, "to advocate democracy is to advocate procedures, to advocate environmentalism is to advocate substantive outcomes" (1992, 168). But Goodin (1996) has also argued that discursive democracy in the public sphere creates a situation in which interests other than one's own are called to mind, including the interests of nature and of future generations.

So it may be that deliberative democracy has the potential to produce more environmentally sound decisions than does interest-group liberalism because it allows citizens to develop a broadly ecological perspective. And that broader perspective is necessary for the adoption and dissemination of those ecocentric cultural views that are key to a green political transformation (Eckersley 1992). Furthermore, if the environment can profit from democracy, it may also be that democracy can gain from its newly won environmentalism. Whereas some have argued that nature has no political lessons to offer and that we should stop looking for any (Saward 1993), others have emphasized the social benefits to be derived from an ecological perspective. Jorge Valadez has argued that ecological consciousness "aids in discerning the actual and potential analogical relationships between the interdependencies in nature and those in the social realm" (2001, 21). Valadez has further argued that a shared ecological vision is one tool for cultivating intercultural solidarity within a multicultural society as well as the moral, cognitive, and affective character traits that are supportive of such solidarity. So even if there were not compelling independent reasons for adopting an ecological perspective, as Valadez acknowledges that there are, that perspective is something any multicultural society would want to encourage strictly for the sake of political unity.

But if environmentalists are to profit from what John Dryzek (2000) calls the "deliberative turn in democratic theory," a better understanding of that turn and its implications is required.

Points of Departure

It is advisable at the outset of any discussion that might become complicated to define one's terms. This practice can be useful either as a mechanism for avoiding misunderstanding or as a means of short-circuiting the entire discussion (depending on one's motivations). Part of our task is easy. "Environmental democracy" can be defined as the making of environmental decisions under conditions described by Winston Churchill as the worst form of government except all those other forms that have been tried. But what are we to make of the term "deliberative"?

Assuming that our search for definitions is a well-intentioned one, it might be useful to continue our search for deliberative environmental democracy by suggesting what the term "deliberative" is *not* intended to describe. The concept of deliberation certainly suggests that democracy is more than simply a matter of securing personal liberty—in Lincoln's famous phrase, to be neither slave nor master. If Lincoln's view is insufficiently sophisticated, perhaps a philosopher might help. For Socrates, democracy was characterized by a "forgiving spirit." It was "a charming form of government, full of variety and disorder, and dispensing a sort of equality to equals and unequals alike" (Plato, *The Republic,* book VIII). Socrates captures something of the egalitarianism commonly associated with democracy, but he also fails to suggest how the form of government might be described as deliberative.

Perhaps more useful is the observation by Reinhold Niebuhr (1944, xi) that "man's capacity for justice makes democracy possible; but man's inclination to injustice makes democracy necessary." The clear implication is that democracy is an expression of the better instincts of humans, of our commitment to transcend private motivations somehow in favor of some form of social even-handedness. This view, linking democracy and justice as it does, certainly seems to suggest some form of deliberation, some collective agreement about how to arrange our social relations. But it also seems immediately to conflict with the interest-group liberalism that is virtually synonymous with democracy today.

The deliberative democracy movement has been spawned by a growing realization that contemporary liberalism has lost its democratic character just as it has also sacrificed its ecological sustainability. Modern democracies, confronted with cultural pluralism, social complexity, vast inequities of wealth and influence, and ideological biases that discourage fundamental change, have allowed their political institutions to degenerate into arenas for strategic gamesmanship in which there is no possibility for genuine deliberation (Bohman 1996, 18–24). Neither true democracy nor environmental protection is possible where citizens become mere competitors with no commitments beyond their own narrow self-interests.

Perhaps this is one reason why it is increasingly difficult to find anyone who defends interest-group liberalism as the best form of government to which we can reasonably aspire—not even the contemporary defenders of pluralism, such as the agonistic democrats who champion conflict in a radically pluralized political culture (Mouffe 1996; 1999; Gabardi 2001). From an environmental point of view, the contest of interest groups for their own advantage is widely seen as a significant contributor to ecological degradation (Ophuls and Boyan 1992). How to move beyond interest-group liberalism is, of course, a matter open to considerable debate. From a more political perspective, Theodore Lowi (1979) criticized this form of democracy for its surrender of legitimate authority to the private administration of a fragmented pluralism and for its tendency to produce policy without law. In short, Lowi accuses interest-group liberalism of squandering that most hard won prize of every free people: popular sovereignty. From a communitarian perspective, the value of pluralism, associated with interest-group liberalism, has been criticized for depriving democracy of its ability to make even the most basic and obvious moral distinctions (Tam 1998, 54–56).

Whereas Lowi's analysis of democracy focuses on the preoccupation with groups, and communitarians are concerned primarily with the reduction of moral values to mere interests, deliberative democrats presume that the essence of democracy is deliberation rather than voting, interest aggregation, or rights. Deliberative democracy has a distinguishing core set of propositions, namely: political equality of participants; interpersonal reasoning as the guiding political procedure; and the public giving, weighing, acceptance, or rejection of reasons (Parkinson 2003, 180). A broadly acceptable definition of deliberative democracy might be a requirement that a society's processes for political choice be so designed and maintained that "outcomes will be continuously apprehensible as products of collective deliberation conducted rationally and fairly among free and equal individuals" (Michelman 1997, 149). In short, "the essence of democratic legitimacy is the capacity of those affected by a collective decision to deliberate in the production of that decision" (Dryzek and List 2003, 1).

It is probably not overstating the case to say that the field of democratic theory has been transformed by the development of the concept of deliberative democracy. For many, deliberation has now become the sine qua non for democratic practice. A deliberative approach to all of the policy problems facing modern democracies seems, to many, to be the only way to overcome the failings of interest-group liberalism.

The theory of democracy may have taken a strong deliberative turn in recent decades, but movement by the many participants in this theoretical dance was hardly synchronous. Various distinct versions or models of deliberative democracy can be identified in the literature, of which three perhaps are most significant: one anchored in the theory of justice of John

Rawls; a second derived from the critical theory of Jürgen Habermas; and a third advanced by Bohman, Gutmann and Thompson, and others, that embraces and seeks to realize the traditional tenets of liberal constitutionalism. In this book we examine each of these variants in depth (chapters 3–6), before undertaking an analysis of the implications of each of them for institutions, citizens, experts, and social movements in an environmental democracy (chapters 7–10).

But any effort to bring the advantages of deliberative democracy to the arena of environmental decision making seems destined to encounter at least one fundamental obstacle. In order to understand this obstacle clearly and to find a path around it, we must begin with a general understanding of what deliberative democracy is and its philosophical foundations.

Although many elements of any definition of deliberative democracy beg definitions of their own, it is evident that deliberative democracy is (at least in part) an effort to realize more fully the dreams of the Enlightenment. Locke, Condorcet, Helvetius, and many of their contemporaries advanced a philosophy of reason through which humankind might throw off centuries of superstition and dogma to achieve a reconciliation with nature and set an upward course of collective progress. This it would do, in part, through institutions of democratic self-government characterized by a system of individual rights, an extensive (and expanding) franchise, and a system of universal education. Thus our modern notions of democracy are as easily recognized as products of the Enlightenment as are the methods of modern science.

Deliberative democrats have no more reason to shy away from democracy's connection to the Enlightenment than do other democratic theorists. In fact, they should be more eager to embrace it. In deliberative democracy, there is a strong emphasis on creating a public sphere in which the competing claims of citizens can be evaluated for their validity rather than their mere popularity. The objective is to move the views of participants toward a reasoned consensus based on sound argument and reliable evidence (Habermas 1997; 1996; 1995). This cognitive quality of deliberative democracy should mean that rational inquiry is more important to this view of politics than to most others. The difficulty arises, however, when one begins to explore the applicability of this more rational and cognitive version of democracy to the problem of environmental protection.

There is a widely shared view in the environmental community that modern ecological problems are nature's revenge on our individualistic, rationalized society for its oppressiveness (Alford 1985). This indictment of our Enlightenment political culture has to do, in the first instance, with its bent toward a technoscientific worldview. Horkheimer and Adorno (1972) traced the roots of the individualism and scientific domination of nature that are characteristic of Enlightenment democracies to their roots in our Greco-Roman past and explored the possible consequences of these trends for modern humans. They foresaw a revolt of human nature against the endlessly delayed gratification that results from the perpetual search for new technological capabilities necessary for continued reproduction of a society whose social relations are fundamentally irrational. The frustration that results from modernity's permanent delay of human gratification makes its domination of nature ultimately unsustainable. So the enterprise of the Enlightenment is thus destined to be thwarted by its own internal contradictions. More recently, it has been argued that another contradiction of the Enlightenment (not discussed by Horkheimer and Adorno) is the revolt of nonhuman nature against its irrational exploitation (Leiss 1972). The unrestrained use of nature destroys the material conditions for its own continuation, as the inexorable expansion of capital at the expense of the environment undercuts our natural resource base (Merchant 1989).

Modern science is also indicted by environmentalists for its mechanistic assumptions and narrow definition of what constitutes a fact (Devall and Sessions 1985), as well as for its cognitive orientation toward the substantive rather than the relational (Valadez 2001). These tendencies, it is argued, operate to blind modern science to ecological concerns (which are rarely mechanical or narrow in scope and are always relational in character). In addition to this cognitive disadvantage, modern science is accused of being ill suited from a political viewpoint to the needs of a truly democratic society. Science, it is argued, is largely closed to the oppressed and disadvantaged (Jennings and Jennings 1993) and is a conceptual element of a patriarchic social structure that represses women as much as it does nature (Evans 1995).

Finally, it is argued that even the scientific detachment that lies at the heart of the research process is ecologically self-defeating. This detached attitude has been associated with an estrangement from human emotion and ethical principle that allows even those whose careers involve the study of nature to participate in its devaluation (Gismondi and Richardson 1994). All of these criticisms have led many to conclude that science, insofar as it applies to intervention in nature, will inevitably lead us to disaster (Dizard 1993). These views have led to a deep suspicion of the scientific establishment among environmental activists, which creates a gulf that is difficult to bridge (Foreman 2002).

A different perspective on science is offered by a number of environmentalists who, while not entirely uncritical of the technoscientific character of modern democracies, are nevertheless convinced of the possibility (and necessity) of bringing both science and democracy to the fight for environmental protection. To begin with, they point out that it is impossible even to recognize an environmental crisis as such without a good deal of technical and scientific sophistication (Kirkman 2002). This remains true even if the production of knowledge arises from technical cognitive interests—the economic exploitation or mechanical control of objects—leading to a risk of "problem closure" that obscures other significant interests (Habermas 1974).

Moreover, the very nature of modern society has changed in ways that move science and technology to the center of our concerns. Since the end of World War II, postindustrial countries (the United States in particular) have experienced a transition from an administrative to a scientific state with an agenda heavily laden with difficult scientific issues. As a result, scientific and technological thought permeates our modern language and cultural processes (Schmandt and Katz 1986). This growing dependency on science and technology has led Habermas (1996) to observe that the challenges to contemporary society make such a high demand on the analytical and prognostic skills of government, as well as government's readiness to act to protect citizens from risk, that the problems of strict statutory control associated with democratic accountability are dramatically exacerbated. We are, thus, confronted with the additional challenge of assessing and amending government utilization of science and technology at a time when controlling those practices is increasingly difficult. And the stakes are high because a society that is unable to adapt its "forms of epistemic authority and institutional practice" to the ecosystem relations on which it relies is likely to fall victim to its own "ecologically irrational" behavior (Dryzek 1987, 245).

Finally, even though there are risks associated with embracing modern science as an essential element of the deliberative process, doing so is probably necessary for entirely political reasons. It very likely is the case that "the authority of science" needs to be brought to bear in the service of ecological literacy if an enlightened perspective on the environment is to "have sufficient credibility to create the general agreement that environmentally sound policies should be adopted" (Valadez 2001, 363). Even so strong a critic of science's bias toward technical interests as Jürgen Habermas (1970; 1971) has acknowledged that traditional social structures are increasingly subordinated to conditions of instrumental rationality and that this subordination extends across the organization of labor and trade, information and communication, and finance and government. Habermas concludes that this trend is so broad and relentless that we must not accept the "pessimistic assertion that technology excludes democracy," even if we discount the optimist's dream of a "convergence of technology and democracy" (Habermas 1970, 60).

But the rationality gained through "specialized and competent fulfillment" of social tasks by experts is no protection against the paternalism and "self-empowerment" of administrative agencies (Habermas 1996, 189). What is needed is a more focused production of information about environmental challenges, goals, and progress that is broadly known, regularly reviewed, and used as the basis for strategy development, tactics formation, and resource allocation by agencies charged with environmental protection (Metzenbaum 2002). And it goes without saying that this process of information generation and deployment must involve frequent and meaningful opportunities for deliberative input from as many interested citizens as can be accommodated. This necessity has both political and cognitive dimensions.

In a democratic society, experts cannot assume that their special knowledge will have an impact on environmental decisions unless "they can successfully take on the lay perspective" (Bohman 1996, 64). The legitimacy of the deliberative process itself requires that citizens should not merely defer to authority or alleged expertise (Dryzek 2000). And if, as theorists of deliberation suggest, democracy is more than simply the aggregation of preferences, then the discursive feature of law-making must be crucial to understanding law's claim to legitimacy. Since the legitimacy of law depends on self-legislation, the sources of democracy must be linked with the formal decision making process (Avio 1999).

Moreover, the scientific worldview has a significant conceptual blind spot, which only the involvement of lay decision-makers can correct. Science and technology can know nature only in instrumental terms, because it is only in this way that science can be effective in securing the material preconditions for human survival (Habermas 1987a). But "as soon as specialized knowledge is brought to politically relevant problems, its unavoidably normative character becomes apparent," setting off controversies that polarize citizens and the experts themselves (Habermas 1996, 351). There is no human experience that abides as a scientific "fact" without an element of valid interpretation having been imparted to it (Polanyi 1964). Science, like any other general view of things, is "highly stable and can be effectively opposed, or rationally upheld, only on grounds that extend over the entire experience of man" (Polanyi 1964, 10). For science to guide environmental policy effectively, it must be constantly subjected to a critical political ecology that "eschews meta-narratives or received wisdom about environmental degradation, and instead adopts a critical attitude to how such supposedly neutral explanations of ecological reality were made" (Forsyth 2003, 267). The empirical-analytical capacities of science cannot themselves attach social and political interpretations to their products. It is in this sense, perhaps, that Habermas argues that "access to the facts is provided by the understanding of meaning, not observation" (1971, 309).

For ordinary citizens to play the role of critical auditor of the social and political meaning of scientific and technological advances would seem to be a tall order. But a hopeful attitude toward the problem is not unreasonable. Enlightenment values may have penetrated mass culture sufficiently to give rise to a "cognitive populism" that makes citizens willing to perform this function (Gunderson 2000, 144–145). In his discussion of the relationship between experts and citizens in the deliberative process, James Bohman optimistically argues that "the layperson can take on the perspective of the expert by becoming a well informed citizen" (1996, 64). If all of this is so, it would seem to sustain the belief advanced by Aristotle (*Politics,* book III, chap. 11) that when average citizens meet together, their perceptions combined with those of the "better classes" are quite sufficient to the public purpose. Determining whether this optimism is justified necessitates examining closely the assumptions and manifestations of differing approaches to the deliberation project and assessing their consequences and significance in terms of democratic institutions, citizenship, expertise, and social movements. We return to a fuller consideration of the implications of the Enlightenment for deliberative democratic practice in chapter 11.

Meanwhile, whether deliberative democracy and ecological rationality might ultimately be reconciled is not obvious. A vast theoretical literature about deliberative democracy has insufficiently confronted three criticisms that get at the heart of its usefulness to practical environmental politics of the twenty-first century. These criticisms are: (1) that deliberative democracy is crippled by utopianism; (2) that it has ignored the implications of potential empirical evidence about its premises and claims; and (3) that it cannot be reconciled with the competing, conflicting imperatives of the natural world, of global market capitalism, and of the administrative state. Those criticisms had left the theory of deliberative democracy at the margins of creative thinking about the politics of the environmental problematique until only recently, when serious challenges to them began to appear in the literature.

In fact, a close examination reveals these criticisms to be less than compelling. The theory of deliberative democracy offers the foundation for a possible and practical reconciliation of rationality, strong democracy, and demanding environmentalism. Much evidence can be found both in a careful reanalysis of basic approaches to thinking about deliberative democracy and in the applied world of contemporary environmental policy and politics.

The rationale of this book is that ecological rationality, substantive democratic governance, and policy reasonableness all require deliberation, both in the sense of contemplative decision making and in the sense of collective inclusive discourse. Our approach in this book is, first, to explore these interrelationships; second, to examine critically three main alternative constructs or models for deliberative democracy and to analyze their potential and implications for ecologically rational and reasonable environmental politics; and third, to explore what these three conceptions of deliberative democracy mean for institutions, citizens, experts, and social movements with respect to any practical reconciliation of democracy and environmentalism. The objectives of this book are important for reasons that are simultaneously theoretical and policy practical. First, there is a need to better establish that democracy, in the form most worth having, is ecologically sustainable. Second, borrowing a distinction of Habermas's, modernity needs to know that environmental protection can (and must) become a norm of culture rather than a mere fact of modern government. Both needs require development of models of ecological deliberation and deliberative environmentalism.

2

From Rationality to Reasonableness in Environmental Democracy

The scientific and administrative state is situated in a physical and ecological context that requires a conceptualization of rationality broader than the instrumental rationality that characterizes most administrative theorizing. Various scholars have contributed to clarifying some aspects of the needed broader conceptualization, particularly with respect to foci (system, substance, procedure) and form (social, legal, political, and ecological). But unlike the classical Aristotelian conception of rationality, the goal-blindness of contemporary rationality distinguishes it from reasonableness. The work of John Rawls and Jürgen Habermas suggests that the recoupling of reasonableness and rationality is possible through political discourse and pursuit of social action that requires reasoning about ends as well as means. Opportunities for deliberative democracy and for furthering environmental justice illustrate how rationality, justice, and ecological sustainability can be integrated by breaking down distinctions between decision-making processes and the substance of decisions.

The concept of rationality is often identified exclusively as instrumental rationality, or rationality of means. For example, as Weber was only the first to argue, the growth and spread of bureaucracy is explained by the way its inherent instrumental rationality meets the needs of modernity. In other words, the peculiar legal and political appeal of bureaucratic administration is that it facilitates practical achievement in a process that is logically structured.[1] Yet the administrative state exists in (and must make use of) an environment that not only must take into account the cultural nuances of its human members, but also the broader physical and ecological realm in which all humans are situated. These are all matters subject, in some degree, to rational understanding and explanation. This complexity requires a corresponding complexity in the idea of rationality, with language distinguishing different kinds and forms of reason, behavior, and principles. Thus ecological rationality is an imperative, and yet as a distinct form of reason it can be understood and appreciated only in the historical context of a larger body of scholarship on rationality in decision making.

In particular, Simon's differentiation between substantive and procedural rationality and Diesing's specification of forms of practical reason are useful tools in mapping and defining ecological rationality. However, the definition and development of ecological rationality is only a step in a broader reorganization of our thinking about what rationality in collective action amounts to. Just as Simon found the proverbs of administration to be internally flawed and to produce unfortunate outcomes (Simon 1976a), so too is rationality, decoupled from reasonableness and ecological context, a faulty guide to administration, policy, and politics. As successful as has been Simon's call to recognize the distinction between and boundedness of procedural and substantive rationality, and as useful as Diesing's account of practical reason may be, alone they are not enough to help us grapple with a richer conceptualization of rationality, or to realize the need for more than rationality narrowly construed.

But there are voices asking us to reconsider our basic commitment to a scientific, technical, or economic view of what constitutes rationality in human decision making. Chief among these disparate voices are Rawls, who calls us back to a more classic understanding of rationality, and Habermas, whose concern for critically informed praxis offers a glimpse of how both procedural and substantive rationality might be reunited in the context of environmental politics and deliberative democracy. To appreciate fully the potential of their insights, it is essential to understand the development of rationality as a theoretical concept and as a form of practical reason. It is also necessary to examine closely the estrangement of rationality and reasonableness in the hands of contemporary social scientists. Only in this way can we begin to grasp the potential of ecological rationality as a tool for the reform of our political structures and the rejuvenation of our politics.

A Brief Tour of the Rational

Of particular importance among the distinctions drawn about rationality are those of Weber, Mannheim, Diesing, and Simon (Weber 1978; Gerth and Mills 1946; Henderson and Parsons 1947; Mannheim 1948; Simon 1964; 1976b; 1978). These distinctions reflect three different foci for application of the concept of rationality: the system, the choice, and the reasoning process.

Functional rationality is the rationality inherent in the functioning of systems, societies, or organizations. The functional rationality of a system is the degree to which system behavior is organized according to particular principles and can be understood by reference to principles of order.[2] Functional rationality does not imply that the principles underlying a given functionally rational system must be known by any individual person; it implies only that they be knowable. Both an organization and an ecosystem, for example, can be highly functionally rational, that is, organized according to rationally calculable principles. Those principles may or may not be understood by anyone.

Substantive rationality applies to individual choices or actions.[3] It is an attribute of the behavior itself and refers to whether behavior is "appropriate to the achievement of given goals within the limits imposed by given conditions and constraints" (Simon 1976b, 130–131). Substantive rationality is a standard for judging and labeling behavior. A behavior is substantively rational if it is appropriate or correct (that is, if it *appears* to be rational). An administrative decision is substantively rational, for example, if given goals appear to have been achieved by "deductive reasoning within a tight system of axioms" (ibid., 147). The actual use of deductive reasoning is not a requirement; indeed, a rational choice may have been arrived at intuitively, by trial and error, or by luck.

Procedural rationality, in turn, refers to the actual processes of reasoning, the cognitive procedures used to choose actions (Simon 1978, 9). It describes an intelligent system's ability to discover appropriate adaptive behavior (Bartlett 1986, 224). Rationality in this sense is an attribute not of an action or behavior but of a deliberative, intellective process; it is synonymous with the commonsense use of the term "reasoning." Procedural rationality refers, for example, to the processes by which an individual or organization thinks through a policy or administrative problem, situation, or course of action.

The relationships between functional, substantive, and procedural rationality can be problematic (Bartlett 1986; 2005). Some individual actions may be irrational (substantively) in the context of a society or organization that is highly rational (functionally). That is, even though some behaviors of some individuals cannot be labeled rational (they are not appropriate to the achievement of the individual's goals within the limits of conditions and constraints), the social system of which these individuals are a part may still exhibit a high degree of functional rationality. A functionally rational economy, for example, may in large part be based on predictable nonrational behavior by individuals. Likewise, individual behaviors may be rational (substantively) even though no reasoning (procedural) was employed by the individual in choosing the behaviors. And, as mentioned earlier, a system may be rational (functionally) without any individual understanding (procedural rationality) its principles of order.[4]

Ecological rationality is manifest with regard to all three foci: procedural, substantive, and functional. So categorizing rationality merely in terms of what it is applied to is not helpful in defining ecological rationality inasmuch as ecological rationality can be found at all levels: in cognitive processes (procedural), in characteristics of a choice (substantive), and in characteristics of a system (functional). Ecological rationality, rather, is a form of practical reason that can be distinguished from, and must be understood in comparison with, other prominent forms, such as technical, economic, social, legal, and political rationality (Diesing 1962; Dryzek 1983; 1987; Bartlett 1986).

Technical rationality seeks efficient achievement of a single goal. Economic rationality entails the maximum achievement of a plurality of goals. Underlying technical rationality and economic rationality is the principle of efficiency; both are based on an order of measurement, comparison of values, and production. The principles of order for both technical and economic rationality are focused almost exclusively on means rather than ends.

Other forms of rationality are inherently less purely instrumental forms of reason. Social rationality seeks integration in social relations and social systems, an ordered social interdependence that makes social action possible and meaningful. Legal rationality refers to the reason inherent in any clear, consistent, and detailed system of formal rules for preventing and solving disputes. Political rationality is a rationality of decision-making structures, a practical intelligence capability for solving problems facing a society. Its principle of order is that of facilitating arrival at effective collective decisions. Ecological rationality is a rationality "of living systems, an order of relationships among living systems and their environments"

(Bartlett 1986; 2005). Underlying ecological rationality is the principle of biogeophysical interdependence.

All of these forms of reason are relevant to an analysis of politics in the administrative state. The narrowly instrumental character of administration and administrative organizations makes technical and economic rationalities dominant; indeed, the dominance of these rationalities is the defining feature of modern industrial societies (Ellul 1964; Mumford 1970; Dryzek 1987). Technical and economic rationality are virtually synonymous with what is commonly referred to as instrumental rationality. But all other forms of rationality persist and are necessary for large modern organizations to survive and flourish.

The various forms of rationality are at least partly incompatible, and they may fundamentally conflict (Diesing 1962; Dryzek 1983; 1987; Bartlett 1986). Nor are they all of the same order of importance. According to Diesing (who did not explicitly consider ecological rationality),[5] political rationality has precedence over other forms "because the solution of political problems makes possible an attack on any other problem while a serious political deficiency can prevent or undo all other problem solving (1962, 231–232). John Dryzek argues, however, that ecological rationality is a still more fundamental kind of reason: "The preservation and promotion of the integrity of the ecological and material underpinning of society—ecological rationality—should take priority over competing forms of reason in collective choices with an impact upon that integrity" (Dryzek 1987, 58–59). The priority of ecological rationality, according to Dryzek, is lexical. That is, it has absolute priority over other forms of reason because long-term, serious conflict between ecological rationality and other forms of rationality will result in the elimination of the other forms. Nevertheless, ecological rationality does not fully preempt or supplant other forms of rationality: rarely is it completely determinative, and it has little relevance to many dimensions of human activity (Bartlett 1986; Dryzek 1987; Hayward 1995a).[6]

But the emergence of ecological rationality as a powerful concept in policymaking and administration strongly suggests that, at a fundamental level, rationality may be at war with itself. Understanding how this could be so is pivotal to our efforts to reinvent democratic theory and reinvigorate environmental politics. And to fully understand the war of rationality with itself, we must look to the estrangement of rationality and reasonableness.

The Estrangement of Rationality and Reasonableness

After so many have invested so heavily in developing the concept of rationality in policy and politics, we might be forgiven for feeling that nothing can challenge its preeminence as the determinant of human behavior. Arrow has argued that in all the social sciences,

> There is no single sweeping principle which has been erected as a rival to that of rationality. To the extent that formal, theoretical structures in the social sciences have not been based on the hypothesis of rational behavior, their postulates have been developed in a manner which we may term ad hoc. Such propositions are usually drawn from introspection or casual observation; sometimes they are of the nature of empirical regularities. They depend, of course, on the investigator's intuition and common sense. (Arrow 1968, 645)

From the opposite corner of the social sciences, Habermas has made an essentially similar, if more mournful, observation. Habermas claims that as a result of the triumph of technical rationality, every single value appears as meaningless, "stamped solely with the stigma of irrationality, so that the priority of one value over the other—thus the persuasiveness which a value claims with respect to action—simply cannot be justified rationally" (1973a, 264). And it is true that the most popular contemporary definition of rationality includes only such elements as value-maximizing behavior, consistency, purposefulness, and bounded choice. Intuitions, value commitments, and higher-order beliefs, such as worldviews or spiritual beliefs, play no part in behavior that is planned, calculated, and directed toward a specific end (Allison 1971, 28–32).

It is not entirely true, however, that rationality of whatever hue has eclipsed all other aspects of human behavior. In fact, Simon argues that rationality does not really determine behavior. Behavior, he says, is "determined by the irrational and nonrational elements that bound the area of rationality" (Simon 1976a, 241). Both rationality and nonrationality are natural; the area of rationality is merely the area of adaptability to nonrational elements. This sounds perhaps like a healthy skepticism toward the idea that technical rationality can answer all of life's problems. But the implications of this view may be far less benign. If our choices as to goals are outside the sphere of rational discourse, what options do humans have for resolving the practical problems of everyday life that come replete with alternative ends and means? In the environmental arena, are we limited to a choice between the tyranny of the free market as an unexamined ideology and the mysticism of the Gaia hypothesis?[7] It was precisely such a dismal choice that motivated Habermas to warn that

> if practical questions, eliminated from knowledge that has been reduced to empirical science, are dismissed . . . entirely from the controlling powers of rational investigation, if decisions on questions touching on the praxis of life must be pronounced as beyond any and every authority committed to rationality, then we cannot be astonished by the ultimate desperate attempt to secure socially binding precommitments on practical questions institutionally by a return to the closed world of mythical images and powers. (1973a, 266–267)

Few who have witnessed the influence of mysticism in the environmental community, or the increasing absolutism and irrationality of politics generally, could avoid being chilled by this warning.[8] Certainly our powers of reason must afford us other, better choices.

The contemporary definition of rationality generally includes the concepts of profit-maximizing behavior, consistency, purposefulness, and bounded choice (Allison 1971). These are the elements of rational choice as most social scientists have come to understand it. But in starting from the basic premise of the instrumental rationality of human actions in the service of egotistic ends, rational choice falls prey to "an individualistic bias that ignores the fundamental role played by cognitive and emotional identification with others in shaping the very self whose interests become the mainspring of human motivation and action" (Wrong 1994, 196–197). In other words, our attempt to employ instrumental rationality to pursue our self-interests undermines the cultivation of precisely the self that is required for us to understand what our interests are. Hence the warning from Habermas that the price we pay for economy in the selection of means is a decisionism set wholly free from the selection of higher-level goals (1973a, 265). Diesing also pointed to the same irony: "Thus ultimate ends, the basic aims of life, cannot be selected or evaluated by rational procedures; they must be dealt with by arbitrary preference, or intuition, or by cultural and biological determinism. And yet it seems unfortunate to have rational procedures available for the relatively less important decisions of life and to have none for dealing with the most important decisions" (1962, 1).

It is precisely this "goal blindness" that led Bellone to conclude that the notion of rationality in administrative theory is conceptually unsound.

Bellone points out that the term rationality, as Simon uses it, has nothing to do with the Aristotelian concept of rationality. Before modernity, the concept of rationality always had ethical overtones. To call a person rational "was to recognize his or her allegiance to an objective standard of values that transcended economizing imperatives" (Bellone 1980, 145). This overarching sense of reason is the element of classical rationality that is missing from the modern concept.[9] Contemporary social structures generally have become "subordinated to conditions of instrumental or strategic rationality: the organization of labor and trade, the network of transportation, information, and communication, the institutions of private law, and, starting with financial administration, the state bureaucracy" (Habermas 1970, 98). Instrumental rationality has become the sole admissible value. And, perhaps most ironically, we fail to see it as a value because it seems simply to coincide with rationality as such (Habermas 1973a, 64).

Of what, then, does the missing element of reasonableness consist? What is it that distinguishes the reasonable from the rational? As Rawls points out, we are aware of this difference in everyday speech and common examples readily bring it out. For instance, we might say, "Their proposal is perfectly rational given their position, but it is outrageously unreasonable from my point of view." This illustrates several facts about reason and rationality. In knowing that people are rational, we do not know what ends they will pursue; we know only that they will pursue them intelligently. But when we know that people are reasonable where others are concerned, we know that they are willing to govern their conduct by some principle from which they and others may reason in common. Thus reasonable people take into account the consequences of their actions for others. The disposition to be reasonable is, therefore, neither derived from nor opposed to the rational. But it is incompatible with egoism, as it is related to the disposition to act morally (Rawls 1993, 48).

The reintegration of reasonableness and rationality is, therefore, a process of weaning people away from their focus on personal means and ends.[10] It is, of course, unfashionable in the social sciences these days to predicate any discussion on the concept of the public interest (unfashionable because the public interest cannot be understood in terms of the substantive, instrumental rationality of individual decisions and, moreover, because it presumes a moral foundation to political analysis). But we need not admit to naiveté in order to revive the notion that political discourse of some appropriate character might allow citizens to act from the deeply abiding public spirit to which eighteenth and nineteenth century democratic theorists, at least, were so dedicated. And we are aided in this ambition by the relentless and inescapable quality of contemporary environmental problems.

In fact, this discourse already exists in nascent form in environmental politics. It is precisely the opportunity for individual empowerment to pursue social action through reasoning that constitutes a potential solution to the valuative concerns of Rawls and Habermas. Rationality thus can transcend the instrumentalist "trap" that swallows up technical and economic rationality, instead allowing and even requiring continual reconsideration of ends and higher values. The environmental justice movement illustrates this.

Rationality and Environmental Justice

For Habermas, a free, responsible, and rational society is one in which as many people as possible can meaningfully participate in the "public sphere." This is the arena in which various interests may engage in free and open discourse about society's normative agenda (Habermas 1974, 49–53). This discourse, however, must meet certain particular requirements if it is to achieve truly inclusive participatory democracy.

At one level there is the dimension of social discourse for which practical action and interpretive reason are relevant. This Habermas refers to as communicative action (or, occasionally, symbolic interaction). Communicative action involves a conversation "governed by binding consensual norms which define reciprocal expectations about behavior and which must be understood and recognized by at least two acting subjects" (Habermas 1970, 92). Clearly, almost any social arrangement wherein participants agree to refrain from arbitrary behavior can meet this basic criterion. Most of our conventional and well-settled social understandings are the results of such processes. This does not, however, guarantee that they are just. The primacy of justice in this regard is best articulated by Rawls, though his formulation is one with which Habermas could be expected to agree: "Justice is the first virtue of social institutions, as truth is of thought. A theory however elegant and economical must be rejected or revised if it is untrue; likewise laws and institutions no matter how efficient and well arranged must be reformed or abolished if they are unjust" (Rawls 1971, 3).

So there must be a form of discourse beyond communicative action that is required to achieve a just and rational society (Hayward 1995a,b). This second level of rational discourse we may refer to as "critical discourse." If communicative action is the level of social reality where conventional understandings are developed and expressed, critical discourse is where those conventions are challenged and sometimes overthrown. Critical discourse tests the truth claims of opinions and norms that participants no longer take for granted. In such a discourse, the force of an argument is the only permissible compulsion and the cooperative search for truth is the only permissible motive (Habermas 1973b, 168). Neither institutional power nor political or economic influence may play a role in such a basic reexamination of accepted opinion.[11] And no truly democratic discourse is complete without this reexamination; in its absence, the norm of full participation has been sacrificed to expediency and majoritarianism. This realization is crucial for both our interest in justice and our commitment to rationality, for there is nothing inherent in the majority viewpoint that renders it either just or logically sound.

In recognizing the connectedness of rationality and justice, we gain an important insight into some of the most vexing aspects of the recent history of environmental politics. It is a commonplace of environmentalism that solutions that seem rational at a technical, administrative, or ecological level are frustrated by the apparent irrationality of the political process. At the top of the list of supposedly irrational manifestations of the larger political and administrative process are the dreaded NIMBYs (individuals or groups who proclaim, "not in my backyard!"). Of course, from the NIMBYs' points of view, as well as that of narrow, instrumental rationality, there is nothing at all irrational about what they are doing. They are merely using what resources they have to pursue what they perceive to be their own individual best interests. In the words of Glaberson, "NIMBYs are noisy. NIMBYs are powerful. NIMBYs are everywhere. NIMBYs are people who live near enough to corporate or government projects—and are upset enough about them—to work to stop, stall, or shrink them. NIMBYs organize, march, sue, and petition to block the developers they think are threatening them. They twist the arms of politicians and they learn how to influence regulators. They fight fiercely and then, win or lose, they vanish" (Glaberson 1988, 1).

And the key to their success or failure is often not the nature of their interests nor the quality of their rationality, but rather the sufficiency of their resources. And herein lies a concern for both justice and rationality: NIMBYs confront powers whose justice and reasonableness are by no means beyond question. But to the extent that the success of NIMBYs depends on their resources, the ability of their criticism to check the positions of others for their justice and truth value is uncertain. Where the NIMBYs have won, have they done so because of the justness of their cause and the merits of their arguments, or have they simply marshaled superior power?

This is an especially important question because NIMBYism has increasingly taken on racial and cultural overtones. For example, in the United States the turning point in the argument over the nature of NIMBYism may have been the publication of the United Church of Christ's Commission on Racial Justice report, *Toxic Waste and Race*. This report found that three of every five black and Hispanic Americans live in a community with uncontrolled toxic waste sites. Predictably, the report resulted in charges of environmental racism being leveled against the U.S. Environmental Protection Agency. The EPA's response was that poverty and a lack of political power, rather than racism, was what attracted polluters (Satchell 1992, 34–45). Apparently, the EPA had succeeded in disentangling powerlessness, poverty, and race in a way that other governmental agencies and the disadvantaged themselves had until then failed to do. And they seemed to expect minorities and the poor to appreciate this improvement in analytical clarity.

Not surprisingly, the grassroots groups associated with the environmental justice movement have continued actively to seek early citizen involvement in decisions to ensure that minority communities are ranked high in priority for cleanup actions (Kriz 1994, 224–229). It is greatly to the credit of these groups that much of the argument about environmental injustice concerns standards of procedure and process (Bullard 1993). Chief among these procedural challenges are lawsuits brought pursuant to the environmental impact statement (EIS) requirement of the U.S. National Environmental Policy Act (NEPA). Litigation under NEPA has been a continuous process from the act's inception. These actions commonly alleged that an EIS was not done but should have been or that an EIS that was done was inadequate. Most significantly, however, the plaintiffs in these cases are typically individuals or environmental groups that might be expected to lack the resources necessary to compete effectively in the political marketplace (Council on Environmental Quality 1993). And whether their competitive disadvantage is traceable to racial or economic factors is (contrary to the EPA) of little importance. The only factor of importance is their access to the judicial system and the seriousness with which business and government must regard them as a consequence of that access.

The use of NEPA by individuals and groups to assert their environmental rights focuses our attention on what Rawls has taken to be the underlying principles of justice. His formulation holds that justice is achieved when each person has an equal right to a fully adequate scheme of basic liberties and when social and economic inequalities are attached to positions open to all and organized so as to be of the greatest benefit to the least advantaged members of society (Rawls 1993, 291). So to the extent that NEPA has created a more politically level playing field in environmental decision making and has allowed us to focus concern on the impact of policy outcomes on society's least advantaged, it has imported a significant element of Rawlsian justice into the environmental arena. And by integrating the views of traditionally underrepresented groups into the policy process, NEPA and environmental impact assessment has made it possible to plug one of the holes that had introduced much substantive irrationality into environmental decision making.

Although much has been said about the war between reasonableness and rationality, it can never be anything other than an intellectual civil war: a conflict between inseparable concepts. In Rawls's words: "As complementary ideas, neither the reasonable nor the rational can stand without the other. Merely reasonable agents would have no ends of their own they wanted to advance by fair competition; merely rational agents lack a sense of justice and fail to recognize the independent validity of the claims of others" (1993, 52). Without both reasonableness and rationality, we are left either without an agenda or without the ability to get others to help us pursue the agenda we have. But when both qualities exist in a relationship of mutual awareness, we can make sense of matters that otherwise would seem paradoxical.

For example, Murphy points out that one of the most interesting aspects of technical rationality as it has come to reshape social and economic organizations is that these rational structures seek durability by having similarly trained people occupy standardized jobs processing mechanically transcribed information. In this way, as also in the market, the importance to the system of any particular individual is radically reduced. Although this is undoubtedly one of the least charming characteristics of administration focused on instrumental rationality, it has generally been accepted as necessary to achieve the cardinal objective of organizational life, namely, survival. And yet it is precisely the survival-driven actions of private and public organizations that have brought us to the brink of ecological disaster, threatening instrumental rationality with self-destruction. A more broadly reasonable form of rationality would reconcile this contradiction by incorporating multiple feedback mechanisms and by requiring reasoning about ends as well as means. According to Murphy: "Sustainability has been an important element of formal instrumental rationality. In terms of this criterion, it would hardly be rational if the efficient use of means to attain ends had the consequence of exhausting those means. The ultimate irrationality would be for the apparently rational industry of post-industrial system to run out of gas or choke itself into extinction" (1994, 43). Thus, as Lewis Mumford (1970, 393) foresaw long ago, all thinking worthy of the name must now be ecological.

Moving Forward

In light of this realization that the only rational organization or society is a broadly reasonable one, explicit application of ecological reasoning to major public and private actions can be regarded as essential to both procedurally rational decision making and substantively rational outcomes. Procedures such as impact assessment, policy appraisal, and environmental audits can enhance expertise in dealing with complex and interdependent policy issues and can have a coordinative effect on policy endeavors (Baber and Bartlett 1989, 152). More important, the consideration of impacts before making policies or taking decisions with ecological implications is an important step toward institutionalizing ecological rationality in political, social, and economic structures, improving the chances that these organizations will produce environmentally sound results (Murphy 1994, 44). But such procedures can achieve their potential only if they also are reasonable, that is, if they institutionalize values and processes that facilitate selection of higher goals, cognitive and emotional identification with others, and ethical action—and if, of course they are fundamentally democratic and operate in the context of an extensively democratic civil society. The task that lies ahead is to imbed such environmentally and otherwise reasonable values and processes in all of our political, social, and economic institutions. As Thomas Spragens (1990, 111) argues, "What the recognition of the politics in reason offers us, constructively, is an avenue for vindicating the essential intuition of the Enlightenment—the intuition that the life of reason is defined by norms of behavior that also play a crucial role in creating a good society."

Options for extending and fundamentally restructuring democratic structures, procedures, and culture in various social choice arenas remain available and may even be adopted in foreseeable circumstances, paving the way for more substantial, perhaps not yet imagined, institutional innovation (Cohen and Sabel 1997; Dorf and Sabel 1998). The coevolution of deliberative politics and policy processes will likely continue, transforming decision making and the reconstruction of reality informally, subtly, and profoundly through cultivation of procedural and substantive ecological reasoning. This restructuring will break down, and irreparably so, both the practical and conceptual distinctions between democratic decision-making processes and the substance of decisions. It was this distinction that allowed Simon to argue that "A man as a behaving system is quite simple. The apparent complexity of his behavior is largely a reflection of the environment in which he finds himself" (1981, 65). But human decisions no longer will seem complex just because humans mirror the complexity that surrounds them. Decision making, democratic and informed by an integrated rationality reconciled with reasonableness, is destined to be as complex as humans' relationship with nature.

3

Toward Environmental Democracy: Three Points of Departure

Appreciation of the imperatives of an ecological understanding of the world has led theorists and would-be reformers to call for the extension of a transcendent rationality to all human affairs. Others, despairing of both the limits of rationality and the consequences of its unchecked ascendency, which are at least partially to blame for the current environmental problematique,[1] call for a radical transition to governance according to some form of strong democracy, abjuring the extension of rationality as unnecessary to, and indeed in conflict with, the moral and consequential merits of practicing democracy. Thus the relationships of knowledge, action, and nature have become core challenges of modernity, demanding a reconciliation that is not merely theoretically possible but practically feasible. The prospect of such a three-way reconciliation, relating human knowledge and action to each other and simultaneously to the unyielding imperatives of the natural world,[2] is still largely unexplored by theorists or reformers.

In chapter 2, we attempted to carve out a space for the concept of environmental rationality within the universe of rationality constructed by social theorists from Max Weber to Herbert Simon and Paul Diesing. Brief mention was made of the roles that Jürgen Habermas and John Rawls might play in arriving at a better understanding of the concept of rationality in relationship to environmental issues. We left unexplored the broader question of how one relates human knowledge and action to the unyielding imperatives of the natural world, a question to which we now turn.

Embracing the argument that ecological rationality requires deeper or stronger forms of democracy and accepting that "shallow forms of democratic politics provide only weak forms of ecological rationality" (Plumwood 1998, 569) still leaves unanswered the question of what must be the democratic substance of concrete manifestations of ecological rationality (Bartlett 1986; Dryzek 1987). Any institutionalized concept of ecological rationality has to have fully developed substantive content. No other concepts of rationality remain entirely formal or procedural; neither can a working concept of ecological rationality be allowed to wander around half dressed.

Three promising points of departure can be found in proposals for a reconciliation of nature and democracy by full liberalism, by consensual normative precommitments, and by mandated discourse. Moreover, these proposals are not merely "ivory tower" fantasies or utopian dreams; existing deliberative institutional innovations in state-associated democratization reach further than is usually recognized. Although their design may not necessarily have been influenced directly by democratic theory, a number of practical policy experiments—major environmental policy initiatives of the last third of the twentieth century—can be identified that correspond remarkably closely with the prescriptions of these sets of theoretical principles.

We develop here these three options for giving substantive meaning to the concept of ecological rationality within the arena of practical democratic politics. We describe theoretical underpinnings, policy examples, and some policy implications. We wind up not with a cheerful synthesis, but rather with a specification of policy contexts within which each of the three orientations is the more appropriate content for the formal concept of ecological rationality. The future policy analyst is charged with a diagnostic task, namely, to determine which of the deliberative theories we describe is indicated by the characteristics of the specific policy problem confronted.

The Dialectic of Enlightenment

The relationship of knowledge, action, and nature is an integral component of the core challenge of our modern age—described by Max Horkheimer and Theodor Adorno as the "dialectic of enlightenment." In their view, the project of the enlightenment is nothing less than "the disenchantment of the world; the dissolution of myths and the substitution of knowledge for fancy" (Horkheimer and Adorno 1972, 3). The object of this historical project is to relieve humankind of *necessity*, the constraints imposed by a natural world existing outside of human control. The freedom of humanity, in this enlightenment tradition, consists in the liberation of the individual from the oppression of necessity. The object of scientific knowledge is thus established. What humans want to learn from nature is how to use it in order to dominate both it and other humans.

This domination is not, however, without its costs. In both relations between individuals and the relationship of humankind to nature, humans "pay for the increase in their power with alienation from that over which they exercise their power." The enlightenment leads humans to behave rationally toward things as a dictator toward subjects, knowing them only insofar as they can be manipulated (Horkheimer and Adorno 1972, 4, 9). Rationality in the service of understanding the world becomes ubiquitous and cannot be decoupled from the exercise of control. The implications of this for relations between humans have received wide attention.

As noted in chapter 2, the foundation of the social sciences in the twentieth century can be located in this principle of instrumental rationality. In the face of this hegemonic rationality, Yehezkel Dror (1968, 151) could only plead that intuitive processes do not have to be regarded as irrational. But the tide has flowed strongly in the other direction. Eric Voegelin (1969; 1975) observed that the classical concept of rationality has always had a significant ethical dimension. But in starting from the basic premise of instrumental rationality as the wellspring of human action, contemporary social science must accept goals as given, assuming that they derive from arbitrary preferences, intuition, or cultural or biological determinism. It is this realization that caused Diesing (1962, 1) to take note of the ironic situation of humankind, possessed of powerful rational procedures for making the relatively trivial decisions among means but utterly bereft of comparable methods for the crucial choice among ends. This is the sense in which Horkheimer and Adorno claim that the enlightenment ultimately abrogates itself by adopting a form of reason that is "as little capable of finding a standard by which to measure any drive in itself, and in comparison with all other drives, as of arranging the universe in spheres" (1972, 91).

The implications of a fully developed rationality of enlightenment for the natural world are no less problematic. When instrumental rationality becomes fully integrated with the dominant mode of production, it loses any capacity it may ever have had to critically evaluate its own agenda.

"Reason has been so thoroughly purged" of any specific order of value "that it has finally renounced the task of passing judgment" on actions and ways of life (Horkheimer 1974, 9). It is in this way that modernity's insensitivity to nature can be seen as a variation on the pragmatic attitude that has become typical of Western civilization as a whole. More than ever before, today we conceive of nature as a mere tool of humans, possessing no objective meaning or aim recognized by reason, and so the legitimate object of human exploitation without limit. Rationality finally becomes incapable of conceiving of any order of reason outside of itself or negates such an order as a mere delusion (ibid., 7, 104–108). The respect of humans for the rational status quo that they themselves unceasingly produce takes on such mythic proportions that it becomes a positive fact in itself, a fortress for the exploiter secure from any form of revolutionary imagination—imagination that ultimately comes to despise itself as utopian (Horkheimer and Adorno 1972, 41). In other words, the very concept of rationality is a construct of class privilege and capitalist power, validated by its capacity to produce a constant stream of goodies and protect the status quo. The result is that any dissenting perspective is labeled, even by those who hold it, as utopian and thus is saddled with an obligation to justify itself through something more than mere reason. That is why "for the old Frankfurt School, nothing short of a reconciliation with eternal nature could dissolve the *aporia* of the enlightenment, however unlikely such a reconciliation might be" (Whitebook 1985, 151).

Thought and Action in the Democratic Context

Viewed from the perspective of the dialectic of enlightenment, a more intelligent and less exploitative relationship between humans and their natural environment might seem well out of reach. This may result, at least in part, from the fact that better environmental decisions are at least as much a matter of power as they are a problem of analysis. Along with the rationality of modern empirical science, the Enlightenment blessed (or cursed) humankind with a new range of concepts for analyzing the relationship between individuals and the state. This development has been captured most trenchantly in the dichotomy between the freedom of the ancients and the freedom of the moderns, and more recently in the distinction between republican and liberal freedom (Sandel 1996).

In its classical formulation, the freedom of the ancients was a matter of personal power. One was free to the extent that one was capable of working one's will in the world. The freedom of the moderns is more concerned with an individual's security. In this view, one is free to the extent that one is protected from the depredations of others and from the arbitrary use of power by the state. This modern concept of freedom is far more consistent with the Enlightenment penchant for system building—applying presumably deterministic principles to building reliable, fully harnessed social machines—than it is with the ancient idea of heroic personal assertion. Thus modern liberalism takes on a distinctly constitutional character, reflecting the assumption that freedom is more a matter of discriminating design than individual initiative.

The contest between these two concepts of freedom is reflected in the contemporary debate over the problem of public deliberation. How, it is asked, can a nominally democratic system of interest-group liberalism be transformed into a civic culture characterized by a genuinely open and participatory form of public deliberation? Moreover, how can the processes of thought and action that characterize this new form of democratic life be managed in such a way that humankind's relationship to the environment becomes more rational (in the classical sense)?

In approaching this debate, we find that several core issues seem to constitute the essential structure of any new form of public deliberation, giving rise to the following questions:

(1) What are the prerequisites for successful public deliberation?

(2) What counts as success? In other words, what level of agreement (a bare majority, a consensus, or unanimity) will we demand for the results of public deliberation to be considered legitimate?

(3) What method of interaction (or style of reasoning) is required for public deliberation? And a related question,

(4) What role is there in the process of deliberation for interests that are particular to an individual or group? And finally,

(5) With respect to the special imperatives posed by the scientific quality of most environmental issues, what role should experts and their knowledge play in public deliberation?

So demanding an agenda can hardly be addressed without playing some constraint on its scope. Accordingly, we focus our discussion of these issues on the three proposed responses that are best developed theoretically: full liberalism, ideal discourse, and consensual normative precommitment. We concentrate on the views of James Bohman, Amy Gutmann, Dennis Thompson, Jürgen Habermas, and John Rawls, who represent three distinctive responses to the problem of public deliberation on environmental problems.

The Prerequisites of Public Deliberation

A useful point of departure for understanding the prerequisites of successful public deliberation is the catalog of constraints on such deliberation provided by James Bohman, Amy Gutmann, and Dennis Thompson. Democratic deliberation is constrained by the social facts of cultural pluralism, large inequities of wealth and influence, social complexity (which is thought to make deliberation obsolete or impossible), and community-wide biases and ideologies that discourage change (Bohman 1996, 18–20; Gutmann and Thompson 1996, 349–357; 2004, 26–29).

Our constitutional rights as given in our modern system, including most prominently the freedom of expression and assembly, are necessary conditions for successful deliberation in that they prevent the worst abuses of bias and inequity. But the political institutions created by this system of rights have become less a forum for deliberation than an arena for strategic gamesmanship. In Bohman's view, and that of most other advocates of public deliberation, rights make deliberation possible, in part by placing limits on it. But these rights tell us nothing about what deliberation is or how it is best conducted under existing conditions and constraints (Bohman 1996, 23–24). For advocates of full liberalism, as for Rawls, public deliberation requires that citizens ground their positions in *public* reasons, limiting themselves to justifications that any reasonable person could accept. Citizens can have whatever private motivations they want, but in public discourse they must limit themselves to intersubjectively reasonable justifications, that is, reasons that do not presuppose some particular conception of the good or some comprehensive moral doctrine. Thus public reasoning includes the capacities and procedures of ordinary reasoning but also "a process of deliberating and judging 'from the standpoint of everyone else'" (ibid., 79). With this basic standard established, it is possible for Bohman to outline a set of conditions under which public discourse might be expected to succeed.

Bohman's core assumption, shared by Gutmann and Thompson (1996, 349–357), is that "a people cannot be sovereign unless they are able to deliberate together successfully and unless they have something to say about the conditions under which they deliberate" (Bohman 1996, 198). Further, the discursive structures of deliberation must make it less likely that irrational and untenable (nonpublic) arguments will determine deliberative outcomes. It is essential that discursive procedures are broadly inclusive, disallowing the creation of permanent majorities and disenfranchised minorities. Finally, to assure the losers in any given public deliberation that their continued participation in collective action is worthwhile, discursive procedures must allow for ongoing revisions that take up compatible features of defeated positions or improve their chances of being heard (Bohman 1996, 100).

The procedural prescriptions offered by full liberalism are designed to achieve two essential goals. They are intended to create the conditions for effective political participation and ensure equality of political capacity for all citizens. These circumstances are taken to be the core requirements for the effective resolution of cultural conflicts by public deliberation. This set of procedures makes social innovation possible, which "begins when a public forms around a piece of critical discourse and successfully frames public debate in such a way that it may reshape democratic institutions" (Bohman 1996, 107–109, 203).

The perspective on public discourse provided by Jürgen Habermas may, at first blush, seem to differ little from that of advocates of full liberalism. For Habermas, public discourses succeed in proportion to their diffusion, and thus only under conditions of broad and active participation. "This in turn requires a background political culture that is egalitarian, divested of all educational privileges, and thoroughly intellectual" in its orientation to public deliberation (Habermas 1996, 490). As if in anticipation of the argument that this formulation is too demanding, Habermas makes clear that "democratic citizenship need not be rooted in the national identity of a people" (ibid., 500). Regardless of the diversity of cultural forms of life represented in a society, Habermas does insist that democracy requires that "every citizen be socialized into a common political culture" (ibid.).

But what does this suggest about the procedural requirements of public discourse?

As Habermas makes clear, the "republican model of citizenship reminds us that constitutionally protected institutions of freedom are worth only what a population *accustomed* to political freedom and settled in the 'we' perspective of active self-determination makes of them" (1996, 499). But what form of deliberation does this model suggest? We shall discuss the form of public rationality advocated by Habermas presently. At this point it is sufficient to observe that, for Habermas, a public agreement counts as rational, that is, as an expression of a general intent, if it could only have come to pass under the ideal conditions that alone create legitimacy. Democratic society can be envisioned only as a self-controlled learning process. This involves finding arrangements that support the presumption that the basic institutions of a society and its basic political decisions would meet "the unforced agreement of all of those involved, if they could participate, as free and equal, in discursive will-formation" (Habermas 1979, 186).

The conditions that Rawls imposes on successful public discourse are far more demanding even than those of Habermas. According to Rawls, "political liberalism looks for a political conception of justice" that may "gain the acceptance of an overlapping consensus of reasonable religious, philosophical, and moral doctrines" in the society to be regulated by it. This requires us to "find some point of view, removed from and not distorted by the particular features and circumstances" of social reality, "from which a fair agreement between persons regarded as free and equal can be reached" (Rawls 1993, 10, 23). This point of view Rawls has characterized as the original position. From this position, decision makers know that there will be a differential distribution of resources in society, but they have no information about their position within this distribution or that of anyone else. The preferred resolution is always one that would be agreed to in principle by rationally self-interested individuals who were unaware of their own position in society. This "veil of ignorance" removes the distorting influence of self-interest on decisions regarding the basic institutions and processes of a society. Together with the assumption of equality of political status, the veil of ignorance in the original position is taken by Rawls to establish the basis of public reason in the fundamental institutions and processes of a democratic society.

The implications of this view for environmental decision making become clearer when we realize that one of the advantages of the original position, according to Rawls, is that it leads to ideally democratic decisions, "fairly adjusted to the claims of each generation" (1971, 288). This intergenerational standard of fairness is required by the fundamental proposition that "what touches all concerns all" (ibid.). The fundamental organizing principle of public reason, within which the other basic ideas about public discourse are connected, is that of "society as a fair system of cooperation over time, from one generation to the next" (Rawls 1993, 15). To establish fairness between generations, the parties in the original position do not know the present state of society. They are faced with the task of agreeing on a principle of just savings that fairly balances the demands of the current generation on society's resources with those of future generations. In conducting this discourse, "the correct principle is that which the members of any generation (and so all generations) would adopt as the one . . . they would want preceding generations to have followed (and later generations to follow), no matter how far back (or forward) in time" one chooses to think (ibid., 273–274). This has clear implications for questions that will be discussed below, but for now it is sufficient to recognize that it imposes a unique set of prerequisites on any public discourse.

Rawls argues that his conception of public discourse, concerned as it is with establishing basic principles of justice that could expect to receive universal assent, is far more limited than the process imagined by Habermas. "Since there is no reasonable religious, philosophical, or moral doctrine affirmed by all citizens" in even the most well-ordered society, the conception of justice affirmed in such a society must be a conception limited to the domain of the political and its associated values (Rawls 1993, 38). The idea is that political liberalism, as conceived by Rawls, establishes a basis for public discourse within the category of the political and leaves philosophy, religion, and other cultural artifacts untouched. It thus escapes the long tradition of development, interpretation, and dispute associated with these controversial aspects of human existence. In comparing his approach to public discourse with that of Habermas, Rawls observes that his position is limited to the political, while Habermas's is comprehensive. This results from the difference between what Rawls refers to as analytical devices of representation. For Habermas, the device of representation is the ideal discourse situation as a part of his comprehensive theory of communicative action. The representation device employed by Rawls, the original position, differs from the ideal discourse situation in that it is restricted to the realm of politics—suggesting no shared cultural values, only the general awareness of limited resources and the likelihood of unequal distribution (Rawls 1995, 132, 134, 138).

This comparison of the two theories by Rawls has not gone uncontested by Habermas (1995). Nevertheless, it is sufficient for our purpose to leave that dispute unexplored and to draw our own comparison of the work of all three theories on the narrower question of what are the essential prerequisites for successful public deliberation. It is probably fair to say that what Bohman, Gutmann, and Thompson require for public discourse is interest-group pluralism at its best. Citizens of their republic are entitled to use public discourse to pursue ends of their own choosing and are entitled to expect that other citizens will hold no more influence over collective processes than they themselves enjoy. Habermas would undoubtedly view this as necessary to but not sufficient for public deliberation. In his view, a shared political culture is necessary for successful public discourse. While this does not have to rise to the level of a national identity, it does require that there exist a shared commitment to the use of public reasons (reasons not derived from particular ethical or religious perspectives) in defense of positions adopted in the arena of public discourse dedicated to testing the truth claims of competing worldviews. Taking a different tack, Rawls requires that fundamental decisions be derived from a particular perspective, the original position, which is purged not only of ethical and religious suppositions but also of any specific information about the position of individuals in the collective arrangement being constructed. Rawls does not reject the "full liberalism" advocated by Bohman, Gutmann, and Thompson. He merely renders it irrelevant to fundamental decisions by banishing from public discourse the specific values and desires that are the very foundation of modern liberalism. Full liberalism, Habermas, and Rawls, therefore, present three fundamentally different visions of what is required for successful public discourse. To some extent, these differences may be explained by examining their contrasting views about what constitutes success in public deliberation.

Legitimating Public Discourse: What Counts as Success?

In full liberalism, success in public discourse is evidenced by its results. When it succeeds, public discourse produces "a shared intention that is acceptable to a plurality of the agents who participate in the activity of forming it" (Bohman 1996, 56). To this "sovereignty" requirement Bohman adds the notion that the success of deliberation should be "measured reconstructively," that is, in light of the observed development of democratic institutions, rather than by some external standard of justification (ibid., 241). Adding this "democratic" standard allows us to synthesize three basic requirements for the legitimacy of collective decisions resulting from public deliberation. To be legitimate, decisions must result from fair and open participatory processes in which all public reasons are given equal respect. Further, decisions must make the public deliberation of the majority the source of sovereign power. Finally, the deliberative process must produce outcomes that give citizens reason to continue to cooperate in deliberation rather than merely comply with the majority will (ibid., 187).

The important point is not that the process merely remains open to continued participation by all (though that is a necessary condition). It is also that the majority accepts the restraints imposed by a "mutually respectful process" (Gutmann and Thompson 2004, 11) never exploiting its position to such an extent that the minority chooses to opt out. This can suggest (1) that the majority is a shifting coalition of interests in which every individual is included with sufficient frequency that none feels permanently disenfranchised, or (2) that a permanent minority is treated by the majority with consideration sufficient to retain its commitment to the ongoing deliberation in spite of its minority status. As a practical matter, public deliberations of an ongoing nature are always going to be sustained by both conditions (representing pluralism and individual rights, respectively). Thus, in full liberalism, public deliberation is successful when the processes of deliberation are fair and open, when the majority position prevails, and when the results are such that citizens seek to continue to participate in the ongoing deliberative process.

As might be expected, Habermas has much to say on the problem of legitimation. In his own words, "the extent of what has to be legitimated can be surmised only if one contemplates the vestiges of the centuries-long repressions, the great wars, the small insurrections and defeats, that lined

the path to the modern state" (Habermas 1979, 193). The general problem of legitimation is compounded in the modern era by the fact that traditional worldviews have lost their power and validity (as public religion,
customary ritual, justifying metaphysic, and unquestionable tradition)
and reshaped themselves into subjective systems of belief and ethics (the
Protestant ethic, for example) that serve to ensure the cogency of modern
value orientations. All of these problems epitomize capitalist production.
Capitalist production also suggests a possible solution. The promise of the
market is that the exchange relationships that have come to dominate society will be legitimate because of the presumed equivalence of position
occupied by parties to transactions— neither party to the market exchange is under any obligation to the other, and neither is presumed to be
more worthy to have his or her needs satisfied. Thus, in principle, the political domination of a market economy can be legitimated "from below"
rather than from above through institutions of traditional culture (Habermas 1970, 96–99).

This form of legitimation, however, is problematic. The internalization
process that "secures a motivational foundation for actors' value orientations is not usually repression-free; but it does result in a certain authority
of conscience that goes hand in hand with a consciousness of autonomy"
(Habermas 1996, 67). A more serious problem results from the fact that,
because the power to control and direct exchange processes has itself come
under political control and state regulation, legitimation can no longer be
derived from the apolitical order constituted by the relations of production
and exchange. So to the extent that the market has become politicized, the
requirement for direct legitimation of social relations, which existed in
precapitalist societies, reappears in the modern era (Habermas 1970, 102).

Loss of the independent power of capitalism to legitimate social relations has created a problem of circularity. Decisive for the legitimation
of the state in the modern era is that the level of justification has become
reflective (Habermas 1979, 185). States justify their actions through presumptions and procedures—namely, all of the presumptions and procedures that constitute interest-group liberalism—that are not themselves
based on any normative order (they can't be because capitalist instrumental rationality allows for none). For example, when we say that electoral
outcomes are fair because the process is procedurally open to all, we offer
a justification of government that ignores the real-world obstacles to po-

litical participation by the disadvantaged. When we defend the distribution of wealth by offering as justification the efficiency of free exchanges as a means for allocating resources, we ignore all of the market flaws that make exchanges in real societies anything but free. Nevertheless, procedural fairness and the efficiency of the market are the bedrock justifications given for Western social structure even though they are grounded in no normative order. Indeed, they explicitly renounce any systemic tendency with respect to differing values and divergent outcomes.

Rather, these justificatory presumptions and procedures exist to satisfy the demands of the legitimation crisis and are accepted, not because they make sense morally or ethically, but because they serve that social function. In this sense, they are reflective (self-validating to the extent that validation is considered relevant by the established order): "The procedures and presuppositions of justification are themselves now the legitimating grounds on which the validity of legitimation is based" (Habermas 1979, 185).

To rationalize this apparently irrational situation is the central challenge to modern legal theory. In Habermas's view, "procedural law must be enlisted to build a legitimation filter into the decisional processes of [bureaucracies] still oriented as much as ever toward efficiency" (Habermas 1996, 440). He hastens to add that participatory administrative practices must not be considered a substitute for legal protections, which are expressions of normative consensus. Participatory administration certainly may produce good decisions and it serves a clear legitimating function. But we should not allow the efficacy and popularity of a decision process to excuse its violation of someone's fundamental liberties. Still, administrative procedures "are ex ante effective in legitimating decisions that, from a normative point of view, substitute for acts of legislation or adjudication" (ibid., 441). On this view, "a legal norm has validity whenever the state guarantees two things at once" (ibid., 448). First, the state must ensure compliance among the population at large, compelled by coercive force if necessary. Second, the state must guarantee the institutional preconditions for the legitimate development of the norm itself, so that it is always at least possible for the citizens to comply out of respect for the law instead of fear of coercion (ibid.).

In the discourse theory of democracy advanced by Habermas, the procedures for the production of law form the only possible source of legitimacy that is not anchored in a metaphysical worldview. Procedures of democratic discourse make it possible for issues and contributions, information and reasons, to flow freely. They secure a discursive character for political will-formation and, thereby, ground the assumption that "results issuing from proper procedure are more or less reasonable" (ibid.). From this perspective Habermas foresees that constitutional democracy will become "at once the outcome and the accelerating catalyst of a rationalization of the lifeworld reaching far beyond the political. The sole substantial aim of this project is the gradual improvement of institutionalized procedures of rational collective will-formation," procedures that do not prejudge participants or their goals (ibid., 489). By rationalizing the power of markets and bureaucracies and creating the possibility that legal commands may be regarded as both social facts and legitimate norms, public discourse allows modern societies to be integrated not only through instrumental rationality but also by shared values and mutual understandings (ibid., 39).

For Rawls, on the other hand, the question of success in public deliberation would seem to have little to do with the problem of legitimacy. For Rawls the key question is not whether basic decisions about social and economic relationships are legitimate, but rather whether they are just. Rawls's classical formulation of the two principles of justice is, by now, well known to most social theorists. Justice requires, first, that "each person is to have an equal right to the most extensive basic liberty compatible with a similar liberty for others," and, second, that "social and economic inequalities are to be arranged so that they are both (a) reasonably expected to be to everyone's advantage and (b) attached to positions and offices open to all" (Rawls 1971, 60). These are the principles, according to Rawls, that reasonable persons in the original position would agree to. Their decision is legitimate because it is reasonable, the result of a general and wide reflective equilibrium.

Rawls contrasts this situation with the view of Habermas, which he characterizes as suggesting that the test of moral truth or validity is full rational acceptance by all parties in the ideal discourse situation with all requisite conditions of procedural fairness satisfied. Rawls specifically denies that the justification of his principles is based in any way on systems of opinion or belief. They are no more subject, he claims, to such preferences than are the axioms, principles, and rules of inference of mathematics or logic (Rawls 1995, 141–142, 144). In offering this justification, he makes no appeal to any source of authority beyond generally accepted forms of reasoning found in common sense and the settled methods and conclusions of science. As for the preferences and values of specific persons, Rawls assumes only the existence of reasonable comprehensive doctrines and the possibility of their forming an overlapping consensus. "A doctrine is fully comprehensive when it covers all recognized values and virtues within one rather precisely articulated scheme of thought; whereas a doctrine is only partially comprehensive when it comprises certain (but not all) nonpolitical values and virtues and is rather loosely articulated" (Rawls 1993, 175; see also 224). Existence of such doctrines is regarded as a fact about the political and cultural nature of a pluralist democratic society. Rawls further assumes that these facts can be used like any others; reference can be made to them and assumptions can be made about them without relying on the religious, metaphysical, or moral content of such doctrines (Rawls 1995, 144).

Rawls further argues that a singular advantage of his approach is that it demonstrates that in a democratic society marked by a reasonable pluralism, stability of the political and social order *for the right reasons* is at least possible. In contrast, when citizens are united by their comprehensive doctrines, their positions are not embedded in, or connected with, a shared political conception (Rawls 1995, 146).[3] In such cases, "there exists only a modus vivendi, and society's stability depends on a balance of forces" in potentially fluctuating circumstances (ibid., 147). The notion of political liberalism, on the other hand, does not rely on the concept of moral truth applied to its own political judgments. It says only that "political judgments are reasonable or unreasonable, and it lays out political ideals, principles, and standards as criteria" for reasonableness (ibid., 149). Rawls concludes his comparison with Habermas with the claim that "legitimacy is a weaker idea than justice and imposes weaker constraints on what can be done. It is also institutional, though there is of course an essential connection with justice. . . . Democratic decisions and laws are legitimate, not because they are just but because they are legitimately enacted in accordance with an accepted legitimate democratic procedure" (ibid., 175). The clear implication, of course, is that the validity as a norm that Habermas claims for the product of his political discourse is genuinely available only when enactments go beyond procedural legitimacy to achieve justice.[4]

For their part, most advocates of full liberalism see more commonalities than differences in the work of Rawls and Habermas. Of greatest importance is that both Rawls and Habermas insist that citizens converge "on the same reasons, rather than agree for different reasons" (Bohman 1996, 182–183). For Habermas, citizens must agree to the same propositions for the same reasons for the outcome to be democratic. This might be said to constitute a strong principle of legitimacy. Laws must meet with the agreement of all citizens in a discursive law-making process that is itself reasonably constituted. For full liberalism, however, convergence is not a requirement of public reason, but merely an ideal of democratic citizenship. From this perspective, legitimacy requires only that a law be the "outcome of a participatory process that is fair and open to all citizens and thus includes their publicly accessible reasons" (ibid., 183–184). Unanimity on outcomes or reasons is not required. The implications of these contrasting views of the basis for legitimating the outcomes of public discourse can be seen more clearly if one examines the competing styles of reasoning advocated by full liberalism, Habermas, and Rawls and the role that particular interests plays in each.

Democratic Reasoning: A Question of Style

Public discourse, as advocates of full liberalism conceive it, may require vast changes in the political status quo in order to ensure a balance of political influence among citizens. But it imposes minimal restrictions on the style of reasoning citizens may employ. Public discourse, simply put, requires the use of public reasons (Gutmann and Thompson 1996). Reasons are public when "they are convincing enough to motivate each citizen, even a dissenter, to continue to cooperate in deliberation even after the decision has been made" (Bohman 1996, 35). The distinguishing characteristic of a public reason is that it is offered to a general and unrestricted audience, rather than a specialized and restricted collective. Nothing about public discourse requires that a reason offered in defense of a position be the most important one in the proponent's mind, or even that it be genuinely held; it requires only that it be public in this particular sense. Ultimately, social practices and forms of discourse are rational to the extent that they promote the acquisition and use of knowledge in the public sphere. Because deliberative politics has no single substantive domain, no more specific concept of rationality can be adduced (Bohman 1996, 46–53).

A clear implication of this view is that the interests of individuals, while not entirely explaining human behavior (Gutmann 2003, 123–124), are the primary motive factor in public discourse. Because the goal of participation in such discourse is to solve problems together with others who have distinct perspectives and interests, public deliberation does not require alteration or abandonment of those individual interests. What is required is a solution to the problem of political inequity. This can be achieved through better organization of existing interests into collectives and through institutional innovations in the areas of voting rights, campaign finance, and regulation of public discourse. Once citizens are successful in forming movements around their shared interests, procedural changes in the decision process (disclosure, public meetings, and hearing requirements) as well as in the balance of resources needed to participate in the process will be required. Distributional equity in the area of political influence is to be achieved by prohibiting both infringements on free speech and deliberative inequalities in governmental processes (Bohman 1996, 55, 134–135, 138–141). In short, full liberalism's formula for controlling the mischief of faction is a carefully engineered discursive system and a perfectly leveled political playing field.

For his part, Habermas has a more demanding theory of public discourse. In his view, the purpose of discourse in the public sphere is to allow citizens actually to resolve their normative differences. Discourses help citizens test the truth claims of opinions and norms that may previously have been taken for granted, but are no longer simply assumed. In such a discourse, the force of one's argument is the only permissible form of compulsion and the cooperative search for truth is the only permissible motive (Habermas 1973b, 168). This dimension of social activity, where practical action and interpretive reason are the core values of interaction, is what Habermas calls communicative action (or symbolic interaction). Communicative action involves conversation governed by binding consensual norms that define reciprocal expectations about behavior and which must be understood and recognized by each actor involved (Habermas 1970, 92). The resulting communicative power "is exercised in the manner of a siege. It influences the premises of judgment and decision making in the political system without intending to conquer the system itself" (Habermas 1996, 486–487).

The concept of communicative reason advanced by Habermas is essentially procedural. But Habermas's communicative reason allows no surrender to the skepticism that presumes the equivalency of particular interests, that makes no distinctions between the values of peoples' preferences. Habermas is attempting to rescue a concept of reason from the disintegration of metaphysical and religious worldviews that has left us only with isolated forms of rationality wherein religion, science, economics, and virtually every other system of thought are glibly reconciled with one another by referring only to aspects of human experience within which they are valid. The object is a concept of reason that is "skeptical and postmetaphysical, but not defeatist" (Habermas 1992, 116).[5] The alternative would be to make do with technical rationality (instrumental reason) as the sole admissible value, which is not seen explicitly as a value at all because it seems to coincide with rationality as such (Habermas 1973a, 264). The price to be paid for doing so is a form of decisionism that divorces reason from the selection of higher-level goals. Value statements are stamped with the stigma of irrationality, so that the priority of one value over the other—and thus the persuasiveness that a value claims with respect to action—simply cannot be rationally justified. Under such circumstances, the values held by those in dominant social positions are not subject to effective challenge. And when questions concerning the practical implications of human values are eliminated from the realm of knowledge (which has been reduced to empirical science and its instrumental correlates), the resolution of differing interests is placed beyond any and every public authority committed to reason.

Whereas this placing of values beyond reason might be regarded by some as a positive turn of events, allowing for the development of individual reason for application in classical liberalism's free market in ideas, it strikes Habermas as more likely that persons would find it frighteningly anomic and would look for something else to help them reconcile competing value claims. The result would be desperate attempts by alienated citizens "to secure socially binding precommitments on practical questions . . . by a return to the closed world of mythical images and powers" (Habermas 1973a, 265–267). The resurgence of various forms of fundamentalism around the world seem to be indicative of just such a process at work.

Although Habermas and advocates of full liberalism may differ markedly on the ultimate role of particular interests in public discourse, they apparently agree on two essentials. First, it is doubtful that either would deny that interests are and will remain the raw material of collective decision making. They differ mainly on how intensively and by what means that raw material should be processed into a finished product. Second, effective public discourse will require substantial changes in the distribution of political resources so that no advantage accrues to those whose arguments are neither persuasive (for Habermas) nor representative of the majority (for full liberalism). Again, they might differ on what the critical resources are and how their distribution might be adjusted, but both Habermas and advocates of full liberalism would agree (we think) that effective public discourse will require new rules for a game that would allow citizens to advocate their particular views with a higher degree of fundamental fairness.

The style of reasoning and approach to particular interests advocated by Rawls, on the other hand, is fundamentally different. In his view, people must be allowed to continue being rational (in pursuit of their own interests), but they must agree to a fundamental political structure that requires them to be reasonable. Neither reason nor rationality (of even a highly technical sort) can be sacrificed because then merely reasonable persons would have no ends of their own worth pursuing, whereas merely rational persons would "lack a sense of justice and fail to recognize the independent validity of the claims of others" (Rawls 1993, 52). In contrasting his view with that of Habermas, Rawls notes that Habermas maintains that political liberalism cannot avoid "the questions of truth and the philosophical conception of the person" (Rawls 1995, 150). Rawls does not see why this is so. For Rawls, political liberalism can avoid both of these ideas and substitute others—such as the reasonable and the conception of persons as free and equal citizens (ibid.). This approach is possible if the agreement reached in the original position is viewed as a joint precommitment to certain principles that then become an irrevocable public basis of justification (Freeman 1990). In this way, societies as well as individuals have found it useful to bind themselves through precommitments (Elster 1984). As Ulysses tied himself to the mast, so citizens in a democracy must resist the siren song of particular interests by tying themselves to the fundamental elements of a political order (e.g., a constitution). For the class of public discourses handled in this way, the interests of particular persons are literally banished from the process. Then, with this structure of reasonableness (fairness) firmly established, citizens may once again be allowed to exercise rationality in pursuit of their own values.

Thus Habermas, Rawls, and full liberalism provide three contrasting views of the nature of public discourse. Full liberalism sees a process essentially similar to that existing in most contemporary democracies, but significantly amended through both procedural and substantive reforms designed to level the political playing field for all parties so that permanent majorities and minorities (permanent winners and losers) do not exist. The object of full liberalism is to produce substantial majorities for important decisions (made up of people who adopt the same position for different reasons) and to ensure that the minority views the decision process in a sufficiently positive light that it is willing to continue in the deliberative process in the hope that some of its perspective will eventually be taken up by the majority. Differences in interest among individuals are not ultimately resolved so much as they are reconciled for the present.

Habermas can be seen as suggesting a two-track approach. Law and political decisions in a complex and pluralistic society can be rational and hence legitimate in the deliberative democratic sense. That is, collective decisions can be rationally authored by the citizens to whom they are addressed if the decision-making process includes two basic elements. First, the process must be open to inputs from a vibrant, informal, and thoroughly intellectual public sphere. Second, the discursive process must be structured so as to support the rationality specific to each type of discourse and to ensure appropriate implementation of decisions (Bohman 1996, 177). This structural approach locates public reason in the discursive structures of a shared political culture. It produces a consensual expression of the general will that links the public and its fully democratic discourse with the legislature and administration pursuing their inherently more elitist tasks.

Rawls's approach is at once more limited and more demanding. It starts from the observation that, in everyday speech, we understand perfectly well the difference between what is rational and what is reasonable. We can easily say, for instance, that "their proposal is perfectly rational given their bargaining position, but it is nevertheless highly unreasonable" (Rawls 1993, 48). This example, beyond showing how the rational can become the enemy of the reasonable, shows specifically where Rawls presumes the divergence of reason and rationality begins. Its source is the interference of particular interests with impartial reasoning. If decision makers can be isolated from the effects of interest, they can, using the precepts of common sense, arrive at a position they can support unanimously for the same (correct) reason. This unanimity can then serve as a binding precommitment on fundamental issues that will result in just arrangements in the realm of social reality. In this way, it is possible to reconcile reasonableness and rationality.

According to Rawls, we know that people are reasonable where others are concerned when they are willing to "govern their conduct by a principle from which they and others reason in common" (Rawls 1993, 49). Thus the disposition to be reasonable is neither derived from, nor necessarily hostile to, specific forms of rationality. "But it is incompatible with egoism as it is related to the disposition to act morally" (ibid.). We are still free, perhaps more so than ever, to have and advance our own preferences and opinions because the limits of public reason do not apply to our personal deliberations and reflections. Public reason governs citizens only as they engage in political advocacy in the public forum and engage each other on issues involving questions of fundamental political arrangements (ibid., 215). But in that limited arena, public reason should govern with an iron hand.

The specific character of these three approaches to public reasoning can be seen more clearly by examing the implications of each for the role of scientific experts. In the course of that discussion it should also be possible to discern what these approaches suggest about public discourse concerning environmental issues.

Experts and the Environment in Public Discourse

Table 3.1 compares the approaches to public discourse advocated by full liberalism, Jürgen Habermas, and John Rawls. In no way have we done full justice to the richness and complexity of these competing views. We have,

Table 3.1
Summary of three approaches to public discourse

	Bohman, Gutmann and Thompson (full liberalism)	Habermas (ideal discourse)	Rawls (public reason)
Prerequisites of discourse	Equality of *both* access and influence	Shared political culture	Reasoning from the original position
Standard of success	Plurality rule with minority acceptance	General consensus for shared reasons	Unanimity for the right reasons
Style of reasoning	Good faith bargaining	Tests of competing validity claims	Search for binding precommitments
Role of interests	Primary motivation for action	Source of competing validity claims	Eliminated from reasoning process
Role of experts	Source of bargaining chips	Practical testing of competing claims	No role in basic decisions

however, presented an outline of each that is sufficient to allow us to take the next step. That is, we are now able to suggest what each of these views implies for the expertise-driven field of environmental policy.

In discussing the role of experts in public discourse, full liberalism begins with the observation that differentiation of functions within deliberative institutions meets some of the challenge to collective decision making posed by the unavoidable fact of social complexity. It is perfectly permissible to have a variety of deliberative roles as well as an epistemic division of labor within deliberation and decision making. In fact, this state of affairs is practically unavoidable: "Neither capacities nor acquired knowledge can be assumed to be evenly or widely distributed" (Bohman 1996, 162). These are scarce resources in complex societies. So citizens inevitably "surrender their autonomy to experts, delegates, and other forms of division of labor" (ibid., 168).

At first blush this might appear to be a rather undemocratic position for an advocate of "full liberalism." But this position is qualified in a significant way. Experts cannot assume that their special knowledge will have practical effect unless they can successfully take on the lay perspective. This is because the division of epistemic labor depends on public trust to be effective. Bohman warns that although science is a tempting standard by which to judge public opinion, that ideal would be difficult to institutionalize given the facts of political pluralism and social complexity. Moreover, appeals to external scientific standards would, all too often, violate the norm of publicity that is central to full liberalism's concept of public discourse (Bohman 1996, 64, 169, 240).

It seems clear that, ultimately, the information provided by modern science has no different role in a system of full liberalism than any other decision premise generated by the citizenry. Bohman suggests that we use "public impact statements" to gauge the extent to which public reasons expressed by those affected by a collective decision were taken up in the decision process (Bohman 1996, 190). An environmental decision would be validated not because its environmental impact had been judged acceptable, but because all participants in the dispute had gotten enough of what they wanted to continue participating in the public discourse. One is strongly reminded of the mitigation process in coastal zone protection, which allows for the destruction of one wetland here if another can be created there. This approach makes perfect sense if environmental values are regarded as essentially fungible resources.

Habermas's view of the role of experts is, perhaps, more subtle and nuanced than that suggested by full liberalism. And it is correspondingly more difficult to summarize. He begins with the observation that neither the optimistic assumption of the convergence of technology and democracy, nor the pessimistic assumption that technology excludes democracy, is in any way warranted. For Habermas, reciprocal communication between scientists and decision makers is both possible and necessary. Experts must advise decision makers, and politicians must consult scientists, in accordance with practical necessity. On the one hand, the development of new scientific and technical capabilities is governed by an order of needs and historically determined interpretations of those needs—in short, by political values. On the other hand, social interests, as reflected in political values, are significantly regulated by being tested against the technical possibilities for their gratification (Habermas 1970, 60–67).

With this general description as a starting point, Habermas describes the empirical conditions that he assumes are necessary for such a pragmatic use of science to develop. These conditions include the development of a more thoroughly intellectual citizenry, a reduction in the secrecy and economic competition that impedes the free flow of information, and an end to the bureaucratic encapsulation resulting from scientific specialization that isolates scientists from us and from each other. These three conditions, if achieved, will turn out to have had a common origin. Given the high degree of division of labor typical of the modern sciences, "the lay public often provides the shortest path of internal understanding between mutually estranged specialists. . . . This necessity for the translation of scientific information, which grows out of the needs of the research process itself," also benefits the endangered communication between the general public and their political representatives (Habermas 1970, 75–78) through the reduction of scientific information into ordinary language.

Ordinary language—with its grammatical complexity, propositional structure, and reflexive character—has all the merits of a multipurpose form of communication. Its capacity for interpretation and range of circulation is practically unlimited. It is superior to the special codes of scientific communication in that it provides a perspective from which the costs of actions take by differentiated subsystems of society can be appreciated and their effects on groups and individuals assessed. From its more universal horizon of understanding, ordinary language can, in principle, translate any proposition found in the exotic tongues of science. But it cannot return messages with operational significance to all types of addresses. For translations into other special codes—such as the languages used by the steering mechanisms of money and administrative power—ordinary language remains dependent on the Rosetta Stone of the law. Thus, normative messages derived from specialized discourses can circulate throughout the whole of society only in the language of law (Habermas 1996, 55–56). Law is the mediating language in which specialized discourse groups communicate with one another.

Finally, Rawls has a view of the role of experts that is different from that of either Habermas or the advocates of full liberalism. For Rawls, the discourse of a civil society is always about political questions of basic justice in which "all discussions are from the point of view of citizens" (Rawls 1995, 139). This discourse will not be the only ongoing discourse, but it will be the only one that fully involves public reason. Other discourses can be important socially, economically, politically, and so forth, but they still will concern less fundamental matters (Rawls 1993, 214). The discourse of a civil society includes all citizens, an omnilogue in which there are no experts. The argument "is normative and concerned with ideals and values"; it is always about principles rather than facts per se (Rawls 1995, 140–141). Thus, decisions in the original position are based purely on "the authority of human reason present in society" rather than appeal to the superiority of an information base or deductions from such a base.

The implications of such a view for environmental problems might seem clear. The implications of just decisions for the environment, whether good or bad, would not seem to matter so long as the decisions *are* just. But that view underestimates the depth with which Rawls has explored the implications of his theory. Rawls allows that the status of the natural world and our proper relationship to it is not necessarily a constitutional essential or a basic question of justice in the sense that he uses those terms. But environmental questions can become constitutional essentials and issues of basic justice when our duties and obligations to future generations and to other societies become involved (Rawls 1993, 246). Under those circumstances, the correct approach is to subject the issue to reasoning from the original position. For example, in approaching a dispute between two societies over an environmental question, the preferred resolution is that which would be agreed to in principle by rationally self-interested individuals who were unaware of which society would eventually be their own. Experts produce necessary information, but they play no special role in resolving basic environmental issues that are properly conceptualized as issues of justice involving basic distributional principles.

Given that most serious environmental dilemmas and contradictions entail conflict over the nature and commitment to be accorded the irretrievable, the irrevocable, the nonrenewable, the long term, and the needs of future generations (sustainable development), the Rawlsian approach to rational environmental allocation between generations is even more instructive. Rawls, following an idea of Henry Sidgwick, argues that deliberative rationality requires persons to attend to their future good viewed in its whole. In the same way, the life of a people is conceived of as a scheme of fair cooperation spread out through historical time. The relationship between its various generations is "governed by the same conception of justice that regulates the cooperation of contemporaries" (Rawls 1971, 289). The essential point, of course, is that the collective will concerning the provision for future generations is subject, as are all other social decisions on fundamental issues, to the principles of justice (ibid., 297, 416–417).

Rawls concedes that it might be argued that a democratic state has no business intervening for the sake of future generations in the deliberations of its citizens, even when the public is manifestly mistaken (on the long view) in its choice of distributional principles. Any constitutional order, even under the most favorable conditions, is only a structure of imperfect procedural justice. People deliberating within its confines may commit injustices that are evident and demonstrable as such by the same conception of justice that underlies the regime itself. Under those circumstances, there is nothing sacrosanct about the public's decision concerning an appropriate level of savings for the benefit of future generations and the bias of the future generation in favor of its own time preference deserves no special respect (Rawls 1971, 295).

It is clear that, in Rawls's view, there is no rational basis for preferring the immediate over the long term. Indeed, other things being equal, we should arrange things at the earlier stages of life so as to permit greater happiness at the later stages. A rising plan of distribution keeps our hands free until more relevant facts allow for better distributional choices. It is also preferable because later activities can increase overall satisfaction by incorporating, binding together, and extending the results and enjoyments of an entire life's experience into a coherent structure as a plan of declining value never could (Rawls 1971, 420–421). Thus Rawls argues in favor of binding precommitments that provide for an increasing level of things of value as one moves forward in time.

A Deliberate Conclusion

Democratic theorists often disdain concern with policy practicalities. In turn, critics have often condemned theories of deliberative democracy as abstract, impractical, and irrelevant (deLeon 1997). Bohman offers the complaint that "Everyone was talking about deliberation, but no one was saying what it is or how it could work under real social conditions" (Bohman 1996, ix). Even more often, political theorists exhibit an unawareness of the extent to which ideas can be found embodied in ongoing political experiments and routines. Dryzek, for example, argues that "any deeper democratization of the liberal capitalist state is often a remote prospect. . . . Once the basic parameters of capitalist democracy have been achieved, the state is peculiarly resistant to further democratization" (Dryzek 1996, 36). His sweeping conclusion, however, is undercut by his own brief empirical analysis of a handful of deliberative institutional innovations in state-associated democratization, which he finds have indeed produced advances in democratic scope (the domains under democratic control) and authenticity (substantiveness), if not franchise (number and distribution of participants) (ibid., 40–42). And the universe of natural experiments in environmental democracy of the state is far richer and more extensive than Dryzek suggests. Collectively, these policy experiments have significantly advanced democratic scope, authenticity, *and* franchise.

Perhaps it is time to take more seriously Paehlke's heretical remonstrance against "an overly theoretical approach to the problem of environment and democracy" (Paehlke 1996, 20). By contrasting the theoretical perspectives of Bohman, Gutmann, and Thompson with those of Habermas and Rawls, we can find empirical grounding in an inventory of wide-reaching institutionalizations of deliberative environmental democracy overlooked or underestimated by Dryzek and others.

The next logical step is to examine the potential of each of these three approaches to public deliberation as policy theories that could explain—and suggest strengthening of—ongoing democractic environmental experimentalism (Dorf and Sabel 1998). The objective is to describe more fully the implications of these theoretical perspectives for deliberative structuring and implementation of environmental initiatives, institutions, and procedures in polyarchic democracies (Cohen and Sabel 1997). Before undertaking such a closer examination of the potentialities of mandated discourse, normative precommitment, and full liberalism, we offer here a few speculations about the range of application that each of these theories might enjoy.

In full liberalism, public deliberation is, to put it a bit crudely, a matter of political logrolling conducted on more level ground. The system of interest-group liberalism we currently experience would be amended primarily to ensure greater openness in decision processes and an equality of whatever resources can be translated into political influence. Full liberalism is, in short, one of fair tradeoffs. The implication for environmental issues is clear. The very idea of tradeoffs suggests the existence of values that can be easily exchanged. To the extent that environmental issues present that opportunity, one could deploy a theory such as Gutmann and Thompson's to guide negotiations among the parties, such as those entailed in the politics of urban brownfields redevelopment policy in the United States. Since 1995 the U.S. Environmental Protection Agency has been providing funding to localities to bring together and involve community groups, investors, lenders, developers, and other affected parties, including low-income, minority, and other disadvantaged communities, to address the issues of cleaning up contaminated sites and returning them to productive use (Zeitler 2000). Certainly the spirit of this program, whatever its actual implementation (so far in more than 100 locations for up to $200,000 each), is consistent with full liberalism's broad prescription for practical measures to realize liberalism more fully.

The approach to public deliberation advocated by Habermas emphasizes an ideal discourse situation in which the positions of contending parties are not merely compromised, but their underlying disagreements are resolved by subjecting their divergent presumptions to a test of validity. Environmental problems arising from a context that is both fact-rich and imperfectly understood might profitably be subjected to such a process. The development and sharing of analytical skills and a broad information base under circumstances of equal status and consensual decision might reasonably be expected to produce results that are both of high quality (perhaps the highest possible) and not subject to derailment at the implementation stage, as often are the results of nominal compromise. At their best, environmental impact assessment (EIA) systems are attempts to institutionalize this kind of public deliberation.

The conversion of scientific information into ordinary language and its propagation throughout society in the form of legal propositions and conclusions is strongly suggestive of the policy theory underlying EIA (Bartlett and Kurian 1999). As a mechanism for enhancing the exchange of ideas between scientists and decision makers, between scientists and citizens, and between scientists in one specialization and those in another, the communication process fostered by EIA can be seen as an attempt to approximate the ideal discourse situation advocated by Habermas.

Where EIA fails to live up to the prescription of Habermas is with respect to the requirement for consensus. In the United States and elsewhere, EIA has not been interpreted as requiring decision by consensus. It produces something approximating consensus only when all the participants possess the resources required to extend and broaden the EIA review sufficiently that the project being evaluated becomes cost-prohibitive without the acquiescence of its critics. Even if this nominal form of consensus is achieved, there is no assurance that the competing claims of the participants have been truly put to a test of validity and those found wanting eliminated from the discourse. This would still trouble Habermas because he is convinced that humankind can recognize nature as another subject in discourse only when humans can communicate without compulsion and come to recognize themselves in each other. If people could do that, they would become able to encounter nature as an opposing partner in a possible interaction instead of as an object of technical control (Habermas 1970, 88). This breakthrough is Habermas's ultimate objective because his underlying motivation is to do justice to the integrity of both the life world and social systems and to show how each presupposes the other (Bernstein 1985, 22).

Finally, the original position of Rawls is the modern prototype of reasoning abstracted from experience. Its power and appeal results precisely from this fact. It offers the possibility of a justification and legitimation for collective decisions that is entirely deontolgical and postmetaphysical. It relies in no way on the comprehensive doctrines and belief systems that divide humanity. And in the environmental context, it provides a decisional baseline that can assert priority over the interests associated with any particular dispute. When an environmental issue poses a value that is absolute, as the extinction of species clearly does, it would be entirely understandable to seek a normative precommitment that would resolve the dispute in a more or less automatic fashion. Unsurprisingly, we find this principle at work in such policies as the Convention on International Trade in Endangered Species (CITES) and the U.S. Endangered Species Act (Sagoff 1988). Both resist the idea of contemporary cost and benefit calculations in favor of a binding precommitment to the long-term protection of biodiversity as a collective value. This provides a conceptually clear illustration of the role of experts in deliberations of justice. No weighing of alternative measures is called for, no close analysis of the interests at stake. Scientists are relied on only to produce the information necessary to trigger the precommitments that have been arrived at by rational decision makers in the original position and thus to set these in motion—steps that can be understood by all because they have been reduced to the language of legal mandates.

This approach has also been applied in other policies aimed at protecting absolute environmental values. Examples are international policies for preserving the protective and regulative qualities of the Earth's atmosphere, namely, the Vienna Convention and (so far much less successful) Framework Convention on Climate Change (Caldwell 1996). The 1985 Vienna Convention was a "constitutional" precommitment: agreement that threats to the ozone layer were a serious problem, covenant to engage in extensive further discussions, and commitment to take meaningful but unspecified action should further research and monitoring and discussion led to the near-consensus conclusion that the absolute value of the ozone layer was threatened. This is exactly what happened in the next thirty months that led to the Montreal Protocol and beginning of successful international policy action to phase out substances harmful to the ozone layer. The 1992 Framework Convention on Climate Change entails the same "constitutional" precommitment, with discourse over the certainty and extent of the problem and the specifics of policy action still ongoing.

These remarks should not be interpreted as the typical attempt to have our cake and eat it too. We do not suggest that environmental rationality is a happy medium, or a cheerful synthesis of all three views we have discussed. Our point is that the environmental problematique and the forms of thought it calls out for are too varied to be slotted neatly into either the categories of rationality in the contemporary social sciences or even the more subtle schools of thought concerning reason in public deliberation. Neither is ours an argument for an environmental variant of contingency theory. We do not advocate a "whatever works" approach because that mentality lends itself too easily to the importation of instrumentally rational but critically unexamined assumptions about the meaning of success (Bartlett 1994).

If the divergent approaches to reasoning we have described are ever to serve as the foundation for development and practice of a distinctly ecological concept of rationality, the choice of democratic procedures for deciding particular issues must be dictated by an understanding of the theoretical demands of problem contexts, in both functional and situational terms. In effect, the niche occupied by an environmental issue and its functional relationship to its policy environment must be identified if the ecology of any environmental problem is to be understood. And that ecological understanding is what will ultimately give substance to the idea of ecological rationality (Hayward 1995b).

4

Normative Precommitment in Environmental Politics and Policy

Probably no philosopher of the twentieth century has had a greater impact on democratic theory than John Rawls. Yet one particular area of political theorizing has remained barely touched by Rawls's groundbreaking work: theorists of environmental politics have seemed strangely indifferent to both *A Theory of Justice* and *Political Liberalism*. A few environmental writers have cited Rawls in commenting on particular issues of special concern to them—animal rights and environmental justice are cases in point. But it is a recurring curiosity in the study of environmental justice that major contributors to the field can compose entire books and omit any serious discussion of the theories of Rawls. In fact, a number of recent volumes (Bryant 1995; Bullard 1994; Camacho 1998; Faber 1998; Lester, Allen, and Hill 2001) do not mention Rawls at all, much less discuss his theories (though one finds room to mention Dan Quayle). Others discuss Rawls, but only in the limited context of the implications of his views for a particular problem of environmental ethics such as animal rights (see, e.g., Wenz 1988). This is made all the more curious by the fact that many in the field concede that moral exploration of environmental issues necessarily involves a process of "reflective equilibrium" that is closely associated with the work of Rawls (de-Shalit 2000, 22). Nevertheless, most environmental theorists—Andrew Dobson (1998) being a prominent exception—have seemed reluctant to embrace Rawls's general philosophical perspective and to explore its implications for environmental politics. Likewise, important collections of scholarship about Rawls typically offer scant attention to the implications of his work for environmentalism (see, e.g., Davion and Wolf 2000).

The first potential problem is that Rawls's approach strikes many as simply a form of philosophical introspection (Dryzek 2000, vi). For democratic theorists generally, and environmentalists in particular, this quality of Rawls's approach seems to involve individuals mulling ethical dilemmas over in their own minds rather than any process of collective social action. To the extent that this is true, it makes Rawls's work particularly suspect in a field like environmental politics where a premium is placed on consciousness-raising linked to social action.

Second, the Rawlsian approach has been criticized as excessively concerned with procedure (Plumwood 2002). A preoccupation with putting the right processes of political reasoning and communication in place is seen as a problematic approach to "hearing the bad news from below." Proceduralism of this sort, it is argued, neglects the intimate relationships between process and product that underlie inequities among individuals as well as unsustainable decisions about the environment.

Finally, Rawls has been criticized for being too much a captive of the conventional liberalism that many hold responsible for the environmental problematique. The supposedly neutral premises advanced by Rawls have been characterized as reproductions of an established political order that reinforce the political disenfranchisement of historically disadvantaged interests, both human and nonhuman (Mouffe 1996).

With these three counts in the environmentalists' indictment of Rawls, what more needs to be said? Perhaps a great deal. In chapter 3, we characterized Rawls's approach as a search for "binding precommitments." Rawls's theory calls for those in a deliberative democracy to agree to constitutional essentials and basic principles of justice arrived at through a process of reasoning that divorces them from consideration of their own interests and preferences. In effect, Rawlsian citizens will agree in the abstract about what is fair before they take account of their own stakes in later decision-making processes. This is obviously a powerful tool within the limited range of its legitimate use—constitutional essentials, basic principles of justice, and fundamental normative choices. Rawls allows that the status of the natural world and our proper relationship to it does not *necessarily* fall into these categories, an assertion that undoubtedly alienates many environmentalists. But Rawls does indicate that environmental concerns *may* rise to this level of significance where our duties to other societies and to future generations become involved (Rawls 1993, 244–246). That is, binding precommitments may be the preferred way of addressing all-too-common problems involving sustainability or transboundary externalities, a large and hugely important category of environmental problems indeed.

Since it emerged as a political force, the environmental movement has repeatedly hit upon normative precommitment as a strategy for achieving its ends, finding it attractive as an approach that combines moral sensibility about the environment and potent symbolic politics (e.g., in the United States, the Title I of the National Environmental Policy Act, the Endangered Species Act, the swimmable and drinkable goals of the first Clean Water Act). Mark Sagoff (1988) in particular has written extensively about this. What has been missing has been any sort of philosophical grounding in terms of governance or democratic theory, thus muting its appeal as a policy strategy. This is what Rawls provides.

Thus it would be well for environmental theorists generally, and deliberative green democrats in particular, to explore Rawls's philosophy in greater breadth and depth in order to understand its significance for, and the policy importance of, binding precommitment as a strategy for achieving deliberative environmental democracy, environmental justice, and ecological rationality.

An "Initial Situation"

Rawls's central concern is to define the most appropriate conception of justice for specifying the fair terms of social cooperation between citizens regarded as free, equal, and fully cooperating members of society over a complete life and from one generation to the next (Rawls 1993, 3). This is crucial to Rawls because, in his view, justice is "the first virtue of social institutions, as truth is of systems of thought" (Rawls 1999a, 3). But Rawls's concern is not abstract or philosophical. In developing his theory of public reason, his self-declared aim is practical. He presents his theory as a conception of justice "that may be shared by citizens as a basis of a reasoned, informed, and willing political agreement" (Rawls 1993, 9). This should be a matter of great concern to environmentalists generally and to those in the environmental justice movement in particular. It is true that this focus on social institutions has led some to complain that he is indifferent to the fate of nonsentient elements of the environment (Wenz 1988). But Rawls's choice of subject should make his views highly relevant to those who are primarily concerned with race and class bias in the distribution of environmental risks in human society. Rawls's conception of social justice should be regarded, in the first instance, as a standard whereby the distributive aspects of the basic structure of a society can be assessed (Rawls 1999a, 8; 1993, 11–15).

His theory on the foundations of social institutions marks Rawls as a philosopher in the contractarian tradition of Rousseau and Kant. Rawls's principles of justice are, in his view, the principles that "free and rational persons concerned to further their own interests would accept in an initial position of equality as defining the fundamental terms of their association" (Rawls 1999a, 10). This reliance on the mechanism of self-interest has raised the ire of some environmentalists (de-Shalit 2000, 201). But it provides a useful starting point in addressing the issues of racial and class bias that animate much of the environmental justice community.

As with contract theories generally, Rawls's approach to developing principles of social cooperation is procedural. He employs the "veil of ignorance" as an initial situation (the "original position" in Rawls's terminology) to ensure that no one is advantaged or disadvantaged in the selection of basic principles by the outcome of natural chance or the contingencies of social circumstance (Rawls 1999a, 11; 1993, 23). In short, "one excludes the knowledge of those contingencies which set men at odds and allows them to be guided by their prejudices" (1999a, 17). In this way, the principles of justice are agreed to in an initial situation that is fair. Moreover, a society satisfying the principles chosen in this initial situation comes as close as a society can to being a voluntary scheme. This is because it meets the standard of fairness that free and equal persons would assent to under circumstances that are themselves fair (1999a, 12).

The role of self-interest in Rawls's theory has been the target of considerable criticism. Some have argued that Rawls's theory of public reason hovers uneasily between impartiality and mutual advantage, not really knowing which stance to adopt (Barry 1989). In fact, Rawls's theory finds solid ground between impartiality and mutual advantage, anchored firmly in the concept of reciprocity (Gibbard 1991, 266). Neither disinterest nor altruism is necessary for fairness, according to Rawls. Because everyone's well-being depends on a scheme of cooperation without which no one could have a satisfactory life, the division of advantages and disadvantages in a society aspiring to fairness must be such as to draw forth the willing participation of everyone, including those less well situated (Rawls 1999a,

13). This concept of reciprocity is so clearly compatible with the environmentalist's concern for the interdependence of humans and their environment that is seems remarkable it has escaped comment until now.

The veil of ignorance has been another target of criticism. Some have alleged that Rawls's method of reflective equilibrium is too limited in that it is essentially a process of private reflection (de-Shalit 2000, 24). There is a sense in which reflection on any subject is a private process. But Rawls structures his initial situation to produce a reflective equilibrium that can be shared. In the "original position" we know that people are rational. That is, we do not know what ends people will pursue, only that they will pursue them intelligently. As we explored at some length in chapter 2, we also know that people are reasonable where others are concerned, that they are willing to govern their conduct by a principle from which they and others can reason in common. This balancing of the rational and the reasonable is inevitably a collective enterprise because, although the disposition to be reasonable is not opposed to the rational, it is incompatible with egoism as it is related to the other-regarding disposition to act morally (Rawls 1999a, 49). Thus the reasonable enjoys a position of priority over the rational (Rawls 1993, 25). This expanded conception of human reason is particularly suggestive of the concept of ecological rationality as it has been discussed in the environmental literature (Bartlett 1986; 2005; Dryzek 1987; Plumwood 2002).

A final criticism related to the original position is that it produces a set of principles that apply only to those who are parties to the original agreement. In particular, it is complained that Rawls's theory "fails to endorse a duty of justice concerning nonsentient constituents of the environment" (Wenz 1988, 233). Rawls admits that his theory fails to embrace all moral relationships in that it leaves out any account of how we are to conduct ourselves toward animals and the rest of nature (Rawls 1999a, 15). But, as Andrew Dobson points out, Rawls is not precluding a concern for animals, it is just that he has not argued that such a concern can be motivated by reasons of justice (Dobson 1998, 181).[1] And given the fact that Rawls describes his theory as limited to the political sphere, the search for a foundation for animal rights was always destined to begin elsewhere (Rawls 1993, 8). So complaints on this score alleging a defect in Rawls's original position (Pritchard and Robison 1981) seek to hold Rawls accountable for failing to do something he never set out to do.

Procedures of Justice

Before describing the principles of justice posited by Rawls and exploring some of their implications, it may be useful to describe more fully the original position and the reasoning process that is to take place there. The approach employed by Rawls is an example of pure procedural justice. This approach is appropriate where there is no independent criterion for the right result. Rather, there is a correct (or fair) procedure such that the outcome is likewise correct (or fair) whatever it is, provided that the procedure has been properly followed (Rawls 1999a, 75). Deliberations in the original position have to do not with specific distributions of goods, but with the relationship between social positions. Social positions are the starting places, properly generalized and aggregated, of people in society. By choosing these positions as subjects of deliberation, we specify a general point of view from which to develop principles of justice that are intended to mitigate the arbitrariness of natural contingency and social fortune (ibid., 82). This general point of view provides the basis for a public justification of the liberal values reflected in Rawls's theory, which avoids disputes over religious and philosophical perspectives by offering reasons that can be shared solely by virtue of citizenship in a constitutional democracy (Evans 1999, 117–127).

So in the original position the parties want to ensure for themselves (and their descendents) the best situation in society. Doing so presumes not only fair procedures in the selection of principles of justice, but also the existence of certain conditions of justice. These may be described as the normal conditions under which human cooperation is both possible and necessary (Rawls 1999a, 109). There are objective conditions of justice, chief among them that natural and other resources are neither so abundant that schemes of cooperation become superfluous, nor so scarce that cooperative ventures must inevitably break down. There are also subjective conditions of justice, circumstances that make it necessary to have a theory of justice, which are present whenever persons possess their own plans of life such that they put forward conflicting claims to the division of social advantages under conditions of moderate scarcity (ibid., 110). What is sought by rational and reasonable persons under these conditions is "a set of principles, general in form and universal in application, that is to be publicly recognized as a final court of appeal for ordering the conflicting claims of moral persons" (ibid., 117).

Designed to yield such a set of principles, the original position is intended to set up a fair procedure so that any principles agreed to will be just. The objective, consistent with the idea of pure procedural justice, is to nullify the effects of specific contingencies that put persons at odds and tempt them to exploit social and natural circumstance to their own advantage (Rawls 1999a, 118). The parties in such a position have no basis for bargaining in the conventional sense. The know nothing of their situation in society or their natural assets. Therefore, no one is in a position to tailor principles to his own advantage. Without these limitations on knowledge, the bargaining problem of the original position would be hopelessly complex, making the required unanimity on a particular conception of justice impossible (ibid., 120–121). But in the absence of this knowledge, the principles of justice agreed to can make manifest, in the basic structure of society, the desire of humans to treat one another not only as means but as ends in themselves (ibid., 156). The veil of ignorance "prevents us from shaping our moral view to accord with our own particular attachments and interests. We do not look at the social order from our situation but take up a point of view that everyone can adopt on an equal footing. In this way we look at our society and our place in it objectively" (ibid., 453).

Having described the original position in some detail, it is now possible to describe the principles of justice that Rawls argues reasonable and rational persons would agree to in that position. We begin with Rawls's second principle, his principle of distributive justice, because it is on that principle that the interest of environmentalists has focused.

The Second Principle of Justice

Rawls's second principle of justice is that social and economic inequalities are to be arranged so that they are both (a) reasonably expected to be to everyone's advantage, and (b) attached to positions and offices open to all (Rawls 1999a, 53). The second clause of this principle (positions and offices open to all) has been the least controversial and is not closely related to our present concerns. We shall concentrate, therefore, on the first clause, that inequalities be reasonably expected to be to everyone's advantage.

There are, according to Rawls, two natural senses in which a distribution could be "to everyone's advantage." The first sense of this phrase is that distributions could be governed by Pareto optimality, that no one can be made better off without making someone else worse off (Rawls 1999a, 58). The second sense of the phrase, referred to by Rawls as the "difference principle," is stated as follows: "Assuming the framework of institutions required by equal liberty and fair equality of opportunity, the higher expectations of those better situated are just only if they work as part of a scheme which improves the expectations of the least advantaged members of society" (ibid., 65).

At least two questions arise naturally at this point. Why are the interests of the least favored the standard of distributional justice and what precisely is subject to distribution under this principle? It should be recalled that those who profit from unequal distributions are expected to earn those profits through contributions to society that benefit all of its members. Use of the "least favored" as a standard for judging this issue is founded on the realistic assumption that when the contributions of those in favored positions spread generally throughout society it is likely that if the least advantaged benefit so do others in between (Rawls 1999a, 71).

As for the subjects of distribution under the difference principle, these fall into several general categories. They include rights and liberties, social and economic opportunities, income and wealth, freedom of movement and occupation, access to the powers and prerogatives of office, and a sense of one's own self-worth (Rawls 1999a, 79; 1993, 181). These things Rawls regards as primary social goods, in the sense that they are of value to anyone regardless of their rational plan for life or their particular concept of the good (1999a, 223; 1993, 307). The effect of this principle is to transform the aims of a society's basic structure so that the total scheme of its institutions no longer emphasizes economic efficiency or other technocratic values. It is, rather, an agreement to regard the distribution of natural talents and other contingent advantages as a common asset. The objective is to ensure that all share in the greater social and economic benefits made possible by the complementarities of this distribution and the social synergy it creates (Rawls 1999a, 87).

In this way, the difference principle expresses a conception of reciprocity according to which the more advantaged, when they view the matter from an appropriately general perspective, recognize that the well-being of each depends on a scheme of social cooperation without which no one could have a satisfactory life. They also recognize that they can expect the willing cooperation of all only if the terms of the scheme are reasonable (Rawls 1999a, 88). Thus the difference principle takes equality as the basis of comparison, guaranteeing that those who have gained more must do so on terms that are justifiable to those who have gained less (ibid., 131). There are, however, certain kinds of social and economic tradeoffs about which this formulation of the difference principle might provide conflicting prescriptions. One is the provision of public goods. The other is the question of distributional fairness across generations.

Publics: Today and Tomorrow

Rawls's theory provides for the existence of public goods. It does not, however, specify a particular quantity of any specific public good. Rawls uses the conventional criteria to identify these goods, namely, publicness and indivisibility. He argues that all citizens must be provided with an equal amount of these goods (whatever they are) and that opting out or purchasing more not be allowed (Rawls 1999a, 235). He also argues that arranging for and financing these goods must be taken over by the state and that binding rules requiring payment by citizens for these services must be developed. From an appropriately general perspective, the necessity of this arrangement should be evident to all, and the use of coercion in the provision of public goods is, therefore, rational from each person's point of view (ibid., 236). This much is relatively uncontroversial. However, Rawls also identifies a class of public harms, the correction of which is appropriately within the purview of a just government.

The single example of a public harm offered by Rawls is the industry that sullies and erodes the natural environment. The costs associated with these harms, Rawls correctly observes, are not reckoned by the market. Commodities produced and sold in these markets are sold at much less than their marginal social costs. It is up to the enforcement arm of government to correct this imbalance between private and social accounting, as a matter of social justice (Rawls 1999a, 237). This is not an infringement on the liberty of the producer of such products. It is merely a recognition of the principle of reciprocity to which all would assent if the matter were viewed from an appropriately general perspective. In Rawls's own words, "to be held accountable to the principles of justice in one's dealings with others does not stunt our nature. Instead it realizes our social sensibilities and by exposing us to a larger good enables us to control our narrower impulses" (ibid., 403).

An important part of this larger good is a certain orientation to the future. From an individual perspective, there is no rational basis for preferring the immediate over the long term. Other things being equal, we should arrange things at the earlier stages so as to permit a happy life at the later ones. This rising (or, at least not declining) plan of life is preferable because later activities can often incorporate and bind together the results and enjoyments of an entire life into one coherent structure in ways that a declining plan of life cannot (Rawls 1999a, 421). At a collective level, a society regulated by a public sense of justice results in an increase over time of forces that tend to produce social stability (ibid., 436).

More concretely, persons in the original position are assumed by Rawls to have no information as to which generation they belong. Thus, questions of social justice arise between generations as well as within them.[2] Chief among these are questions of the conservation of natural resources and the maintenance of an environment capable of sustaining a just human society (Rawls 1999a, 118–119). The life of a people, in Rawls's view, is appropriately conceived as a scheme of cooperation spread out across historical time. It is to be governed by the same conception of justice that regulates the cooperation of contemporaries (ibid., 289). So the appropriate expectation in applying the difference principle is that of the long-term prospects of the least favored extending over future generations. "Each generation must not only preserve the gains of culture and civilization, and maintain intact those just institutions that have been established, but it must also put aside in each period of time a suitable amount of real capital accumulation" (ibid., 252). This combination of the difference principle with his principle of just savings significantly obviates the complaints of critics who charge that Rawls's principles provide insufficient guidance in establishing a savings rate (Paden 1997).

If all generations are to gain, the parties in the original position must agree to a savings principle that ensures that each generation receives its due from its predecessors and does its fair share for those to come (Rawls 1999a, 254). The objective of this accumulation is not to enrich later generations, but to maintain a society with a material base sufficient to establish effective and just institutions within which all the basic liberties can be realized (ibid., 256–257). The proper rate of savings for future generations is inherently problematic. Rawls describes a series of stages through which societies may pass, each of which suggests its own rate of savings (ibid., 286–288). But he recognizes that there is nothing sacrosanct about public decisions on this matter. Our current biases with respect to time preferences deserve no special respect and, in fact, the absence of the injured parties (future generations) makes present decisions all the more open to question (ibid., 261). The criterion for this decision is, however, somewhat easier to state as a general matter. It is that we require the parties to agree to a savings principle subject to the constraint that they would wish all preceding generations to have followed the very same principle (ibid., 111; Rawls 1993, 274). This standard gives substance to Rawls's claim that the fundamental organizing idea of public reason "is that of a society as a fair system of cooperation over time, *from one generation to the next*" (Rawls 1993, 15, emphasis added).

Among the background supporting institutions needed to achieve distributive justice is a guaranteed "social minimum" of material support (Rawls 1999a, 243). As Taylor (1993, 270) points out, any social minimum is dependent on maintaining some base level of environmental quality: "Because each member of every generation is entitled to the social minimum, social institutions must be arranged to sustain the level of environmental quality required to provide the social minimum into the indefinite future."

These questions of distributive justice have preoccupied environmentalists to the virtual exclusion of other aspects of Rawls's work. In particular, Rawls's first principle has been virtually ignored in the environmental literature. This may be a result of the fact that the first principle is described by Rawls as procedural in character and widely regarded by others as having little importance outside of the strictly political realm. This attitude is regrettable because, in Rawls's theory, the first principle is very nearly absolute and enjoys a clear priority over considerations related to the second principle. For this reason alone, environmentalists would do well to consider the implications of Rawls's entire theory before dismissing it as a foundation for environmental justice.

The First Principle of Justice

Rawls's first principle of justice is that "each person is to have an equal right to the most extensive scheme of basic liberties compatible with a similar scheme of liberties for others" (1999a, 53). While no one of these liberties can be absolute, owing to their reciprocal character, they are to be adjusted to form one system that is to be the same for all (ibid., 54). Important among these are political liberties, freedom of speech and assembly, liberty of conscience and freedom of thought, freedom of the person (including freedom from psychological oppression and physical assault), the right to hold personal property, and freedom from arbitrary arrest (ibid., 53). Not included in this list is the right to own certain kinds of property (notably, the means of production).

This first principle of liberty enjoys priority in the total system of justice envisioned by Rawls (1993, 294). The priority of liberty means that "whenever the basic liberties can be effectively established, a lesser or unequal liberty cannot be exchanged for an improvement in economic well being" (Rawls 1999a, 132). This is true even when those who benefit from the greatest efficiency, or together share the greater sum of advantages, are the same persons whose liberties are limited or denied (Rawls 1993, 295). Denial of equal liberty can be defended only where it is essential to change the conditions of civilization (as in a revolt against totalitarianism) so that in due course these liberties can be enjoyed. Within the realm of equivalent arrangements of liberty, that structure should be chosen which maximizes the worth of liberty (particularly political liberty) to the least advantaged within a complete scheme of liberty shared by all (ibid., 179). This standard is critical inasmuch as one of the main defects of constitutional government historically has been the failure to insure the fair value of political liberty (ibid., 198).

Rawls's principle of liberty is not, however, a prescription for license. There is a right vested in government to maintain public order and security. This is an enabling right, in the sense that it is a right government must have if it is to carry out its duty of impartially supporting the conditions necessary for all to pursue their interests and to live up to their obligations to others as they understand them (Rawls 1993, 187). This right of government can be seen as a natural extension of the right of self-protection. Justice does not require that persons stand idly by while others destroy the basis of their existence. It can never be to citizens' advantage, from a general point of view, to forgo the right of self-protection (ibid., 192). Also, it is rational for citizens to wish to protect themselves against their own irrational or unreasonable inclinations by consenting to a scheme of prohibitions and penalties that may give them the necessary motivation to avoid foolish actions. They may also wish to accept certain impositions designed to undo the unfortunate consequences of their imprudent actions (ibid., 219). These measures are not impositions on freedom because they do not reduce the value of the overall scheme of liberty enjoyed by citizens. By acting from these principles to impose limitations upon themselves, citizens express their nature as free and rational beings subject to the general conditions of human life (ibid., 222).

Rawls's first principle has significant implications for the environmental justice movement. If, as Rawls argues, it is never to anyone's advantage to forgo the right of self-protection, then one of the most basic liberties must be the freedom from being put at risk by the actions of others. Rawls argues that social institutions may be evaluated by how effectively they guarantee the conditions necessary for all equally to further their aims, or by how efficiently they advance shared ends that will similarly benefit everyone (Rawls 1999a, 83). Thus it may be plausible to argue that our obligations to the future include maintaining not only a fair savings rate but also a nondiminishing range of choices and opportunities to pursue valued interests and activities (Norton 1999, 132–133). It is arguable that this obligation is not merely distributive, but also an issue of basic liberty inasmuch as it serves to guarantee the equal value of basic liberties. This is critically important because the basic liberties may be equal in a formal sense although their worth, or usefulness, may not be the same for all (Rawls 1999a, 132).

This more substantive view of basic liberties allows us to develop a more ecologically meaningful version of Rawls's first principle. In his discussion of health as a social good, Manning points out that the primary social good of self-respect is damaged if health protection is not provided (1981,

159–160). But perhaps even a stronger statement of the matter is warranted. Beckerman observes that in a just society institutions do not humiliate people (1999, 86). Because it would never be in anyone's interest to forgo the right of self-preservation, it is only reasonable to assume that health risks are always imposed on people involuntarily (either in direct ways or through the imposition of falsely dichotomous choices). This loss of liberty cannot be justified as can other losses in liberty, as a temporary condition essential to the transformation of civilization into a more equally just society (Rawls 1999a, 132). Such a sacrifice can never be imposed by equal citizens in a well-ordered society because in establishing basic institutions they are motivated by their fundamental capacity for social cooperation (Rawls 1993, 306). Involuntary abridgements of liberty can play no role in such institutions.

Furthermore, it is essential to a just society that the full and fair value of basic liberties is assured. Beyond the issue of imposed health hazards, this requirement reaches the protection of environmental capital in the form of natural resources and genetic diversity. Contrary to the complaint that Rawls fails to address the issue of the effect of environmental policy on the distribution of primary goods (Miller 1999, 156), this focus on ensuring the full value of basic liberties brings resource conservation into the priority discussion of basic liberties. This eventuality has led Rawls to argue that although questions regarding the status of the natural world and our proper relationship to it are not ordinarily constitutional issues, "they may rise to the level of constitutional essentials and *basic justice* once our obligations to future generations and to other societies are involved" (1993, 246, emphasis added).

Rawls and the Environment: Integrating the Dialogues

Rawls (1993, 10) has argued that it is normally desirable that the comprehensive philosophical and moral views we are inclined to use in debating political issues should give way in any deliberations about fundamental political values—such as constitutional essentials and basic questions of justice—to a minimalist form of debate grounded on the limited premises to which all reasonable citizens could subscribe. These public reasons should be easily accessible to any citizen and anyone should (at least potentially) be able to accept them. Rawls offers three examples of appropriate public reason arguments for environmental policies: "To further the good of ourselves and future generations by preserving the natural order and its life-sustaining properties; to foster species of animals and plants for the sake of biological and medical knowledge with its potential applications to human health; to protect the beauties of nature for purposes of public recreation and the pleasures of a deeper understanding of the world" (1993, 245). But environmental policies and actions are not limited only to those that can be justified solely by the use of public reasons.

Having discussed in some detail a few of the central features of Rawls's theory of public reason, we can suggest how these insights might enhance our discourse on environmental theory and empower the movement for environmental justice. As there is a priority to Rawls's principles of justice it is, perhaps, appropriate to begin with the first, preferred principle—that specifying an equal scheme of basic liberties.

Rawls recognizes that the provision of basic liberties is only the starting point of a just society. He acknowledges that whereas, from a formal point of view, the basic liberties are the same for every citizen, the worth, or usefulness of liberty is not the same for everyone (Rawls 1993, 326). The poignancy of this observation is clear in the disproportionate exposure in the United States of poor and minority communities to toxic hazards. Neighborhoods already struggling against crime, illiteracy, drugs, and hopelessness are regularly subjected to health hazards that differ from the other risks they confront in that they are powerless to protect themselves from them either individually or collectively (White 1998). The historical indifference of "mainstream" environmentalism to this relationship between pollution and powerlessness is evocative of Rawls's observation that a reasonable society is part of our ordinary human world, not something to which we attach great virtue, until we find ourselves without it (Rawls 1993, 54).

The challenges of environmental injustice are different from those with which most environmentalists have grappled. Species preservation, habit conservation, resource management, and other technical aspects of environmental protection yield most readily to reasoned arguments divorced from the moral and philosophical doctrines that have driven the civil rights movement. This would seem entirely appropriate to someone aspiring to the level of generality and reflective equilibrium advocated by Rawls. In discussing the abolitionist and civil rights movements, however, Rawls argues that the comprehensive religious and philosophical views to which they appealed were required to give sufficient strength to the political conception they advocated so that it could subsequently be realized. Given those historical conditions, it was not unreasonable to act as these movements did for the sake of the ideal of public reason itself (Rawls 1993, 251). Allowing the use of these more comprehensive views is justified because "the worth of political liberties to all citizens, whatever their social or economic position, must be approximately equal" (ibid., 327). The political disenfranchisement reflected in numerous empirical studies of the distribution of toxic sites and their correlation with race and class arguably merit a similarly expansive treatment. The potential utility of Rawls's approach for crafting environmental justice arguments lies in its ability to address the implications of inequitable distributions of ecological risk from both the limited viewpoint of public reason and the richer perspective of widely held comprehensive doctrines (Bell 2002).

Beyond the question of basic liberties and their environmental implications, Rawls's second principle of justice raises a number of significant environmental issues. That principle requires that inequalities in the distribution of primary social goods should work to the benefit of those occupying the least advantaged positions in society. As a general matter, inequality that does not meet this description would have to be imposed on the less advantaged, damaging the most important of primary goods—self-respect (Rawls 1999a, 386). Moreover, the appropriate burden of proof in these matters favors equality: it defines a procedural presumption that persons are to be treated alike (ibid., 444). Here we have a prima facie case that productive activities that provide profit for some while imposing environmental losses on others are unjust.

Beyond this general point, Rawls has argued that if social stability is to be more than a simple modus vivendi, it must be rooted in a reasonable political conception of the right (1999b, 16). Should the cooperative arrangements agreed to as part of that political conception have unjustified distributive effects between peoples, these effects would have to be corrected by the agency of government (ibid., 43). This leads Rawls to conclude that an important role of government is that of the representative and effective agent of a people who take responsibility for a territory and its environmental integrity, as well as for the size of the population (ibid., 38–39). His reasoning begins with the argument that the institution of property is recognition that unless a definite agent is given responsibility for maintaining an asset and bears the loss for not doing so, that asset tends to deteriorate. In the present case, the asset is the people's territory and its capacity to support them in perpetuity; and the agent is the people themselves as politically organized (ibid., 39).

The question of supporting a people in perpetuity returns us to another of Rawls's arguments with significant environmental implications. Early in *A Theory of Justice,* Rawls states that parties in the original position want to ensure for their descendants the best endowment of genetic resources possible. In pursuit of that goal, the parties would adopt policies in this regard that they would desire earlier generations to have followed (1971, 92). This is a biological (one might say environmental) version of the just savings principle described earlier. In addition to financial resources, educational opportunity, and social infrastructure, those in the original position would adopt policies designed to pass on to their descendants a biologically richer world than they inherited from their predecessors. They would adopt these policies not out of altruism or some sense of familial connection but, rather, because these are the policies they would have willed generations before them to adopt.

Subsequently, Rawls relates the just savings principle to the principles of justice by interpreting the just savings principle from the standpoint of the least favored in each generation (1999a, 292). Such application of the just savings principle should result in patterns of savings for future generations sufficiently generous that the least favored will benefit. Failure to so interpret the just savings principle according to the difference principle would allow just constitutions to produce unjust results over time. This is because a just constitution, even under the most favorable conditions, is a case of imperfect procedural justice. The people of a given time may decide wrongly. The injustice may be perfectly evident according to the conception of justice underlying the regime itself. So there can be nothing sacrosanct about the public's desires concerning the level of savings, and its bias in favor of its own historical perspective deserves no special respect (ibid., 296). The collective will concerning provisions for the future is subject, as are all other social decisions, to the principles of justice (ibid., 297). For Rawls, the conception of justice can no more be voted on than the axioms, principles, and rules of inference of mathematics or logic (Rawls 1995, 144).

This is no imposition on the citizens of a just society. Citizens in a well-ordered society are fully autonomous because they freely accept the constraints of the reasonable, and in so doing their political life reflects the conception of a person who takes as fundamental her capacity for social cooperation (Rawls 1993, 306). Thus a sense of justice shows itself in two ways. First, it leads us to accept the just institutions that apply to us and from which we and our associates benefit. Second, it gives rise to a willingness to work for the setting up and maintenance of just institutions and for the reform of existing institutions when justice requires it (Rawls 1999a, 415). The reach of this logic may extend beyond the nation-state if the implications of Rawls's approach for the distributive justice of global consumption are followed to their conclusion (Hill 2001).

So although Rawls has stated that the natural world and our proper relation to it is not a constitutional essential or a basic question of justice, these issues may become questions of constitutional essentials and basic justice once our duties and obligations to future generations and other societies are involved (Rawls 1993, 246). It now remains only to suggest a response to one final complaint that has been lodged against Rawls's theory of justice. Some have alleged that public reason is inadequate to the needs of environmentalism because it offers no defense for the nonsentient members of the biosphere (Wenz 1988, 233).

Rawls both brings this complaint upon himself and, ultimately, offers his own best defense. He argues that the capacity for a sense of justice and of moral feeling is an adaptation of humankind to its place in nature (1999a, 440). Because this adaptation is unique to humans, our conduct toward animals is not regulated by the principles of justice, or so it would seem (ibid., 441). True to his contractarian roots, Rawls maintains that it is moral persons who are entitled to equal justice because "justice is owed to those who have the capacity to take part in and to act in accordance with the public understandings" arrived at in the original position (ibid., 442). The capacity for a sense of justice is sufficient in order to be owed the duties of justice, which suggests, according to Rawls, that we are not required to give strict justice to any species lacking that capacity (ibid., 448).

Although that might appear to end the matter, Rawls leaves the door ajar for further analysis of this problem. He allows that it is certainly wrong to be cruel to animals and that the destruction of an entire species is a great evil. "The capacity for feelings of pleasure and pain and for the forms of life of which animals are capable clearly impose duties of compassion and humanity in their cases. . . . They are outside the scope of the theory of justice, and it does not seem possible to extend the contract doctrine so as to include them in a natural way" (1999a, 448). But Rawls recognizes that peoples' moral instincts extend beyond the human species and that these impulses must be accounted for by a more general theory of moral obligation. He concludes his discussion of the issue by saying that "how far justice as fairness will have to be revised to fit into this larger theory it is impossible to say. But it seems reasonable to hope that if it is sound as an account of justice among persons, it cannot be too far wrong when these broader relationships are taken into account" (ibid., 449).

Perhaps without meaning to, Rawls may have pointed the way to this broader theory. In his most recent book, *The Law of Peoples* (1999b), he extends his theory of public reason from the relationships within societies to the interactions between peoples. Rawls uses the term "peoples" to emphasize that he is not concerned with states as traditionally conceived but, rather, with societies and their moral character as reasonably just or decent regimes (1999b, 27). From this perspective, Rawls describes five orders of peoples, three of which are not relevant here because they are described by Rawls as being in some sense unreasonable.

The first order of peoples is the *reasonable liberal society*. What distinguishes liberal peoples is that they have a reasonably just constitutional order, its citizens are united by a government that serves their fundamental needs, and its citizens share a moral commitment to be both reasonable and rational in their relationships with one another (Rawls 1999b, 23–25).

The second order of peoples is the *decent people*, or the *decent hierarchical society*. These societies are characterized by nonagression toward other societies, and an internal legal regime that is driven by a shared conception of the good. This second characteristic is evidenced in a concern for basic rights, a sense of moral obligations and duties, and a public-minded administration of the shared conception of the good through a system of rules reasonably believed to be consistent with that conception (Rawls 1999b, 64–66). These decent but not liberal societies, together with the reasonable liberal societies, make up Rawls's category of well-ordered societies.[3] Members of well-ordered societies owe each other a duty of toleration (ibid., 88).

To most environmentalists the question will now occur: is there any place in the fellowship of well-ordered societies for species of higher animals? The great apes live in tightly knit social groups and display an evident commitment to an order of rules that, from the perspective of the animal behaviorist, clearly contribute to the well-being of the group's members. The behavior of members of these "societies" makes plain that they are aware of and subscribe to these rules. Their consciousness of themselves as a group is revealed by their general reluctance to accept outsiders of the same species. Their recognition of the voluntary nature of group membership is evident in their occasional willingness to accept new members in spite of this general rule. The dominant males, while sometimes high-handed by human standards, seem to enforce the rules within self-imposed limits that suggest a realm of personal autonomy to which even the most junior member of the society is entitled. Does this not answer, at least in broad outline, to Rawls's general description of the decent hierarchical society?

Some may consider the reasoning suggested above to be a stretch. And there may be a danger in adopting the anthropocentric assumption that animals must rely on human mental constructs like justice for their status in the world. But the implications of this argument are compelling. If we can stretch our conception of "moral personhood" (Garner 2003), might we not owe certain classes of animals both the courtesy of noninterference in their way of life and a certain respect for the territorial integrity of their society? Might we not have found a philosophical warrant for habitat protection as deep as the underlying logic of our own social order?

Andrew Dobson has defended Rawls's position with respect to the rights of animals by claiming that Rawls does not preclude a concern for animals; "it is just that he thinks such concern cannot be motivated by reasons of justice" (Dobson 1998, 181). But perhaps both Dobson and Rawls himself have sold public reason short. One might recall at this point a remark Rawls himself made in connection with humans of diminished capacity: "While individuals presumably have varying capacities for a sense of justice, this fact is not a reason for depriving those with a lesser capacity of the full protection of justice. Once a certain minimum is met, a person is entitled to equal liberty in a par with everyone else" (1999a, 443). In this use of the word "person" what matters more, the character of an individual's society or a vanishingly small fraction of his DNA?

Certainly the answer to this question is not empirical. Neither is it political in the sense that everyday public debate will produce a stable consensus on the subject. Our conception of the person in this context is unavoidably a matter of ethical precommitment, just the sort of question for which Rawls's original position was designed.

Conclusion

Public reason organizes the environmentalist's instinct toward ethical precommitment in a particularly useful way. Rawls's principles are serial in order. They give an absolute precedence to the basic liberties that should render disproportionate impacts of environmental hazard impermissible. On this foundation provided by Rawls's first principle, the just savings concept (appropriately interpreted through the difference principle) mandates a concern for the environmental circumstances of future generations that requires (at least) a "no net loss" policy toward natural resources that also has a highly egalitarian character. His most recent effort to extend the reach of justice-as-fairness into the realm of relations between societies allows us to formulate a rationale for noninterference in (at least) the living groups of higher animals. Although these issues do not exhaust the range of concerns under the heading of environmental justice, a coherent solution to them would certainly point the way to continued progress.

Rawls's theories are most useful to us in thinking about the big questions of environmental politics and policy, those involving fundamental considerations—constitutional essentials, basic principles of justice, and profound normative choices. Rawls's work can be seen as the most demanding account of what "public" means when it comes to reasoning about political questions, because it requires participants to forgo any attempt to base their ethical and institutional choices on their own interests. "Public reason" is, for Rawls, a process, an outcome, and a set of justifications, all of which are shared by the entire reasoning citizenry. Rawls recognized that some environmental matters may rise to that level and should be dealt with through public reasoning and collective ethical precommitment. Progress in environmental science and philosophy may mean that over time the need may emerge for more such public reason policies on environmental matters.

Rawls's approach will always require too much of society and its citizens to be fully applicable in deciding ordinary or "normal" matters. To reconcile interests with justice by exiling interests altogether is hardly a workable way to conduct normal politics, those everyday but nevertheless important social choice activities that occur within the constitutional, principled, normative bounds already determined under Rawls's just procedures. Yet even if Rawls's version of public reason does not give us an operational methodology, it can still be the source of an important regulative norm. It is important to remember that Rawls's full prescriptions may be limited to justifying basic, fundamental environmental policies having to do with sustainability and environmental justice, but they do not prohibit additional green policies that go beyond those of fundamental normative choice. In ordinary everyday politics, "Rawls's account allows appeal to biocentric, ecocentric and aesthetic arguments where constitutional essentials and questions of basic justice are not at issue" (Bell 2002, 707). Nonpublic reasons, or comprehensive arguments, may still justify a most broad spectrum of environmental policies supported by a majority, so long as they are not contrary to constitutional essentials and matters of basic justice.

5

Deliberative Environmental Democracy: From Public Sphere to Biosphere

Of all the philosophical schools with some preeminence since the emergence of environmentalism as a social phenomenon in mid-twentieth century, critical theory has the greatest potential to be useful, not only in explaining sources of the environmental problematique but also in bringing political philosophy to bear on environmental ethics and reconciling democratic politics and environmental values. This is because critical theory confronts existing power relationships in a reflexive way that promotes reexamination of the industrial and commercial processes of social reproduction, leading inevitably to a greater environmental consciousness. An environmental consciousness spawned in this way is thereby already focused on the key determinants of successful environmental interventions, namely, whether those interventions address problematic power relationships in markets and bureaucracies. An attack on environmental degradation launched from this platform also serves to empower groups that are historically disadvantaged (both politically and economically) with potential for beneficial democratic reform beyond environmental issues. And, significantly, the broadly participatory character of a critical theory approach offers the best available (though not perfect) insurance against antireform and anti-environmental backlash (Brulle 2000). Yet, "reflecting a larger disjoint between social theory and environmental thought, scant attention has been paid to the environmental possibilities in critical theory," as DeLuca (2001, 309) notes—this despite a burgeoning literature on democracy and environment that nominally cites critical theorists or seems to be inspired by critical theory (Mathews 1996; Doherty and de Geus 1996; Lafferty and Meadowcroft 1996; Hayward 1998; Wissenburg 1998; Dobson 2000; Barry and Wissenburg 2001; Minteer and Taylor 2002). The exceptions tend to lament what is seen as the failed promise of critical theory (Eckersley 1999a, b).

Jürgen Habermas's theorizing has several strengths beyond those of early critical theory for thinking about environmentalism and democracy. It also avoids some of the same blind spots of the ecocentric critique of critical theory; for example, it acknowledges the perseverance of pluralist complexity and the intransigence of political structures. Missing from these critiques and alternative trajectories for critical theory (DeLuca 2001) are discussions of "how elements of the political system that frustrate democratic participation would protect the environment when processes of democratic will formation fail to do so" (Baber 2004, 261). Habermas has made it a central focus of his career to link his philosophical insights to the concrete problems of governance, and in his more recent writings he has emphasized the linkage between deliberation and action. He has embarked upon a reconstruction of critical theory through the translation of his theory of communicative action and discourse ethics into a social and political theory of democracy (Shabani 2003). Inasmuch as the central challenge to environmental philosophy—showing how the concrete problems of environmental protection and democratic politics may be reconciled—remains substantially unresolved, closer attention to Habermas's work, particularly as it relates to environmental democracy and governance, is warranted. As Robert Brulle notes, "It is in the democratic conversation about our fate and the fate of nature that Habermas and green political theory converge" (Brulle 2002, 17). No other theoretical approach of any philosophical school has as much potential for bridging the existing gap between theory and practice with respect to both democratic theory and environmental ethics.

The writings of Jürgen Habermas on deliberative democracy provide a way to make sense of environmental initiatives that are sometimes denigrated as being merely procedural (sometimes even just symbolic). Habermas calls for the recovery of a public sphere in which an informed citizenry can participate in a free, equal, and open exchange of empirical and normative validity claims, with the consensual outcome determined solely by the merits of the arguments made. This discourse would take place outside the confines of administrative agencies, but it would both limit and direct the exercise of administrative power in a way that a legislature never could (although legislative deliberation is central to Habermas's model as well). This optimistic view leads to the conclusion that an administrative regime constituted along the lines of Habermas's discourse ethics would create precisely the counterflows of knowledge that would empower traditionally subordinated groups (Simon 1994).

If the quality of the discourse is the key to more democratic outcomes, then procedure is substance and the ideal discourse situation described by Habermas is a true advance for democracy. If realized, an ideal speech situation would be the source of habits of mind that would establish the basis for a more enlightened and participatory form of democratic citizenship, one in which the risks associated with faction are less severe than those of interest-group liberalism. That is especially important in the environmental arena, where the general interest so often falls prey to the special. So Habermas's procedural theory of democracy has substantive implications for environmental rationality (Dryzek 1987). Habermas helps us make sense of, among other things, impact assessment, right-to-know, and other public involvement environmental innovations, initiatives, and incipient institutional designs. And, as these are built into law, organizational norms, and social expectations, they make possible a pragmatically grounded analysis of the potentiality of Habermas's theorizing for constructing deliberative environmental democracy.

For Habermas, just decisions, indeed any decisions that can appropriately be called democratic, must be the result of free and open discourse carried out in an "ideal speech situation." This is a circumstance where all who wish to participate in a political discussion are free to do so on equal terms and the decision that results is an uncoerced agreement on the part of everyone involved, with people yielding only to the force of the better argument. How does Habermas arrive at this position and how it might give rise to a form of deliberative environmental democracy?

Habermas and the Public Sphere

Habermas's first major book, *The Structural Transformation of the Public Sphere,* was originally published in German in 1962. In this early work, Habermas is primarily concerned with describing the social conditions necessary for a rational-critical debate about public issues conducted by private persons willing to let the strength of arguments rather than status or power determine the outcome (Calhoun 1992, 1). To understand the scope of this challenge, it is necessary to examine, at least briefly, Habermas's views on the origin of the public sphere.

The public sphere evolved in the "tension-charged field between state and society" (Habermas 1998b, 141). The separation of the state from society initially involved the disengagement of the elements of "social reproduction" from "political power." These elements, which had been welded together through the Middle Ages, separated when the development of a market economy broke the forms of domination based on landed estates, thus making necessary the creation of new forms of administration possessed of state authority (Habermas 1998b). In an extended historical discussion of the evolution of European society, Habermas describes the development, through the seventeenth and eighteenth centuries, of a bourgeois public sphere devoted to the idea of rational-critical argument, in which the merits of the better argument prevail over issues of power and status.

This process of social evolution is not without its own contradictions and tensions. For one thing, the public sphere has not, as a practical matter, always been fully inclusive in practice (Kale 2002). Moreover, the principle of a critical public is inevitably watered down as it expands into wider areas of life. The reading public (that is, the educated and informed public), which prefigured the politically active public, has declined into minorities of specialists who put their reason to use publicly (but often in languages that are not publicly accessible). The remaining masses no longer consider their culture critically, but merely consume it. For its part, the press no longer mediates the public reasoning process. It simply reinforces consumption (Habermas 1998b, 175, 188). The small number of party activists who remain politically engaged become isolated from the mass electorate. Public opinion then ceases to be a source of critical judgment and becomes a social and psychological variable to be manipulated for strategic purposes. The result is a gap between public opinion as a constitutional fiction (the myth that an autonomous public opinion is the final arbiter in modern democracies) and its role as a tool of mass manipulation (ibid., 230–244). In fact, the disintegration of the public sphere as an institution of ongoing participation in rational-critical public debate concerning the use of public authority can be measured by the increasing effort required for the parties to generate periodically something like a public sphere within which to conduct elections. But the public sphere created periodically solely for the sake of elections is inadequate to the maintenance of democracy because it is unrelated to any ongoing debate over the use of public authority (ibid., 211–212). It is insufficient to the maintenance of a genuinely democratic discourse over the use of public authority because it is meaningless outside of the context of the particular election (popularity contest) for which that public space is created. The use of authority cannot be discussed in any genuine way because the entire enterprise is calculated to achieve electoral success, not common understanding. Moreover, it serves only to sustain a politically active core of individuals who are themselves disinclined to submit their views to critical discussion (ibid., 213).

This process of social development is the basis for an evolutionary movement toward the conditions of modernity we observe today, where money in the economy and bureaucratic power in the polity become society's primary "steering media" (Giddens 1985, 108). In a parallel development that is particularly troublesome to environmentalists, the empirical–analytic sciences have come to be dominated by an interest in technical control over their objects of study—over nature in particular (Habermas 1971). As discouraging as Habermas's analysis may seem, he is not convinced of the impossibility of the recovery of a public sphere capable of effective rational-critical discourse in the political realm (Habermas 1974). What is required is a minimizing of bureaucratic decisions and a "relativising of structural conflicts of interest according to the standard of a universal interest everyone can acknowledge" (Giddens 1985, 235). A tall order, certainly. But by "postulating the availability of a non-exclusive public sphere of deliberation where a rational consensus could obtain," Habermas holds out the possibility that the gap between political legitimacy and rationality can be closed (Mouffe 1999, 756–757). Although this approach has been criticized for being insufficiently sensitive to the prospects for the promotion of an alternative, proletarian public sphere (Negt and Kluge 1993), the willingness to confront modernity on its own terms has always been a particular strength of Habermas's work. Still, for many, this second part of Habermas's argument is the least satisfying. This is because in his early work he could not find any effective way to ground his hopes for the recovery of a bourgeois public sphere in the social institutions of advanced capitalism (Calhoun 1992, 29).

Democracy and Communication

For Habermas to develop a more useful (and more hopeful) version of the public sphere, one in which it would be possible to believe that practical discourse about the use of public authority could achieve some level of consensus, it was necessary for him to add a theory of social communication. If one remains focused on the ideal speech situation, a circumstance in which all interested parties participate equally and only the force of the better argument determines the outcome, it is possible that Habermas's perspective could yield nothing beyond an especially well motivated internal dialogue. Although Habermas (2001a) has denied that the ideal speech situation is merely a regulative principle, the risk is clear. The principle of a discourse ethics, if left ungrounded in any institutional framework, could seem like little more than a regulative principle for our own moral judgments, indicating that we should bear in mind what we think an ideal communicative community would say about the matter before us (Benhabib and Dallmayr 1990). If we fall into this trap, we will fail to achieve Habermas's goal of developing personally autonomous participants in deliberative discourse who are "free and equal," each of whom is "required to take the perspective of everyone else" and who thus projects himself "into the understandings of self and the world of all others" (Habermas 1995, 117). We will not only have failed in our social obligations, we will have failed to fulfill the promise of our own autonomy. Participation in the forms of practical reason is as important to our private autonomy as it is to our political autonomy. Both are "as much means for each other as they are ends in themselves" (Habermas 2001b, 780).

This possibility has occurred to Habermas. In order to ground discourse ethics, he argues that two assumptions are fundamental: first, that normative validity claims have cognitive meaning and are subject to rational and empirical evaluation like any other truth claim; and second, that the grounding of normative claims requires an actual dialogue rather than an argumentative process run hypothetically through a single mind. This dialogue, Habermas concedes, must be formal (elevating form over substance). It specifies no orientation as to content, but rather a procedure: practical discourse (Habermas 1990).[1]

The first assumption, that normative claims have cognitive meaning, is classic Enlightenment philosophy. At the heart of the Enlightenment was the view that rationality could discover the good. In other words, ethics were thought to be a matter of discovery from careful observation of cause and effect. For Habermas it is clear that "by observing language in use in particular cultural formations and by committing ourselves to what he calls communicative action" (action aimed at understanding), we can discover, uncover, or reveal what is true and good (Elliot 1994, 393–398). It is in this sense that Habermas posits a "world-disclosing" function of language that can transcend the structural constraints of communication in everyday life (Habermas 1987b, 204). Here, then, is the nexus between communication and the formation of political norms: only practices that permit truly undistorted and uncoerced communication are capable of generating legitimate controls over conduct (Simon 1994).

The second assumption, that internal dialogues are insufficient, takes us one step further. It establishes a principle of universalization that is distinct from that provided by Kant. It shifts our attention away from what each of us might will (without contradiction) to be a universal law and focuses instead on what all might will in agreement to be a universal norm (McCarthy 1978). This would seem to be, at minimum, a necessary requirement to call discourse ethics a rational pursuit. Rationality, after all, presumes communication, "because something is rational only if it meets the conditions necessary to forge an understanding with at least one other person" (Giddens 1985, 99). This idea of a rational, informed discussion of public policy is one that runs through the whole of Habermas's more recent works (Holub 1991). It describes a form of practical reason that provides rules of discourse and forms of argumentation that, rather than expressing universal human values or the ethical life of a particular community, derive their normative content from the validity claims that are sustainable in an actual process of communicative action (Habermas 1997).

Even more about the nature of a recovered public sphere may be inferred from the concepts of communicative action and discourse ethics. The concept of communicative action "implies a readiness to learn to discover our own values, both individual and common, by careful listening and conscientious exposition" through which we seriously examine our own experience (Elliot 1994, 397). The very idea of communicative rationality could be said to express the assumption that anyone who advances normative validity claims must understand the internal relationship between raising claims of intersubjective validity and the commitment to the giving and receiving of reasons.

Further, communicative rationality implies a conception of communication that does not allow for any validity claims to be exempt in principle from possible critical examination (Wellmer 1985, 52–53). This radically open form of communication fits well within the contours of what Habermas has identified as "postmetaphysical" thinking. Habermas's procedural concept of communicative reason attempts to recover a concept of reason that is skeptical and postmetaphysical, but not defeatist (Habermas 1992, 116). By this it is meant that communicative rationality will eschew reasons based in religious or ideological dogma owing to their inaccessibility to the public at large. But in so doing, communicative reason does not accept the conclusion that practical discourse can produce only compromises among preferences, for normative validity claims are subject to testing in much the same way as are empirical generalizations of the nomological disciplines. This importation of the argumentative standards found in the natural sciences is characteristic of the contemporary move to exclude metaphysics from discussions of ethics and politics, a movement with which Habermas is clearly associated (Williams 1999, 125). According to Habermas, both modern science and autonomous morality place their confidence solely in the rationality of their own approaches and their procedures (Habermas 1992, 35). This is the truly novel feature of his theory of communicative action, according to Habermas: the same processes of redeeming validity claims through appropriate types of argumentation is implicit in practical (moral and legal) disputes, as well as disputes about aesthetic judgments and scientific generalizations. All anticipate and, indeed, presuppose noncoercive and nondistortive argumentation. This assumption, in fact, is built into our everyday, pretheoretical communicative interactions. Without it, no one would agree to discourse in the first place (Bernstein 1985, 19).

Certain other characteristics of communicative action and discourse ethics are also ascertainable. First, because communicative action is radically open, it is also radically open to failure. Consequently, any moral insight gained in the process "has to be held open for revision and adaptation" (Elliot 1994). Just as communicative action can arise from no form of dogma, neither may it produce one. Second, the process of consensus building will inevitably involve the construction of bridges between lifeworlds, the semiautonomous language minorities that various opinion groups and professions have become. A key objective of communicative action, therefore, will be to break down the polarized and polarizing language that reflects entrenched ideology (Plevin 1997). Third, any political system structured in accordance with the concept of discourse ethics will be characterized by a wide diversity of institutions and organizations through which citizens will be able to challenge the use of the steering mechanisms of advanced capitalist societies—money in the private economy, and political power in administration. Widely varied combinations of participatory movements, occupational and nonoccupational groups, economic units, mass party organizations, and state bureaucracies will exist in abundance. Within these combinations, democracy and rationality will vary depending on the features peculiar to their structures. More orientation toward consensus, procedural equality, and social rationality will characterize local and occupational levels of participation, whereas at the level of party politics and administration, which necessitates less consensual decision making and more compromising of interests, less procedural equality and less social rationality will be evident (Ingram 1993).

A fourth implication of communicative action for democratic practice is that consensus must be a standard of decision making. Bohman has argued that Habermas must revise his principle of democracy to remove the strong condition of unanimity if he is to solve the problems of social complexity he has set for himself. Only then will the resources of public communication, particularly in the form of well-intentioned dissent, provide a basis for radical democracy in a complex and pluralistic society (Bohman 1994). But McCarthy sees this as an option that would be hard for Habermas to accept. The assumption that consensus is possible is, for Habermas, not merely a normative or regulative ideal of argumentative discourse but one of its constitutive presuppositions. Were it not for this presupposition, our communicative behaviors would lose their focus on rational argumentation and take on the characteristics of tactical maneuvers designed to force opponents into losing positions. Ultimately, McCarthy (1997, 51, 65) concedes, strict adherence to the principle of consensus is not possible. Compromise is the second best alternative, acceptable only when discourse has shown that there is no common interest to be found. Even Habermas has had to concede that some use of representative mechanisms is inevitable in a large and complex society. He has, thus, substituted for active popular sovereignty a somewhat more republican version of consensus-producing public reason (Abraham 1994, 939–946).

As for consensus, however, a more difficult problem is presented. Insofar as we believe that rational (and noncoercive) argument about practical

matters or norms is possible, granting equal rights and liberties to everyone, including equal rights of political participation, is tantamount to accepting a principle of consensual action (Wellmer 1985, 60). This would
seem to be an essential element of the "reconstruction" of human knowledge, defined as the reinstatement of a form of knowledge detached from
particular interests (Habermas 1973b). Indeed, Cronin (2003) has argued
that Habermas's political theory provides the foundation for a "constitutional patriotism" that can serve as a source of political identification in
culturally pluralistic democracies. But Habermas realizes that as a practical matter, in a highly complex and pluralistic society there will often
be circumstances in which no generalizable interest can be discovered
through any amount of ideal discourse. Under those circumstances, compromise is fair and acceptable if it is more advantageous to all concerned
than no arrangement whatever, if the free rider problem can be avoided,
and if no party in the arrangement is exploited due to its position (Habermas 1996, 165–167).

But for a compromise to be legitimate without satisfying generalizable
interests (or being acceptable to all) it must be a strategic agreement arrived at in a balance of power among the parties that ensures the maximum possible harmonizing of the divergent interests involved (Ingram
1993, 302). Habermas thus confronts a significant problem. In the words
of an entirely sympathetic commentator, how can the "apparently utopian
notions of emancipatory knowledge and practice, of ideal communicative
situations and of communicative action and discourse ethics cope with
the grubby reality of self-interested conduct, self-serving institutions and
political horse-trading?" (Outhwaite 1994).

Deliberative Democracy and Law

Habermas himself recognizes these problems when he observes that normative theories are generally open to the suspicion that they take insufficient notice of the hard facts of the modern institutional state (Habermas
1996). To overcome this difficulty, it is necessary to appreciate both the
normative and positive aspects of law—in Habermas's terms, the existence
of law as both norm and fact.

In Habermas's view, the existence of law as a positive enactment of some
legislature means that a consciously adopted framework of norms has

given rise to an artificial layer of social reality (Habermas 1996, 38). Ideally, this layer of social reality is artificial only in the limited sense that it is an instrumental creation in service of the norms that have developed from the more natural (or, perhaps, authentic) relations among private individuals acting in the public sphere. The development of the constitutional state can be understood as an "open sequence of experience-guided precautionary measures" against the possibility that illegitimate power relations will overpower the legal system that expresses society's normative self-understanding. In this sense, Habermas views even the most basic documents of modern democracies, their constitutions, as projects to be fulfilled through a cross-generational learning process (Ferrara 2001). Thus, modern societies are integrated not only through the steering mechanisms of money and administrative power but also through values, norms, and mutual understandings expressed (albeit imperfectly) by a legitimate legal order (Habermas 1996, 39). But the legal order does more even than this for the society based on communicative action.

As noted in chapter 3, Habermas (1996, 55) argues that discourse ethics and communicative action both rely on ordinary language with its "grammatical complexity, propositional structure, and reflexivity," to perform a wide variety of functions. With its virtually unlimited capacity for interpretation and its wide range of circulation, ordinary language is superior to the special codes of disciplines and ideologies in that it provides a "sounding board" for the external costs of the highly differentiated subsystems of advanced capitalism by remaining sensitive to problems affecting the whole of society. The utility of ordinary language as a translation matrix is, however, unidirectional. Ordinary language supplies a universal ground for understanding and can, in principle, translate everything from all languages into a common form. But it cannot in return operationalize its message in a way that is effective for all audiences. Ordinary language is insufficiently precise to exactly express thoughts that are grounded in the specialized languages of the various sciences. (That is why we resort to analogies to explain scientific propositions to lay audiences.) For the translation of normative insights into special codes, ordinary language (and, thus, discourse ethics) remains dependent on positive law for its communication with the steering media of money and administration. So normatively substantive messages can circulate throughout an entire society only in the language of law (ibid., 55–56).

Furthermore, law provides a basis for the predictability of social behavior that allows normative understandings to guide individual behavior. The process of internalizing social norms is imperfectly understood, but certainly it is not perfectly free of coercion. The motivations that make it possible to anticipate that others will respect social norms do not have to be completely understood in order for one to conclude that the existence of a legitimate legal order must at least be among them (Habermas 1996, 67–68). And the legal order is a legitimate order (that is, accepted as worthy of respect) because, although laws do not fit interests and ideas together in any seamless way, they do "interpret interests through ideas, thereby making reasons and validity claims factually effective" (ibid., 70). The legal order's legitimacy flows from the democratic character of the collective will it expresses. Because that will is subject to change over time, it is the participatory character of the political institutions that matters most, not the content of the law at any given moment. For the legal order to remain legitimate, more is required than initial legitimacy. In a normatively pluralistic society, positive law derives legitimacy solely from the political procedures in which the convictions and commitments of citizens find representation (Gregg 1997, 927). And if, as Habermas contends, democracy is more than the simple aggregation of interests, then the discursive features of law will be crucial to our understanding of law's claim to legitimacy. Since the legitimacy of law depends on self-legislation, the informal discursive sources of normative ideas in a democracy must be linked with the formal decision-making processes (Avio 1999, 524). Only in this way can modern legal systems provide the source of social integration needed by complex and diverse societies (Flynn 2003).

This linkage of discursive features of law with institutionalized decision making raises a problem that must be dealt with before the Habermasian view of law can be applied to the question of achieving a deliberative form of environmental democracy. That problem is the role of experts in the public sphere. Habermas recognizes that modern societies depend on the "rationality of a specialized and competent fulfillment of tasks by experts" (Habermas 1996, 188). However, given the need for functional coordination in such complex societies, the simple division of labor between experts and laypersons is no longer sufficient. Constant adjustments to the direction of policy processes through subtle regulatory intervention on the part of the administrative system seem to be the only alternative to a critical overburdening of democracy's problem-solving capacity. And, yet, this alternative carries with it the imminent danger that "cognitive" problems of functional coordination will displace the moral and ethical issues that should be the focus of discourse ethics. Furthermore, as soon as specialized knowledge is brought to bear on politically relevant problems, its unavoidably normative character reveals itself, setting off controversies that polarize the experts themselves (ibid., 320, 351).

A further challenge is revealed when one examines high-risk circumstances, such as threats to the environment serious enough to require a regard for the interests of future generations. Weighing the dangers in such a "risk society" makes such high demands on the analytical and prognostic abilities of experts that the problems of statutory control and legal certainty afflicting the regulatory state in general are dramatically exacerbated (Habermas 1996, 432). With the detailed control of policymaking by elected officials lost to this complexity imposed by high levels of technological and environmental risk, procedural law must be enlisted to build a "legitimation filter"—participatory requirements—into the decision processes of the administrative state, which is and must remain oriented toward efficiency. These participatory administrative practices must extend beyond the symbolic or manipulative, beyond merely information gathering. They "must not be considered merely surrogates for true legal protection but as procedures that are ex ante effective in legitimating decisions that, from a normative point of view, substitute for acts of legislation or adjudication" (ibid., 441). Thus, for Habermas, the claim to legitimacy of legal and political institutions is redeemed by means of informal process of public deliberation protective of generalizable interests and universal human rights and a model of democratic politics entailing an open public sphere together with related institutions of liberal democracy (Fairfield 1999).

What are we to conclude from this about how a deliberative form of environmental democracy could be developed?

Deliberative Democracy and the Environment

The status of the environment in Habermas's work is profoundly ambiguous. At one level he views our separation from nature as merely a consequence of our disenchantment with it after the birth of modern science. He accepts this disenchantment with nature as the price of modernity, a price well worth paying in light of the freedom from necessity that results (Hayim 1992). Unlike members of the older Frankfurt School, Habermas seeks no all-encompassing reconciliation of humans and nature as a means of dissolving the aporia of enlightenment. For Habermas, the natural world is unalterably constituted as an object of instrumental rationality (Whitebook 1985). Habermas makes this argument even though he identifies the pursuit of a technological mastery of the "threatening evils of nature" as the problematic point of departure for modernity (Habermas 1973a, 51).

On the other hand, we have the recognition by Habermas that environmental risks present special difficulties for the problem-solving capacities of democratic institutions. We also have the observation that one possible result of Habermas's work is that "the disastrous dynamics of the capitalist production process, which at present leads to an increasing destruction of the human habitat," could be brought to a halt (Wellmer 1985, 66). So what role does environmental protection play in Habermas's deliberative democracy—act, norm, or mere interest?

At a minimum, Habermas regards environmentalism (as he does the antinuclear campaign) as one of the new social movements, which he sees as primarily defensive in character. This can be regarded, from the environmental perspective, as a weakness in Habermas's theory. Social movements lack the long-lasting financial resources and loyalty enjoyed by political parties. Because it relies heavily on constant participation of activists and enjoys no privileged position in the decision process (Alario 1994, 340), environmentalism is vulnerable. Focused on defending nature and creating new communal relationships, new social movements are centrally concerned with protecting the lifeworld from further colonization by instrumentally rational systems (Giddens 1985, 111). Thus Habermas might be seen as consigning the environment to be a poor stepchild in a society where the interests represented by money and political power have more or less permanent control over social choice. Environmental protection remains a mere preference and capitalist production is the constitutive institution of the society.

If the environment occupied no more essential role than this in his thinking, Habermas would not offer environmentalists much of an advance from interest-group liberalism. Indeed, Habermas rejects the Frankfurt

School's hope (shared by many environmentalists) of a liberation of nature, transformed from an object of human domination into the other subject in dialogue with humanity (Theunissen 1999). In Habermas's view, to play a role in moral discourse, one must have been "socialized into a communicative form of life" that is found only in human communities (Habermas 1987a, 29). But there may be aspects of discursive ethics, and its implications for policy processes, that hold out more hope. Of particular value, perhaps, is his general theory of law and political legitimacy.

Modern law, in Habermas's view, has two distinct faces. It allows citizens to regard its imperatives in two different ways. They may consider legal norms merely as commands, as factual constraints on their personal scope of action to which they respond strategically by comparing the possible costs of a violation with possible gains. Or, they may adopt a performative attitude in which they regard legal norms as socially validated precepts with which they comply out of "respect for the law" (Habermas 1996, 448). This second view of the law would result most naturally from the use of democratic procedures for the production of legal norms. Truly democratic procedures make it possible for issues, viewpoints, information, and reasons to combine and recombine in unrestrained and undistorted ways. Thus, democratic procedures provide the only postmetaphysical source of legitimacy for law. They do so by "securing a discursive character for political will formation." In this way, grounds are provided for the assumption that results of processes of policy formation are more or less reasonable. So a legal norm has validity (in part) because the state has ensured that preconditions exist for the legitimate genesis of the norms themselves, holding out at least the possibility that one might comply with the law's demands out of a warranted respect for the law (ibid.).

At this point, Habermas's analysis of the legal foundations of political legitimacy becomes open to the complaint that he has provided some criteria for judging decision-making processes and administrative institutions without really describing them in any detail. Habermas has, however, provided some additional insights. As noted earlier, the communicative power that would be exercised in a reinvigorated public sphere has the character of a siege. It seeks to influence judgment and decision making in political institutions without intending to conquer the system itself (Habermas 1996, 486–487). In Habermas's view, the sole legitimate aim of the democratic project in modern states is the gradual improvement of institutionalized procedures of rational collective will-formation, procedures that do not (perhaps to the frustration of some environmentalists) prejudge the concrete goals of any participants as more legitimate than others. Prejudgment of goals by special knowledge groups would prevent communicative power from performing one of its most important functions. Only if such concentrations of power in special knowledge groups are avoided can discourse ethics (and public participation generally) act as a limit on use of administrative power. Public discourses find a good response only to the extent that they result in diffusion of influence under conditions of broad and active participation that is egalitarian and divested of educational privilege (ibid., 489–490).

Arriving at this point reminds us of Habermas's earlier (1979, 186) general prescription for a democratic society, which is worth citing at length: "I can imagine the attempt to arrange society democratically only as a self-controlled learning process. It is a question of finding arrangements which can ground the presumption that the basic institutions of the society and the basic political decisions would meet with the unforced agreement of all those involved, if they could participate as free and equal, in discursive will-formation."

This remark is, for an environmentalist, suggestive of, among other things, a number of analyses of the U.S. National Environmental Policy Act (NEPA) that have emphasized the act's cognitive potential (Taylor 1984; Bartlett 1998; Boggs 1993). It is also suggestive of an observation by Lynton K. Caldwell that NEPA's central objective of integrating environmental values into administrative decision making requires a process of *social learning* (Caldwell 1998, 78). These views of the role of NEPA bring to mind a wide range of similarly discursive elements in other major environmental statutes. In the United States, for example, the notice and comment requirements of the Endangered Species Act and the Coastal Zone Management Act, the right-to-know elements of the Superfund Amendments and Reauthorization Act, the public involvement requirements of the National Forest Management Act, the Federal Land Policy and Management Act, and the Nuclear Waste Policy Act—all reflect a latent commitment to the kind of discursive will-formation imagined by Habermas's discourse ethics. Processes and institutions that facilitate or require dialogue about ecological norms can be identified in the environmental policy and civic politics developments of many other countries, both developed and developing (Weidner and Janicke 2002), as well as in transnational public spheres (Dryzek 2000, 159). And much more is possible in cultivation of institutional arrangements that "bring democratic values directly to bear" (Cohen and Sabel 1997; Dorf and Sabel 1998).

This "political capacity building for environmental democracy" (Mason 1999) is critically important to the success of discourse ethics for two fundamental reasons. First, discourse ethics assumes that normative claims have cognitive meaning and can be treated just like any other truth claim (Habermas 1990, 68). The dialogue that leads to democratic will-formation must, therefore, take adequate account of the scientific information base out of which policy questions arise. This can be facilitated by embedding participatory procedures within political and policy processes, not because they necessarily lead to better quality decisions (which they certainly should) but rather because they produce more genuinely democratic decision making. Here we find the outline of a solution to alleged irrationality among community environmental activists, condescendingly referred to as NIMBYs. The widespread belief that NIMBYism results from a lack of scientific information misses the point entirely (Dietz and Rycroft 1987, 60). Environmental activists, when confronted with evidence that does not conform to their views, are generally unmoved simply because they doubt the veracity of government experts who produce the information (Brooks 1984, 48). The solution is not more suspect information but, rather, public involvement in the production of information through a process of discursive will-formation.

Second, discourse ethics assumes that for norms and prescriptions to be adequately grounded they must result from an actual social dialogue, as opposed to a hypothetical or monological process of argumentation (Habermas 1990, 68). And for genuine social dialogue to take place, society must be brought into the discussion (Dryzek 1990; 2000). This is particularly important in the case of environmental dialogues, wherein the rights-based individualism of modern industrialized society often confronts the communitarian claims put forward by representatives of non-Western cultures (Flynn 2003). The opportunity for that kind of public involvement is much greater for local, administrative, and civic arenas of decision making than in national legislatures. Ultimately, this is the only credible response to suggestions from within the environmental movement that there is a fundamental and irresolvable tension between participatory democracy and a sustainable ecology (Ophuls and Boyan 1992). It is simply not possible to protect the environment from human degradation in the absence of a human commitment to do so (Brulle 2000). The public discourse required for the task must be decentralized and fundamentally democratic because the policy goal involves uniting the normative and empirical reality of law, the "is" and the "ought." Habermas characterizes the problem as reconciling law as fact and law as norm. Public discourse designed to achieve this goal is well received only in proportion to its diffusion and only to the extent that it is carried out under conditions of broad and active participation (Habermas 1996, 490). Public discourse will advance the substantive objective of environmental protection only to the extent that it is comprehensive in character. We are reminded of his dedication to this kind of discourse when we review the wide spectrum of social theories Habermas employs in *The Theory of Communicative Action* (1987a), which seeks to explain the emerging contours of modern society in distinctly holistic ways.

When procedures, driven by mandates and directives, are implanted in decentralized political systems, a final imperative of discourse ethics is served. Decentralized will-formation is far more amenable to the involvement of socially and economically disfavored groups than are the more resource intensive processes of elite choice at the highest levels of government. It is for this reason that Habermas characterizes discourse ethics as a universalistic morality capable of bridging the division between "in-group" and "out-group" morality (Habermas 1976, 87). Decentralized will-formation, under Habermas's ideal speech conditions, produces agreement that is rational because it is a genuine (though never perfect) expression of the general interest. Such agreements are also legitimate, not because they are rational, but precisely because of the ideal conditions under which they were produced (Habermas 1979, 186). So while the rationalization of social norms does not lead per se to better functioning of social systems, it would furnish members of society with the opportunity for further emancipation and progressive individuation (Habermas 1970, 119). This would complete the disentanglement of economic and political power characterized by Habermas as the structural transformation of the public sphere (Habermas 1998b). Thus, a discourse environmental ethics serves both the cognitive and political needs of environmental policymaking in a society wishing to remain democratic and the necessity for environmental equity in a society that aspires to be both democratic and just.

Conclusion

The idea of deliberative democracy was given an enormous boost in credibility by the declarations of John Rawls (1993) and Jürgen Habermas (1996) that they consider themselves to be deliberative democrats. Nevertheless, the convergence of Rawls and Habermas, "respectively the most important liberal theorist and critical theorist of the late twentieth century" (Dryzek 2000, p. 2), poses a significant difficulty. Although perhaps not so vastly at odds as some might think, the rights-based proceduralism of the classical liberal and the culture-based will-formation of the critical theorist are not entirely consistent either. A major effort to bridge these differences, and to clarify what cannot be reconciled, is contained in the works of advocates of full liberalism, to which we turn in chapter 6.

6

Environmental Governance and Full Liberalism

Some of the most valuable work being done in the area of deliberative democracy involves efforts to give concrete form to the groundbreaking work of Jürgen Habermas and John Rawls. Many of these second-generation theorists have found it necessary to diverge from the approaches that are the foundation of their own work. James Bohman, for example, is a Habermasian by background. But throughout his work there is woven the view that deliberative democracy must be assimilated to, rather than attempt to displace, liberal constitutionalism (Dryzek 2000). Likewise, Amy Gutmann and Dennis Thompson owe much to the work of John Rawls. Yet they seek a basis for "agreement on substantive moral principles" beyond the choice among basic principles that concerned Rawls (Gutmann and Thompson 2004, 92).

Thus the work of theorists identified with the approach we characterize as "full liberalism" can be interpreted as an attempt to synthesize the theories of Habermas and Rawls in a way that reconciles their divergent approaches to deliberative democracy. Whether this "realism" is ultimately positive, for democracy or for the environment, is a matter of critical concern. The abandonment of impartiality in public discourse, the elevation of diversity to the level of a primary deliberative value, and the treatment of preferences as (to some extent) cultural givens are problematic, especially from environmentalists' points of view. But nevertheless the work of advocates of full liberalism have highlighted several important questions that must be answered if a genuinely deliberative model of environmental politics is to be developed.

Complexity, Pluralism, and Deliberation

The special contribution of Bohman and Gutmann and Thompson to thinking about deliberative democracy, it might be argued, is that they have forced grand theory to confront the mundane fact that modern societies are complex, multicultural, and populated by individuals who are often quite sensitive about their personal rights. These societies exist in a modern world that has been variously described as "post-metaphysical" (Habermas 1992) or "disenchanted" (Bennett 2001). The disenchanted world is dominated by reason and alienation, a world in which ethics has become a code to which one is obligated rather than a source of affective commitment (Bennett 2001). Without fighting labor and class warfare through to their conclusion, our managerial century has found a way for power simply to prevail. Workers and citizens alike are now fully adept at imposing on themselves the language of self-discipline, regulation, and subjugation to professional power (Cawley and Chaloupka 1997).

This poses an especially difficult problem for Habermas, whose "theory of the state insists that citizens identify with the norms that govern them" (Bennett 1987). The danger is that in a disenchanted world, it is easy for liberals to lose faith in the distinction between power and legitimate authority, resulting in a pervasive cynicism that undermines the legitimacy of government action and the affective commitment of citizens to the law (Chaloupka 1999). Bohman's approach can be viewed as an effort to carve out some space in this disenchanted world for political discourse that is still based on personal rather than public meanings, offering a counterweight to this pervasive cynicism.

The complexity and individualism of contemporary Western societies also casts serious doubt on the view of Habermas that deliberative democracy involves a search for consensus approaching virtual unanimity. Only if he revises this principle, Bohman (1994) argues, can Habermas solve the problems of complexity in a way that will allow the resources of public communication (particularly in the form of well-motivated dissent) to create the basis for radical democracy.

The theories of Rawls are challenged, in Bohman's view, by the cultural pluralism of modern societies. Multicultural societies give rise to what Bohman calls "deep conflicts." These are disagreements that go beyond disputes over material interests to include differences over the legitimate grounds for adjudicating disputes. Deep cultural conflict, in Bohman's view, "makes public reason itself essentially contestable, especially when moral and epistemic standards are inextricably intertwined" (1995, 254). The result is that any unitary version of public reason, like that advocated by Rawls, must be so restricted in scope as to be irrelevant for most political disagreements.

Bohman (1996) begins his own account of deliberative democracy with these very issues. He recognizes that deliberative democracy is potentially constrained by cultural pluralism, the existence of large social inequities, the complexity of modern societies, and community-wide biases and ideologies that discourage political and economic change. He also recognizes that setting loose the beast of collective will-formation is, at best, a risky necessity. He emphasizes (as would Rawls) that modern constitutional rights are necessary conditions for successful deliberation, even if the institutions they have created are less often forums for deliberation than arenas for strategic gamesmanship. Bohman also points out (as would Habermas) that although rights may make deliberation possible, in part by setting limits on it, they tell us neither what deliberation is nor how it is best conducted under currently existing constraints.

As might be imagined, the specific elements of Bohman's theoretical approach differ somewhat from those of Rawls and Habermas. Rather than requiring that public reasons be of a nature that all could accept (as does Rawls), Bohman insists only that public reasons be sufficiently convincing that all citizens, including dissenters, are motivated to continue cooperative deliberation even after decisions are reached. The only intrinsic characteristic a public reason must possess is that it be offered to a general and unrestricted audience, rather than to a restricted and specialized collective. Both Rawls and Habermas insist that citizens converge on the same reasons, rather than agree for different reasons. Bohman, however, views such convergence merely as an ideal of democratic citizenship, not as a requirement of public reason. In a pointed reference to Rawls, Bohman declares that public reasons in a pluralist society will not presuppose some particular conception of the good, or some comprehensive moral doctrine, since it is reasonable to assume that they lack public scope. Furthermore, a unitary view of public reasons would run counter to the new "politics of identity." Bohman's culturally rich politics, it could be argued, hold the promise for more effective environmental action because "the idea of the specificity of cultural identities seems to meld easily with the site specificity of ecology" (O'Connor 1999, 165).

Bohman (1996) also has his own specific standard of rationality. Social practices are rational to the extent that they promote the acquisition and use of knowledge. Because deliberative politics has no single domain of discourse, no more specific conception of rationality is possible. The use of knowledge is vitally important because the goal of public deliberation is to solve a problem together with others who have distinct perspectives and interests. Deliberation must begin with the fact-dependent process of arriving at a shared definition of the problem. The process may not allow for universal participation or unanimous agreement. Deliberative democracy succeeds, for Bohman, when it produces a shared intention that is acceptable to a plurality of the agents who do participate in the activity of forming it. This might sound like it holds the potential for the creation of information elites and the disenfranchisement of ordinary citizens. But Bohman argues that the deliberative process will be so broadly participatory that experts cannot assume their special knowledge will have practical effects unless they can successfully take on the lay perspective. Similarly, the layperson can take on the perspective of the expert by becoming a well-informed citizen. For the environmentalist, this broader vision of rationality might carve out space in the public discourse for a concept of ecological rationality that could do battle with the instrumental rationality so often associated with industrialism and its threat to the environment.

To ensure this broadly participatory character, Bohman (1996) takes great pains to specify institutions and procedures that will redress the imbalance of political resources among various groups within the general population. He begins by identifying several conditions that allow ongoing cooperation to exist. First, the discursive structures of deliberation must make it unlikely that irrational and ultimately untenable arguments will determine outcomes. Second, discursive procedures must allow for constant revisions in the discourse that take up features of defeated positions or better their chances of receiving a fair hearing. And, third, procedures must be broadly inclusive, producing no permanent majorities. Finally, and perhaps most important, when deliberation requires the resolution of conflicts that are deeply rooted and culturally based, the parties must be guaranteed equality of political capacity in relation to one another and the conditions for effective participation must be equally secured by all. To those conversant with the literature on environmental impact assessment (EIA), this list of participatory prescriptions might seem familiar. It is a concise and general summary of the requirements cited in EIA research for impact assessment to achieve its analytical potential without stunting democratic participation (Baber 1988; Baber and Bartlett 1989).

How this political equality is to be achieved is, obviously, the most serious question Bohman (1996) confronts. The answer, generally speaking, is a more open public sphere. This is to be produced by the organization of challenges to prevailing opinion into collectives (by the state if necessary) and institutional innovations designed to open political processes—voting rights and campaign finance reforms legislation, for example. Once citizen movements are formed, procedural changes will be required to promote equality of opportunity to define problematic situations. Disclosure and public meetings requirements are obvious steps. Where necessary, the state must also act to equalize the resources necessary for groups to participate fully in deliberative processes. And the courts should begin to interpret free speech rights to prohibit both infringements on speech and deliberative inequalities.

Other steps may be indicated as well. The production and distribution by government of policy-relevant information is the most obvious solution to the problem that neither capacities nor acquired knowledge can be assumed to be evenly or widely distributed in the deliberative environment. The efficacy of this epistemic division of labor would depend on public trust. That trust would increase rather than deplete through use, as ordinary citizens are successful in using information supplied by government to redirect the course of government. There will also be a need for institutional reforms that would create new forms of bureaucratic organization more consistent with participatory deliberation. For example, administrators might be held accountable through "public impact statements" that would detail how the public reasons expressed by those affected by agency decisions were taken up in the decision process.

Whatever specific shape these innovations take, Bohman (1996) is convinced that democratic forms of government generally are more consistent with the complexity of modern multicultural societies than are nondemocratic alternatives, which tend to reduce social complexity rather than preserve it. In several ways, liberal democracies are already on the right track. Differentiation within deliberative institutions (e.g., separation of powers) meets some of the challenges of complexity. It permits a variety of deliberative roles as well as an epistemic division of labor within deliberation. Moreover, the structure of the constitutional state generally preserves complexity by functionally limiting the scope and use of hierarchical power and establishing mechanisms for the dispersal of democratic power. This may be why a theory of deliberative democracy, now come of age, sees liberal institutions, once shunned in favor of more participatory alternatives, as themselves an increasingly attractive home for deliberation (Bohman 1998; Cohen and Sabel 1997; Dorf and Sabel 1998; Gutmann and Thompson 1996). This more positive view of existing public institutions may have an ecological significance beyond its political importance. These institutions are the necessary home for a diverse and complex "social ecology" that confronts the difficult questions of agriculture, technological change, political decentralization, and the development of new social relations (Bookchin 1999). These issues neatly frame the first question that must be answered in the development of a model of deliberative environmental politics: Just how democratic does the model have to be?

Synthesis or Surrender?

It is a particular strength of Bohman's approach that it allows the sympathetic reader to more easily imagine that actually existing governments could be moved in a deliberative direction than does the work of either Rawls or Habermas. This difference is more than that between the relatively accessible style of Bohman and the densely philosophical styles of Rawls and Habermas. Although Habermasian in origin, Bohman's approach to deliberative democracy is distinct from that of Habermas in important ways.

Bohman (1996) demands less of deliberative democracy than do other advocates of the theory and, perhaps, less of the world as well. He allows us to cling to our ideas about individual rights for whatever reasons we hold them, rather than requiring that rights be derived from the logic of deliberative politics, as does Habermas. Unanimity on outcomes and reasons is not required by Bohman for the outcomes to be legitimate. For political decisions to be regarded as legitimate, Habermas requires that they be rationally authored by the citizens to whom they are addressed through a decision process that is open to input from a vibrant and informal public sphere and structured to support the rationality of all relevant types of discourse and ensure implementation of the policy. Habermas also requires that laws meet with the agreement of *all* citizens in a discursive lawmaking process. Bohman requires only that a law be the outcome of a participatory process that is fair and open to all citizens and thus includes their publicly accessible reasons, that it be of a nature that citizens may continue to cooperate in deliberation rather than merely comply with the law, and that the deliberative conclusion of the majority be recognized as the source of sovereign power.

So it is clear that Bohman shares the basic assumption of all deliberative democrats that a people cannot be sovereign unless they are able to deliberate together successfully and unless they have something to say about the conditions under which they deliberate. However, he also insists that any concept of deliberative democracy should recognize and address four concrete challenges: first, that the existence of cultural pluralism undermines the existence of a general will, unitary common good, or single public reason; second, that social inequities, if uncorrected, lead invariably to a cycle of permanent exclusion from effective participation in public deliberation; third, that the complexity of modern society imposes a requirement for decision making in the context of large-scale public organizations; and fourth, that community biases restrict communication by narrowing the scope of feasible solutions and recognizable problems.

So does the theoretical work of Bohman (1998) represent a "coming of age" for deliberative democracy as he suggests, or does it simply mean that the more radical aspects of deliberative democratic theory are destined to be gradually squeezed out by accommodationist thinking (Dryzek 2000)? There are (at least) three issues that deliberative democrats of the Rawlsian or Habermasian persuasion might wish to raise at this point. First, has Bohman given up prematurely on the idea of impartiality in public deliberation, and will that choice ultimately deprive him of the possibility that arguments in the public sphere might be improved (or at least moderated) by knowledge? If so, the consequences for environmental discourse (grounded as it so often is in science) cannot be positive. Second, has Bohman abandoned the idea that the process of deliberative democracy can actually change people's political preferences? In other words, has he fallen into the same fundamental error that renders social choice theory implausible? The implications for the environment of treating citizen preferences as givens would be difficult for environmentalists to accept. And, third, has he elevated the value of cultural diversity over those of reason and sustainability in a way that would ultimately deprive deliberative democracy of its ability to reconcile popular government and environmental protection? Each of these issues is worthy of extended exploration in its own right.

The Death of Impartiality?

In what sense could it be fairly said that James Bohman has abandoned the idea of impartiality in public deliberation? That complaint, it seems, could arise most readily from Bohman's argument that cultural conflicts can be so deep as to preclude adjudication and that, under such circumstances, "democratic arrangements may only exacerbate the problems of pluralism" (Bohman 1995, 253). This goes beyond the traditional view of deliberative democrats that all cultural groups must enjoy equal access to public deliberations. That view is troubling enough to those who worry that such a significant leveling of the political playing field could unsettle, if not subvert, existing understandings about the dimensions of political conflict (Knight and Johnson 1994). But Bohman's extension of the idea seems to suggest that some groups within society will, for cultural reasons, find themselves so at odds with the prevailing discourse that their claims cannot even be fairly weighed by government processes.

If deliberative democracy is to redeem its promise as "the procedure of a revived pluralism" (Schlosberg 1998, 605), it seems impossible that any group could be judged to be so alien that the normal processes of government would not serve it adequately. It may well be that in a deliberative democracy some group may be so disadvantaged that the state would wish to promote in some way the organization of its available resources (Cohen and Rogers 1992). It may even be true, as Michael Walzer (1991) has argued, that civil society itself is in such a degraded condition that it makes sense to call the state to its rescue. In Walzer's (1994) view, state-sponsored associations for social groups are necessary not just to afford them fair representation, but as an antidote to rampant individualism and its receptivity to demagogues.

This argument of Walzer's is reminiscent of Habermas's desire to purge rhetoric from deliberation on the grounds that rhetoric can open the door to demagogues, manipulators, deceivers, and flatterers (Chambers 1996). But why this preference for cool and impartial communication? Several possible reasons come to mind. First, one might want to rule out in advance arguments that deny political equality and those that fail to respect the principles of human integrity (Gutmann and Thompson 1996). Second, one might want to encourage a generally impartial tone because of the possibility that discursive relationships among vastly different social groups are as likely to involve questioning of each other's legitimacy as they are deliberation (Fraser 1992). Finally, setting any group outside of the normal legal process risks undermining the legitimacy of the entire structure. This is especially true of highly diverse liberal societies. Lacking a monarchy, official religion, or unitary worldview, the normatively pluralistic society depends solely on the universal representation of its citizens in the legislative process for the legitimacy of its positive law (Gregg 1997).

Beyond these "process" justifications for impartiality, there are some substantive (and admittedly normative) reasons for preferring a form of deliberation that requires participants to "step out of themselves" to some degree. To begin, there is the assumption that partiality renders one's thinking both less just (as Rawls would argue) and less rational (as Habermas would claim). If other participants in deliberation come to question my commitment to behave justly, they will eventually decline to yield to even my just demands because they will have no confidence that I will honor their just arguments in the future. In this way, deliberation requires not only solidarity within groups but across them as well (Miller 1995). This solidarity must be based on a mutual expectation of just behavior. Particularly in the context of environmental issues, the relationships between groups in and out of power must be reciprocal. Winona LaDuke (1999) has argued persuasively that indigenous peoples need the help of those in power to protect the ecology on which their cultures depend and that industrial society and the dominant culture it supports need the help of indigenous peoples to find new concepts of how to survive on the land.

As for rationality, it has been forcefully argued that deliberation is justified only to the extent that it produces more rational policy outcomes (Estlund 1997). It is not sufficient that deliberation merely bring reasons into play. It must sort good reasons from bad ones. If it fails to do so, deliberative democracy may produce the same Arrowian aggregation problems that every state manifests in the absence of some broadly shared notion of the common interest (Grofman 1993). To avoid this outcome, all participants in the deliberative process must be willing to subject the reasons they offer in support of their position to the "critical tribunal" that both Rawls and Habermas have seen at the core of any progressive social theory that would challenge the instrumental forms of rationality that have been so ecologically disastrous (Eckersley 1999a).

These considerations may explain, at least in part, why a strict limitation to public reason is, for both Rawls and Habermas, a primary requirement for deliberative discourse. It is precisely because arguments couched in terms capable of acceptance by all members of the political community eliminate both self-interests and partial worldviews as reasons and motives that Rawls urges this stringent requirement (Benhabib 1996). So it can be argued that out-group identities must omit from their public reasons elements of their identities that are repugnant to the self-understanding of other groups within the political community. Members of those other groups must themselves be willing to embrace an inclusive identity and in the process shed elements of their values that are at odds with that principle (Miller 1995). Although this seems like asking much, it may be that historically disadvantaged groups have the most to gain in the bargain. It is argued that administrative regimes constituted along the lines suggested by Habermas's discourse ethics would create precisely the counterflows of knowledge that would empower traditionally subordinated groups (Simon 1994). By exempting certain groups from the normal requirements of deliberative politics on the grounds that they are too culturally diverse to meet those requirements, we may do little more than institutionalize their marginal political status. We may even undermine the legitimacy of the entire political community in the process. We certainly would have given up on one of the deliberative democrat's fondest hopes—that the deliberative process might produce consensus by actually changing minds through reasoned argument. And we would have to abandon the environmentalist's dream of promoting the growth of ecologically sound attitudes and preferences in the population at large. So we confront a second issue that must be resolved if a deliberative model of environmental politics is to be developed: How important is it that our deliberations achieve a normative consensus?

Is Deliberation Just Better Aggregation?

The rational choice theorist David Austen-Smith (1992) has argued that speech by an actor can never change the preferences of another actor, but can only convey information and play a purely strategic role in the political arena. Bohman may be open to the criticism that he operates on the same assumption because his view of democratic legitimacy allows people to arrive at strategic agreements for their own divergent reasons, without requiring them to come to a meeting of the minds. But how severe a criticism would this be? Gerry Mackie (1998) has criticized Austen-Smith's assumptions that political interaction is always a one-shot affair, that information communicated verbally cannot be proved or disproved, and that political discourse is limited to two participants. Perhaps such criticism does not wound a rational choice theorist. However, it should mortify a deliberative democrat if it can be laid at his door.

Resting near the heart of deliberative democratic theory is a rejection of the assumption that preferences are determined prior to political interactions and do not change as a result of that interaction (Offe 1997). The possibility of such change is the only alternative to the permanent disenfranchisement of some opinion groups, because not everything in oppositional civil society represents discursive democratic vitality. Neo-fascists and the radical religious right, as examples, are not committed to the fulfillment of modernity's potential and, so, will remain estranged from the deliberative mainstream by their inability to offer public reasons for their positions (Offe 1985). Only the possibility of a change in their views suggests that they may some day enter fully into the democratic project.

The problematic nature of Bohman's position is also evident in his views on voting and consensus decision making. Bohman (1994) has challenged Habermas to abandon his requirement of unanimity in order to address the problems of complexity and pluralism. Other deliberative democrats view voting as a distinctly second-best procedure, to be accepted only when best efforts to achieve consensus have failed (Cohen 1989). Certainly the search for consensus assumes that minds can be changed, and the failure to do so represents a setback to be avoided if possible.

Furthermore, there is at least some evidence that deliberation does have the potential to change opinions. Adolph Gundersen (1995) has reported that in a series of deliberative interviews about ecological topics with forty-six subjects who did not initially identify themselves as environmentalists, every individual became more committed to environmental values by the end of the interview. Moreover, one of the most significant findings reported by Kai Lee (1993) in his study of the Northwest Power Planning Council is that involvement in structured opportunities for public participation sponsored by the Council helped to promote ecological awareness among participants from widely varying backgrounds. It is easy enough to dismiss these reports as proving only that talking with trained researchers can change the attitudes of ordinary citizens toward the environment, but that is precisely the point most deliberative democrats would want to make.

It is certainly true, as Bohman (1996) argues, that science is a tempting standard by which to judge public opinion. However, as he explains, such an ideal standard is hard to institutionalize and too often appeals to highly specialized language that violates the standard of publicity. Fair enough. But science can be a powerful force for reshaping public opinion in ways that promote ecological rationality. For example, Albert Weale (1992) and others have argued that the essence of the new environmental politics is "ecological modernization." Based on the environmental sciences, policy elites, the business sector, and average citizens are becoming convinced that a clean environment is good for business. This is more than a random process involving the mundane concerns of people in the business community. It is a concrete example of the more general phenomenon of engagement across divergent discourses (Young 1990a). Such engagement is likely to succeed only where one form of discourse (in this case, free enterprise) is confronted with a problem that it cannot solve within the limits of its own tradition. Under such circumstances, solutions can be proposed by a competing tradition (here, environmentalism), but only if they are couched in language that the discourse in crisis can accept (MacIntyre 1988).

This practice of engagement across discourse traditions holds one additional advantage. One of the most telling criticisms of deliberative democracy is that some citizens are better at articulating their arguments in rational and reasonable terms than are others (Sanders 1997). The tendency of well-educated males to dominate heterogeneous juries is offered as evidence of this problem. Thus it is argued that the deliberative virtues of civility have a sedative effect that curbs the unruly behavior of the disadvantaged, depriving them of their only opportunity for genuine participation in decision making.

It appears this dynamic can be overcome, however, when the scientific community and the underrepresented engage across the boundaries of their respective discourses. The environmental justice movement is the most significant development in environmentalism of the last two decades and the fastest growing part of that movement (Bullard 1999). It is not the product of state sponsorship. It flourishes not because its proponents are held to a lower standard of reasoning than other citizens. It is a movement whose strength arises from a multiplicity of local struggles that have merged into a political network with an associated discourse that presents a perspective on environmental risk that is both scientifically valid and culturally significant (Hajer 1995). And it is an example of the deliberative democrats' hope for an aggregation of local movements into a larger politics of identity and difference that can be both radical and plural (Mouffe 1996) without abandoning the rationality and publicity advocated by Habermas and Rawls. It is also an example of how marginalized groups can engage in mainstream political discourse without losing their critical edge, a fear Dryzek (2000) has expressed in discussing Bohman's approach. It is this critical edge that holds the promise that deliberative democracy may work fundamental changes in the relationship between the state and civil society that will ultimately yield environmental decisions that are more reasonable and sustainable. Here arises the third question that must be answered if Bohman's approach is to be fully understood and a deliberative model of environmental politics is to emerge: How important is it that deliberative reasons be public, and what does the concept of publicity really imply?

Reason and Sustainability in the Balance

A larger corollary of the view that deliberative politics can change individual attitudes and opinions is the notion that their members can consciously and intentionally change political communities. A nation, in this view, does not have an intrinsic and permanent character. Rather, a nation is an "imagined community" that is built on such elements as symbols, historical narratives, customs, and institutional structures that create, reinforce, and (sometimes) alter national identity (Anderson 1983). Therefore, a deliberative approach to public planning would be open to the power of cultural ideas, metaphors, images, and stories of all kinds (Healey 1993). But how should a deliberative democracy imagine itself? In particular, how should its relationship to the environment be discussed?

From the work of Rawls and Habermas, it is possible to conclude that political discourse should be directed toward (among other things) a recoupling of the concepts of reasonableness and rationality. More specifically, a reasonable conception of the relationship between nature and the polity can be fashioned by integrating a primary commitment to justice and a dedication to the value of sustainability with a suitably ecological concept of rationality (as discussed earlier in chapter 2). The objective is to produce a mutualistic, cooperative view of nature, to which human social, economic, and political life can be reconciled (Bookchin 1982).

Confronted with Bohman's facts of complexity and pluralism, what deliberative democracy may need is a "moral, conceptual, and affective framework" (Valadez 2001, 353) that produces something close to the kind of solidarity that religion engenders without the divisiveness that religion can create. A broadly held ecological consciousness may be the only framework that could come near to satisfying that need. That consciousness need not involve a return to metaphysical or enchanted patterns of thinking. Because human beings have the capacity to embrace imagination and understanding simultaneously, a world of reason (appropriately inclusive in character) need not be a disenchanted world (Bennett 1997). As an example, Jane Bennett (1994) has characterized Henry David Thoreau's rejection of the politics of his day as a pause in attention to the political on behalf of the project of crafting an individual sensibility. That sensibility may ultimately provide the foundation for a reintegration of "wilderness" and "civilization" as we come to realize that the wild exists in the unexplored and unexpected dimensions of the objects of everyday experience. Furthermore, these startling experiences are intrinsically social and political, consisting of a recalcitrant remainder generated by the human propensity to contain and categorize reality (Bennett 1995). Thus an environmentalism of both reason and individual sensitivity may provide a central focus for a more reflective and more deliberative style of social interaction.

In fact, there is much to recommend the environmental movement as a center for any deliberative renaissance. For one thing, political communities must at some point confront the fact that human political and economic decisions are exacerbating environmental dilemmas (Valadez 2001) and that they are doing so in ways that may render those communities themselves unsustainable. An ecological perspective as a central feature of the political culture would allow us to hear what Val Plumwood has characterized as "the bad news from below" (1998, 578) in time to avoid the worst of its consequences.

Moreover, this common concern for survival has the potential to unite multicultural communities despite the divergent values of their members. This common concern for survival can be reinforced by the knowledge that the world's ecosystems are interconnected to such a degree that environmental degradation in one area will have an impact on the rest of humanity (Valadez 2001). That realization would create the foundation for a structure of "nested territorial units" from local to global across which popular sovereignty can be dispersed and yet remain adequately focused (Pogge 1992).

An ecological perspective can also expand the moral vision of a multicultural society by broadening the range of beings that should be granted moral consideration (Valadez 2001). This allows deliberative democrats to take account of nonhuman nature without attributing communicative capacities to the natural world, a step that would raise more controversies than it would settle and render less secure the foundation of political democracy (Dobson 1996). This arrangement does not complicate the deliberative democrat's effort to derive and justify the main rights and equalities central to a fair and open liberalism from the logic of public reasoning among equals (Cohen 1996).

Finally, adopting an ecological perspective may have certain cognitive implications conducive to engendering social solidarity in a multicultural society (Valadez 2001). Environmentalism has the potential to correct (or at least counterbalance) the tendency in Western thought and scientific tradition toward orientations that are material rather than relational. The resulting awareness of the interconnection within social ecologies would help us see that progress in one area can be accompanied by consequences in other areas that are not nearly so positive. For example, rapid economic growth may lead to increased mobility resulting in the loss of any sense of place or a decline in social solidarity resulting from increased economic competition. In short, adopting the holistic perspective inherent in ecological consciousness would provide us with a better understanding of what we need to do to nurture the civic environment in which democracies can flourish.

This understanding of the requirements for a healthy democracy would allow civil society to better play the role, laid out for it by deliberative democrats, of fostering public action in response to failures by either the state or the economy (Janicke 1996). Significantly, most new social movements (environmentalism in particular) tend to be characterized by simultaneous and sustained action both in the state and in civil society (Rucht 1990). This reflects the deliberative democrat's assumption that genuine democracy is built from the ground up by citizen associations (Hirst 1994) and that only a continuation of politics in both the state and civil arenas will provide the necessary limits on the dominant classes and interests in society (Fisk 1989). It also demonstrates an awareness that the key to representing nature in politics is the encapsulation of environmental interests, internalized and represented by sympathetic individuals (Goodin 1996). And it suggests that the achievement of goals related to ecology and equity requires decision-making processes of the most deeply democratic character (Wainright 1994). Interest-group liberalism has been unable to achieve these goals because it takes the dominance of entrenched interests and the existing contours of public opinion as givens. This is something that deliberative democracy must never do. If Bohman's approach leads us to replicate this error in the development of a deliberative democracy, the search for deliberative outcomes that are both democratic and sustainable will prove fruitless. How this can be avoided is a final question that must be answered as we move toward a deliberative model of environmental politics.

Conclusion

Bohman's work can be viewed as an attempt to synthesize Rawls and Habermas in a way that reconciles their approaches to deliberative democracy (the liberal theorist on one hand and the critical theorist on the other) by accommodating deliberative democracy to liberal interest-group constitutionalism. His approach may ultimately prove to be unsatisfactory. His abandonment of the ideal of impartial public discourse, purged of culturally specific reasons, threatens to reintroduce the divisive elements of liberal politics that have prevented us from approaching consensus on even such universal issues as endangered species protection. His elevation of cultural diversity to a preeminent position in the constellation of deliberative values may undermine the goal of achieving environmentally rational policy outcomes, based on the unitary concept of ecological sustainability. And his treatment of preferences as, to some extent, cultural givens could sacrifice the environmentalist hope of developing a new pattern of personal preferences in the general population based on a heightened ecological awareness. But Bohman does advance our thinking about deliberative democracy by demonstrating convincingly the need for a deliberative approach that is practical in orientation but maintains its critical edge. That his approach may have been, in some ways, a misstep does not alter the fact that his project represents what must be our next step in bringing the insights of the deliberative democrat to bear on the challenges of contemporary environmental politics. His work has highlighted several important questions that must be answered before a fully operational deliberative model of environmental decision making can emerge. For this reason, if no other, his contributions should continue to receive the most serious attention from theorists and environmentalists alike.

Clearly, deliberative democrats still have a few things to work out. But this continuing theoretical project is one of the most promising alternatives yet suggested for bridging the gap between democracy and the environment. Without minimizing the conceptual points that still divide deliberative democrats, we turn next to developing a fuller account of the kinds of institutions and processes that might improve our environment while reforming our politics. Such institutions and processes must at a minimum provide workable roles, rights, and responsibilities for three types of inhabitants of the deliberative landscape: individual citizens, experts, and interests (social movements).

7

Institutional Strategies for Advancing Deliberative Democratization

A generation ago, William Ophuls pronounced democracy dead. Citing the growing pressures of ecological scarcity, he declared, "The golden age of individualism, liberty, and democracy is all but over" (Ophuls 1977, 145). According to Ophuls, democracy had gone wrong at two levels. First, it had assumed that rational self-interest was all there was to human beings. Second, it had assumed that interest-group liberalism was all there was to democratic politics. But the relentless and impersonal constraints of the environment were proving these assumptions to be, if not mistaken, at least unsustainable.

It has been clear since Ophuls's declaration of doom that any attempt to reconcile the demands of environmental sustainability with a recognizably democratic politics would have to address at least these two issues. Optimism that democracy can coexist with a healthy environment arises from efforts in exactly these two areas. There must exist a conception of rationality that does full justice to the personal integrity of individuals and yet allows for the emergence of "postmaterialist values" (Paehlke 1989, 169). Such values could provide the foundation for a progressive and environmentally friendly politics. This "environmental democracy" can be linked explicitly to the deliberative democracy movement in contemporary political theory. But what are the participatory institutions that are appropriate to this conception of democracy in a large, plural, technologically complex society for which money and bureaucratic power are the primary steering mechanisms (Giddens 1985, 108–110)? "The challenge for normative political theory . . . is to assist in designing institutions and procedures through which fruitful deliberation over sustainable environmental policy can take place" (Vanderheiden 2001, 218).

Environmental Deliberation

The deliberative democracy movement has been spawned by a growing realization that contemporary liberalism has lost its democratic character in much the same way that it has sacrificed its ecological sustainability. Modern democracies, confronted with cultural pluralism, social complexity, vast inequities of wealth and influence, and ideological biases that discourage fundamental change, have allowed their political institutions to degenerate into arenas for strategic gamesmanship in which there is no possibility for genuine deliberation (Bohman 1996, 18–24). Neither true democracy nor environmental protection is possible where citizens become mere competitors with no commitments beyond their own narrow self-interests.

How to move beyond interest-group liberalism is, of course, a matter open to considerable debate. Since what John Dryzek (2000, 1) calls "the deliberative turn" in democratic theory about fifteen years ago, a great deal of ink has been spilled describing, defining, and elaborating the concepts that are thought to be fundamental to deliberative democracy. Not surprisingly, and fully in the spirit of democratic practice, there have emerged conflicting and contending views about what deliberative democracy permits and demands. Clearly, deliberative democrats still have a few things to work out. But this continuing theoretical project is one of the most promising alternatives yet suggested for bridging the gap between democracy and the environment. Moreover, it has the potential to be of profound significance for policymaking and administrative theory, inasmuch as deliberative norms "can help us distinguish between more and less democratic forms of public administration, thereby guiding institutional experimentation and reform" (Hunold 2001, 152). This potential and significance notwithstanding, it is remarkable how little attention that the ongoing ferment about deliberative democracy in the theoretical literature has received from the more practical world of administrators and administrative scholars—even less attention, it would seem, than applied and practical concerns of all sorts have received from the theorists.[1] So, without minimizing the conceptual points that still divide deliberative democrats, it is our expectation that this project can be moved forward in useful ways via more attention by metapolicy analysts and administrative reformers to the kinds of institutions and processes that might improve our environment while deliberatively (and deliberately) democratizing politics.

Such an exploration need not be entirely, or even mostly, a speculative enterprise. Theorists may sometimes exhibit little awareness of real-world manifestations. "Empirical literature on deliberation is thin" (Cohen and Rogers 2003, 243), and "the evidence is no more than suggestive" (Smith 2004). But there are natural experiments in environmental democracy available for analysis (e.g., Fung 2003; Fung and Wright 2003; Smith 2003). Presuming the context of existing institutions of capitalist liberal democracy and the administrative state (and it is fair to say that Bohman, Gutmann, Thompson, Habermas, and Rawls are all theorizing in response to the reality of the established administrative state in liberal capitalist protodemocracies), strategies are available for advancing democratization of a deliberative nature. At least five possible strategies can be identified: (1) controlling the administrative state directly through mass politics; (2) fragmentating the administrative state through decentralization; (3) improving the administrative state through reformed administrative politics; (4) bypassing and constrainting the administrative state through expanded civic politics and cultivation of alternative social institutions; and (5) transcending the administrative state through metapolicy, constitutional restructuring, or cultivation of transstate arrangements and institutions.

These possible strategies are not mutually exclusive, and neither is any one strategy an exclusive means for realizing the democratic vision of one or another deliberative theorist. The constrasting theoretical perspectives of Habermas, Rawls, and advocates of full liberalism are, however, helpful in illuminating the potential and limitations of each strategy. We must recognize that "our deliberation over potential solutions is intended not just to aggregate our existing preferences, but to form and even transform them in the process" (Vanderheiden 2001, 218). A full cataloging and inductive analysis of these strategies is a task for another book, but here we offer a quick and superficial survey to provide a foundation for further theorizing about democracy and the environment.

Background Institutional Conditions

The implications of ecological necessity for democratic practice are not easily explored. In fact, it is not universally agreed that the effort is well conceived. In Robert Goodin's view, the two issues are essentially different because to advocate democracy is to advocate procedures, whereas to advocate environmentalism is to advocate substantive outcomes (Goodin 1992, 168). Robyn Eckersley, on the other hand, argues that green values and democracy are bound together at the level of principle. In her view, the two are linked by the concept of autonomy. She suggests that democratic values apply to nonhuman as well as to human beings and that authoritarianism is ruled out at the level of green principle (Eckersley 1996, 222–223). Regardless of whether one sees the marriage of ecology and democracy as impossible or inevitable, time spent exploring the courtship options can be fruitful in understanding the relationship.

What are the essential conditions, the background institutions or circumstances, that are required to sustain environmental deliberation? On most lists would probably be a minimal level of access to resources—enough to sustain health and the time needed for political participation. At the top of almost any list of such conditions, one would expect to find the idea of equality, that is, equality of wealth, education, and political access. It is a commonplace of environmental thinking that resource inequality has prevented the environmental movement from achieving more significant results. In the words of Mark Dowie, environmentalists are "losing ground" because they are outspent and outgunned at every turn by development interests (1995, 192–195). Although there might be broad agreement that the unequal positions of those supporting environmental protection and those supporting environmental exploitation is a problem, it is less clear what should be done about it.

One view is that simple disclosure is the key. As Louis Brandeis once wrote in another connection, "sunlight is said to be the best of disinfectants" (1932, 92). Open meetings acts, campaign finance disclosure rules, and other "sunshine legislation" are clearly derivative of this view. Although the approach is helpful (as far as it goes), this traditionally progressive reasoning has also provided cover for those who oppose more aggressive efforts to level the political playing field. It is enough, they argue, that the associations of decision makers and the interests of lobbyists be made public so that citizens may judge for themselves. Were the voting public constantly attentive to such matters, ever vigilant to punish their representatives for selling influence to the highest bidder, the situation of environmentalists would no doubt be significantly improved. The actual state of affairs is, of course, very different.

Another approach is to reduce the inequity of influence among interests through campaign finance reform. In the United States, the McCain–Feingold–Shays–Meehan law is just the latest in a long line of campaign reform efforts designed to level the political playing field. As with sunshine legislation, campaign finance reform—were it to work as intended—should not be dismissed simply because it is not the entire answer to a given problem. But the usefulness of this approach is limited in the environmental arena for several reasons.

First, leveling the playing field in Washington, D.C., or any other capital, is only to the advantage of those who play there. The environmental movement is, of course, represented in the capitals. But empowering that group of representatives has its disadvantages. The accusation that national groups engage in "corporate environmentalism" hits dangerously close to home for organizations that play the lobbying game at the national level. With their organizational success comes the pressure to protect their budgets and respectability, a certain orientation toward efficiency, and a predisposition toward bureaucratically rational decision making that conflicts with the core values of environmentalism and democracy (Bosso 2000, 68; Dryzek et al. 2003).

Second, advantaging national environmental groups will inevitably overlook environmental interests for which there is no national constituency. Among the most important of these interests are the community groups that make up the environmental justice movement. These organizations tend to be small. They rarely have any paid staff. They usually import their leadership from local civil rights organizations, churches, and other groups with little background in environmental issues. Their concerns, while generalizable in principle, rarely extend beyond the borders of their local communities. Reducing the inequities in political influence at the national level is of little use to these groups because they are represented at that level in only the most mediated and indirect ways.

Finally, a more level playing field in a nation's or province's capital will do little for environmental interests that are nearly unrepresented. The animal rights movement, for example, has begun to exercise limited influence at the national level. But its field of interest is generally limited to the animate elements of the biosphere (and, cynics would say, only the cuddlier parts of that). The inanimate elements of nature are often of significant concern only to a few scientists and policy specialists who wield no influence either individually or collectively. It is necessary to recognize that environmentalism is a diverse social movement composed of more than just conventionally organized groups (Taylor 1992; Pepper 1996; Dryzek et al. 2003).

So if disclosure rules and campaign finance reform are incomplete solutions to the problem of the unequal status of environmental interests, what else is there? To find an answer to that question, it is necessary to ask why equality among interests is desirable in the first place. In discussing the general situation of the economically disadvantaged, Gutmann and Thompson emphasize that the point is not for the poor to take their place among the other interest groups jostling for position in the democratic arena. It is, rather, that "an increase in political power—an enhanced opportunity for political participation—is necessary to ensure that their views receive fully informed and vigorous representation in democratic deliberation" (Gutmann and Thompson 1996, 305). The objective is not so much to advantage one group as to ensure that all those involved in a deliberative process are able to take appropriate account of all relevant views.

In this way, the "right" to equal status in political deliberation is analogous to the right to an attorney in court. The right is not designed to privilege one party or to bias the outcome in one direction. The objective is to improve the performance of the decision-making system. This could be achieved in two ways. First, some basic income support is necessary to enable citizens to participate in politics and more generally to make effective use of their political liberties (Gutmann and Thompson 1996, 277). But to depend entirely on this approach would be roughly equivalent to ensuring that every citizen had a salary sufficient to secure the services of a lawyer in case of need. A more practical alternative would be to provide income security sufficient to a generally active civic life and to facilitate active participation in political deliberation directly. In the same way that a citizen's due process rights are made real by the provision of a public defender, the right to petition one's government could be made more real if organizations and individuals could be provided financial support, distributed by an independent and nonpartisan board upon the showing of both a public interest rationale and need (Aron 1980, 54–69).

This kind of public support might be thought inconsistent with the idea that the "marketplace of ideas" should be allowed to flourish without the state acting to privilege particular groups. Habermas has anticipated this sort of objection and has developed a plausible response. In his view, the ideal discourse situation allows for the existence of such "privileged parties" so long as they are confronted with the necessity of demonstrating to what degree their advantage can be justified discursively. They must also show that their advantage is in accordance with the standards of procedural equity, participation, nondeception, and nonmanipulation (White 1988, 76–77). In short, interests should be provided support where that support is defensible in terms of its contribution to the improvement of the political discourse. It must be to the advantage of all participants in their pursuit of positions that are justifiable to each other.

Without some sort of public support for policy intervenors, it is difficult to imagine how fully democratic deliberation is possible. If democratic citizens are to value political liberty as more than a means of pursuing self-interest and if they are to weigh the interests of others and to guide their actions by a sense of justice, then democratic societies must take positive steps to encourage the give and take of argument about controversial political issues. Forums for deliberation must abound (Gutmann and Thompson 1996, 37), and all voices in these forums must be heard equally. But where should these forums be located, and how should they be organized?

Strategy 1: Mass Publics and the Environment

In large and complex democracies, it is impossible for direct forms of political participation to be used to the exclusion of representative mechanisms. Even for deliberative democrats, there is an irreducible minimum of representative politics. From the deliberative perspective, this is not only necessary but also desirable. After all, the number of people who at the same time can have even a simple conversation, let alone an extended moral argument, is very limited (Gutmann and Thompson 1996, 131).

Yet the probability that representative institutions will respond to environmental challenges in appropriately forceful ways is reduced by the variability and ambivalence of public opinion on environmental questions. The history of mass political support for environmental initiatives is mixed at best. In a November 2003 CBS news poll, the environment was not among the issues cited by 1 percent or more of U.S. respondents as the most important issue facing the country (PollingReport.Com 2003). Polls also show broad public support for environmental protection as an abstract matter. But support wavers when particular environmental initiatives are cited, and the number of respondents with no opinion grows markedly when questions become at all specific. These are the hallmarks of an issue possessed of low salience. Low-salience issues may exhibit consistent patterns of opinion, but the opinions themselves are not strongly held and the issue itself is of lesser importance (Guber 2003; Bosso and Guber 2003). This is crucial because it has long been recognized that the connection between public opinion and policy outcomes is more uncertain in the case of low-salience issues like environmental protection (Downs 1972).

The low salience of environmental issues helps explain some of the characteristics of environmentalism as a political movement. It makes clear why, despite environmentalism's high level of general support, there would be so little evidence of a green voting block similar to that found in the case of antiabortion and pro-gun groups (Dunlap 1991, 33; Guber 2003). It also offers an explanation for environmentalism's "negative" power in the political arena. The salience of environmental issues fluctuates, but general support is sufficient to make environmental protection a "consensus issue," which generates little open opposition (Dunlap 1995, 536; Guber 2003). That profile of public support might be expected to allow for more effective defense against unwanted policies (which engages the abstract environmentalism of the public) than the initiative necessary to carry specific policy proposals. That is precisely the history of the environmental movement in American politics (McCloskey 1993, 83; Duffy 2003).

So what is to be done in the arena of mass political participation? Can environmentalism become a positive force, more successfully converting its public support into progress on specific policy initiatives? One answer might be found in a reconceptualization of how political influence is acquired and put to use. A conventional view on this matter has it that lobbying is a sequential process. One first gains access to decision makers and then one exercises influence (Milbrath 1963, 297–304). A more sophisticated view would be that influencing public officials is an unceasing and often subtle process. It begins with talking to officials frequently so as to actually gain their attention to the discussion. One then reinforces, on a continuing basis, the importance of the issue at hand and the policy proposals being presented (Baumgartner and Leech 1998).

This is a demanding process, no doubt. But why should environmentalists be unequal to the task? Other good government and public interest lobbies have played the game successfully (Berry 1997, 233–236). In the particular case of the environmental movement, the path to improved results is already clear. It has long been recognized that decision makers find a lobbyist more persuasive if the lobbyist is also an opinion leader with the ability to influence others (Katz and Lazarsfeld 1955). For environmentalists, whose most significant political advantage is the high level of public support they enjoy at a general level, the appropriate strategy is obvious. They should employ the "outside" strategy of lobbying the public at the same time they pursue the "inside" strategy of influencing decision makers directly. In addition to playing to the movement's strength, this approach is consistent with the imperatives of deliberative democracy. Lobbying the public has the potential to bring forward policy alternatives that otherwise might not have been understood or even considered (Mansbridge 1983; Duffy 2003).

An insight into one possible technique for pursuing this multidirectional strategy is provided by James Fishkin's (1995) discussion of "deliberative polling." In 1996, several Texas utility companies asked Fishkin to conduct deliberative polls for them. Fishkin brought together 250 citizens for a weekend to read reports and listen to presentations from a variety of environmental, industry, and government experts regarding alternatives for increasing power supplies. Participants showed a marked willingness to change their positions, including increased support for efficiency programs as well as higher energy costs for the sake of cleaner air (Levine 2000, 199–200). Such a procedure is not, of course, polling in any conventional sense. It more closely resembles an effort at democratic deliberation. It is also suggestive of the sort of multidirectional lobbying (Brown 1998) that environmental groups should be able to do especially well. Although the results of such deliberative polling do not constitute policy decisions in themselves, they would seem to be the kind of opinion leadership to which decision makers often respond. Perhaps the boldest public deliberation idea, one that builds on deliberative polling experiments, is a proposal for a new national holiday, Deliberation Day (really two days), in which every citizen will take a day off to participate actively in deliberative citizenship activities (Ackerman and Fishkin 2004).

Many other techniques and institutional designs might be creatively employed and combined to contribute to a greater degree of mass deliberative democratization. Graham Smith (2003) analyzes, among others, citizens' juries, consensus conferences, and citizen referenda and initiatives. He concludes that all have weaknesses but also differing strengths that can be complementary and reinforcing. Graham's conclusion is the same as that of Torgerson (1999, 138): "The examples of discursive design that can be brought to bear are no doubt sparse and imperfect, but they nonetheless indicate that communicative contexts can be designed and developed to supply incentives for a significantly better approximation to communicative rationality than is usual in policy deliberations."

The openness of these procedures to the involvement of a wide range of citizens may offer an approach to another challenge confronting the environmental movement. Robyn Eckersley (1992, 185) has argued that the cultivation of an ecocentric culture is crucial to achieving a lasting solution to the environmental crisis. This will require the widest possible assimilation of the core values of environmentalism, identified by Robert Paehlke (1989, 4) as the interdependence implied by the concept of ecology, the status of health as a primary social good, and the concept of sustainability as a transformational force in industrial society. When broadly interpreted, these core values, long familiar to environmentalists, offer an opportunity to reach out to other groups in society. For example, fiscal conservatives are increasingly critical of tax subsidies that encourage unsustainable resource-extraction activities. The poor show a growing concern for the health risks being imposed on them by locally unwanted land uses as well as a growing determination to resist them. And Christian evangelicals are showing an emerging commitment to the protection of the entire biosphere, which they take to be an interdependent web of God's creations (Kelly 1997). Support from these groups not traditionally affiliated with environmentalism is likely to be crucial to the movement's future success (Gottleib 1993). But they are unlikely to be available unless environmentalists adopt a significant commitment to decentralized politics. Just such a trend has already been detected in mainstream national environmental organizations (Graham 1990; Duffy 2003).

Strategy 2: Decentralization

For the environmentalist, decentralization has at least two distinct faces. First, it has been argued that the frequent emphasis on geographic decentralization characteristic of "back to nature" environmentalism carries with it a number of difficulties. Environmentalists have too often advocated a bucolic vision of human beings in small communities living lightly on the land in a manner said to be typical of our ancestors. In addition to being bad history, this vision is also bad environmentalism. On balance, high-density urban living is the least environmentally damaging way for human beings to exist in significant numbers (Paehlke 1989, 244–251). From this perspective, at least, decentralization would appear to be inherently problematic.

Another face of decentralization is political. It is often argued that decentralized decision making in small institutions is more in step with the core values of environmentalism than regulatory schemes devised in and implemented by national political institutions (Kriz 1995, 1419). But the assumption that decision making carried out "closer to the people" is somehow more environmentally friendly is open to serious question. Any survey of policymaking in this area suggests that not all provinces, states, or local governments are responding appropriately to environmental problems within their boundaries (Lowry 1992; Rabe 2003). Reasons for this disparity are numerous. Variations in state political culture and social capital suggest that there will be significant differences in likely reactions at the state level to environmental improvement efforts (Rice and Sumberg 1997). Moreover, a comparison of Canadian provinces and American states shows that those that experience less involvement by the national government have far less innovative policies on pollution prevention and regulatory integration (Rabe 1999a).

Subnational decision making is problematic in other ways as well. In the United States, states are constantly confronted with the temptation to trade environmental protection for economic development in their pursuit of business investments (Donahue 1997). Decision making at the state level also exhibits a tendency to follow the path of least resistance, as when one state seeks to export its environmental problems to another (Gormley 1987, 298–299). States also face serious fiscal pressures, resulting in spending decisions that crowd out environmental protection in favor of education and criminal justice (Brandl 1998, ch. 2). Finally, studies of resurgent "state-house democracy" show that policymaking at the state level has proven highly responsive to the dominant public opinion within each state (Erickson 1993; Bartlett, Baber, and Baber 2005). Where environmentalism is a "dominant" force in public opinion, this tendency would obviously prove helpful. But it is clearly a barrier to environmental improvement in the more common instance where other interests predominate. To the extent that provincial-, state-, or local-level decision making, whether carried out in voluntary groups or elected legislatures, exhibits these limitations, environmental concerns are unlikely to prevail and may not even be heard. Even when deliberative institutions are designed to favor arguments advocating general environmental interests, they may not prevail—instrumental rationality in pursuit of predetermined self-interest is not readily or easily overcome (Zwart 2003).

Still, the potential for redesign of local democratic institutions has hardly been exhausted. An example of real-world experiments—really, a range of experiments—are Habitat Conservation Plans under the U.S. Endangered Species Act (Thomas 2003). HCPs are messy and peculiar political compromises that cannot be directly transplanted to other contexts (Vanderheiden 2001; Raymond 2004), but they do exhibit many of the principles and design properties that Fung and Wright (2003) identify with a family of "empowered participatory governance" innovations. Karkkainen concludes: "These institutions are locally devolved (relative to the *status quo ante*), practically oriented, collaborative, and 'deliberative' in the practical problem solving sense of that term. Consistent with Fung and Wright's central claims, these institutions set out self-consciously to transform state power by reassembling and fusing its elements into new configurations that transcend established jurisdictional, territorial, and functional boundaries" (2003, 223).

Strategy 3: Policy and Administrative Reform

If decentralization is, by itself, an inadequate answer to the deliberative dilemma, what else is called for? Administrative agencies would seem to be poor ground in which to plant the seeds of deliberation. Commenting on Habermas's ideal discourse theory, William Scheurman has observed that the nature of administrative power conflicts with the logic of communicative power, which is ultimately based on relations of mutual recognition and respect (1999, 157). Yet Gutmann and Thompson caution us in setting up deliberative institutions to avoid the temptation to designate some institutions as forums for reason and others as arenas for power (1996, 358–360). The democratic potential of formal policymaking and implementation is vast; as Schneider and Ingram (1997) note, policy designs of nearly all kinds have significant implications for democracy and democratic possibilities, whether intentionally or no. So what might be the prospect for administrative agencies to serve as actual forums for ecological deliberation?

An obvious first answer is that administrative practice is open to reform through the adoption of deliberative procedures. In recent decades in the United States, a broad array of processes that promote deliberation, including policy dialogues, stakeholder advisory committees, citizen juries, and facilitated mediations, have come to play an increasing role in policy implementation and administration. The traditional roles of public hearings and public comment have been expanded (Beierle and Cayford 2002). Perhaps the best example of this sort of administrative reform is the U.S. National Environmental Policy Act (NEPA). The central achievement of NEPA has not been to make administration more scientific but, rather, to democratize administration by making it more vulnerable to protest and challenge in the courts if it uses science in legally indefensible ways (Caldwell 1982, 58). Furthermore, NEPA has had a significant feedback effect on the discipline of ecology, forcing it to grow from a science that was largely theoretical and descriptive into one that is increasingly integrative and practical (ibid., 100). Both of these developments have served to open environmental decision making to broader political participation and to make it more likely that the decision-making process will actually attend to the arguments put forward by the citizens who do participate. The greater the rigor with which the courts review environmental impact statements for legal adequacy, the more the entire decision process will tend toward the consensual decision making to which deliberative democrats aspire. Unfortunately, Supreme Court decisions have dampened enthusiasm among the district courts for careful review of environmental impact statements (McSpadden 1995, 247).

Another possible strategy is suggested by the U.S. Coastal Zone Management Act (CZMA). The complexity and importance of estuaries and

tidal areas and the challenge involved in protecting them would be difficult to overstate (Johnson 1987). A significant problem faced by environmentalists in this regard is the fragmented jurisdictions that control these
vulnerable areas (Platt 1985). Under the provisions of CZMA, financial
assistance is offered to encourage states to adopt federally approved
coastal management plans. Those state plans provide the specific criteria
land- and water-use proposals must meet before a federal permit can be is-
sued. In an inversion of the usual pattern of federal–state interaction, the
act requires federal agencies to comply with state coastal zone plans once
they are approved. The federal government will override the state's decision only after determining that "the activity is consistent with the objectives of [CZMA] or is otherwise necessary in the interest of national
security" (Barnes 1999, 124).

The policy theory underlying CZMA is clearly an innovative departure
from the administrative approaches of the past. The act has been well received by real estate developers, small business operators, and property
owners, largely on economic grounds (Renner 1995). It has also been ap-
plauded by environmentalists as a mechanism to protect against the further loss of wetlands (Millemann 1991). The Coastal Zone Management
Program created under CZMA is a voluntary partnership between the federal government and coastal states and territories (Duff 2001) that com-
ports well with the criteria for institutionalizing deliberative democracy.
Supporters of the act, however, have had to contend with judicial interpretations that have weakened the "consistency" provision that requires
federal agencies to respect state coastal plans (Kuntz 1990; LaLonde
1993). This problem strikes at the very heart of CZMA's attempt to reconcile the breadth of viewpoint and consistency of approach that is possible with national policymaking with the depth of detail and intensity of
public participation that is available at the state level. To achieve this goal
through a voluntary arrangement that has been characterized as "contractual federalism" (Duff 2001) creates important new opportunities for the
devolution of decision making that deliberative democracy requires without surrendering the policy process to elite-dominated local politics. Continuing disputes between national and state interests over issues of
consistency are nearly inevitable (LaLonde 1993, 476). But that is only an
indication of the vitality of deliberative processes at both levels of government. Such confrontation merely creates opportunities for the testing of

validity claims called for in the ideal discourse situation described by Habermas, integrating participatory administrative practices with clear legal protections expressed in statutory law (1996, 440–441).

Strategy 4: Civic Politics

Mass politics, decentralization, and administrative reform all presume government—deliberative democratization means making government more deliberatively democratic. But politics and government are not synonymous. The boundary between the governmental and the nongovernmental is a socially negotiated one, just as the boundary between the political and the nonpolitical is socially defined. The "rediscovery" of civic politics in recent years (De Tocqueville 1961; Putnam 2001) has been manifested in thinking about environmental politics as much as anywhere (Wapner 1996; Lipschutz 1996; 2004; Bryner 2001; Weber 2003; Dryzek et al. 2003). This attention to nongovernmental (or extragovernmental) politics implies that conceptually broadening the category of the political can be fruitful in deepening our understanding of where and how deliberative democracy can be manifested in the public sphere. It suggests a dual strategy: first, of recognizing that some responsibilities often thought of as governmental, for example, environmental protection, can also be served, sometimes even best served, by social institutions other than state-linked government; and, second, of securing the democratic character of those institutions.

Even though civic groups and associations can be huge, most are either small or organized in subgroups or chapters that facilitate face-to-face interaction. Although civic politics is not inherently democratic (organized crime is, after all, both an arena and actor in the realm of civic politics), the voluntary character of most associations, and their continuing need not only for near consensus but for member identification, high participation, and symbolic if not tangible rewards, means that civic politics is fertile soil for the seeds of deliberative democracy.

The number of nongovernmental organizations (NGOs) in the United States and around the world, including in Third World countries, continues to show remarkable growth—two million in the United States and "India has at least one million NGOs that work on development projects alone" (Bryner 2001, 70). The best-known and best-studied of these tend to be organizations aimed at influencing government, but probably most have mostly nongovernmental primary purposes that are political only in a broad sense of the word. An example are land trusts, of which there are hundreds in the United States (Raymond and Fairfax 2002; Brewer 2003; Fairfax et al. 2005). The largest and best-known land trust organization is the Nature Conservancy, a national NGO that eschews lobbying, suing, campaigning, or other traditional, overtly political activities. Although the Nature Conservancy often cooperates and collaborates with government, its basic approach is nongovernmental (but nevertheless political), namely, the protection and preservation of specific pieces of real estate through gifts, purchase, and legal reservation. Most associations contributing to civic environmentalism are, however, small and local, with aims ranging from urban planning to economic redevelopment (Shutkin 2000).

Civic politics offers the possibility that the government's stranglehold on authoritative decision making might be broken. This possibility is attractive on both deliberative and environmental grounds. Gutmann and Thompson warn against structuring deliberative institutions in ways that confine deliberation to government institutions and impose so strict a division of deliberative labor that representatives give all the reasons and citizens merely receive them (1996, 358–360). To do so would be to surrender the possibility, discussed by Habermas, that a broad discourse, juxtaposed with administrative power and parliamentary politics, might allow for the working out of an effective public control of the policy process (1998b, 234). Thus, John (1994) argues that "civic environmentalism" at the subnational level stimulates stakeholders to make creative collective decisions that are independent of, and often more demanding than, parallel government policies.

An intriguing example of how nongovernmental environmental decision making could work is provided by recent experience with "watershed partnerships." Watershed areas present serious challenges that are both environmental and political. These ecosystems are large and incredibly complex. To fully understand the hydrology, geology, and biology of such vast and diverse areas is daunting enough. But these two characteristics, scale and complexity, pose political difficulties as well. Watershed areas often cross jurisdictional boundaries (Blatter and Ingram 2001). The resources they contain are exploited by farmers, miners, ranchers, timber companies, recreation enthusiasts, native communities, manufacturers, and urban water consumers. It is hardly surprising that American water policy is among the most politicized in the world (Switzer and Bryner 1998, 145–148). With the contending interests, ideologies, and lifestyles present in America's watershed areas, it is difficult to imagine a policy arena more in need of political consensus, or less likely to produce it.

Into this maelstrom of political contention comes the concept of the watershed partnership. These voluntary groups convene at the local or regional level to discuss issues of common concern related to watershed resource management. Membership is open to all interested parties. Members have no power to issue binding regulations. But these groups often include large landowners and corporations that can moderate their behavior, environmentalists who can forgo their right to sue, and government officials who can take these voluntary agreements into account in their management of watershed resources (Clark 1997).

These groups vary considerably in structure and approach. At the very least, they offer neutral forums for civil discussion of important environmental issues. This is in itself an important service for the participants who learn mutual respect and build social capital (Clark 1997, 3). Some of these partnerships have proven their capacity to endure the vicissitudes of water politics in the West. Others have fallen victim to the politics they have promoted. But the watershed partnership approach has been promising enough that over seventy such groups have been convened across the West (Natural Resources Law Center 1995). Successes have hardly been limited to water or watersheds (Weber 2003; Weber and Herzog 2003). Peter Levine suggests that the U.S. Congress should consider delegating the authority to devise resource conservation plans to such voluntary groups instead of executive branch agencies. Once local groups had developed acceptable plans, Congress could then direct federal agencies to implement them (Levine 2000, 196).

Strategy 5: Think Locally, Act Globally

Although the theorist often assumes the tabula rasa design or wholesale redesign of social institutions, the policy analyst and the administrative reformer usually neglect to take things that far, largely because of professionally internalized norms of avoiding the impossible. But the impossibility of fundamental institutional change is itself an assumption unwarranted by experience. To be sure, constitutional or metapolicy is not common or routine and certainly never easily accomplished, but neither is it wholly rare. Nor is it limited to changes in written constitutions—perhaps it is an obsession for written constitutions that blinds Americans to changes in their unwritten constitution (unwritten constitutions being near-consensual, binding precommitments about what may be done and how it may be done).

Perhaps the most dramatic example of this kind of change is represented by the civil rights revolution of the last half of the twentieth century. But there are other examples as well, many of which have considerable relevance to environmental democracy: precommitments about government and business openness, about citizen participation before government action, about the right to pollute. Thirty years after its adoption, the implementation and cost of the Endangered Species Act are still controversial, but its basic premise—that the extinction of species should be avoided—is not.

And no discussion of deliberative institutional alternatives can be considered adequate if it omits any comparative or international perspective. How could the comparison of citizen juries in Great Britain and deliberative polling in the United States (Laslett 2003) fail to yield useful insights? The concept of reciprocity that is central to deliberative democracy knows no logical limit. It "extends to all individuals, not just to citizens of a single society" (Gutmann 1999, 309). Moreover, environmental problems (among many others) depend for their resolution on far more "cross-national deliberation" than can be accomplished within any single set of domestic political institutions (Gutmann and Thompson 2004, 61). This imperative reflects back on the ability of individual states to achieve their domestic environmental objectives. Environmental ends can be ensured to a national population only if its government "negotiates and consistently maintains agreements with other governments for the purpose" (Laslett 2003, 217).

Comparative analysis of deliberative democratic experience serves at least two important goals. First, it provides a body of analytical comparisons that should aid both theorists and government officials as they try to work out the institutional details of a more fully democratic society. As an example, the state of Oregon established a Health Care Services Commission to set priorities for health care services under Medicaid. Meanwhile, halfway around the world, the British government created the National Institute for Clinical Excellence to provide assessment and treatment guidelines for that country's National Health Service. Both of these bodies sought to incorporate expert and lay opinion into a system of rational priorities for husbanding limited health care resources. They were intended to be deliberative institutions in that they were supposed to provide an "analytical filter" (Gutmann and Thopmson 2004, 14) for public opinion that would justify policy outcomes through the imposition of a form of procedural rationality. But the public outcry that resulted in both cases required each group to engage in significant participatory back-filling and ultimately resulted in legislative intervention in both instances. Certainly a careful comparison of these cases would be of interest to public health planners in the future who wish to avoid making the same mistakes thrice.

A second use to which comparative analysis of deliberative institutions can be put is somewhat more theoretical, even normative. A comparison of the Canadian and U.S. experience has allowed DeWitt John (1994) to conclude that institutions for applying the notion of sustainable development are relatively underdeveloped in the United States. On the basis of this evaluation, he suggests that the American states follow the example of Canadian provinces in establishing environmental roundtables to bring together environmentalists, corporations, and government officials to discuss how economic and environmental values might be integrated. Such parallel development might encourage greater transnational environmental cooperation. This could occur under the auspices of the International Joint Commission, which operates as part of a binational and multi-institutional system of regional governance incorporating more than 650 stakeholders in the Great Lakes Basin (Rabe 1999b).

The South African Truth and Reconciliation Commission represents a form of deliberative institution with even greater normative potential. Unlike a trial court, the commission achieves an "economy of moral disagreement" by eschewing definite binary choices between guilt and innocence in favor of accommodations of conflicting views that fall within the range of "reasonable disagreement" (Gutmann and Thompson 2004, 185). Truth commissions of this sort are not entirely rare. An examination of this form of deliberative institution may provide the model for a normative stance that international environmental monitoring groups might adopt in support of deliberative bodies, like the Green Parliament in the Czech Republic, when they find themselves at odds with their own national governments (Axelrod 2005). It might also lead deliberative democrats in the direction of thinking about how their insights into democratization at the domestic level could be applied to the international arena.

Deliberative democracy's emphasis on justifying collective decisions to the people who must live with the consequences of those choices would seem to argue for extending the requirements of democratic deliberation to the international arena. Yet "most theorists of deliberative democracy apply its principles exclusively to domestic systems of government" (Gutmann and Thompson 2004, 36). This is, to say the least, ironic. Although the aggregation of interests across boundaries is hard to conceptualize, "deliberation across boundaries is relatively 'straightforward' and deliberative theory would seem to be more useful in the international system precisely because it lacks "alternative sources of order" (Dryzek 2000, 116). If we can set aside, for our purposes at least, the fact that introducing democratic principles abroad can be used to legitimate dubious military adventures (Zolo 1997), there would still seem to be two fundamental reasons to limit deliberative democracy to the national stage.

First, it could be argued that the justification of preferences through the public reason demanded by deliberative democracy is owed only to those who share with us the burdens of a common citizenship. Second, the absence of sovereignty at the international level might be thought to deprive deliberative democracy of the background conditions for success that a stable legal order provides. But we agree with Gutmann and Thompson (2004) that these objections are largely unpersuasive. The differences between domestic and international society are often exaggerated, particularly with respect to the reliability of legal institutions. The argument about shared citizenship, while it may apply to matters such as taxation, is far less convincing with respect to issues such as war, trade, immigration, economic development, and (most especially) the environment. After all, environmental damage can occur virtually anywhere, and "environmental liability affects every single citizen of every single state in the world, along with other humans who do not belong to nation-states at all" (Laslett 2003, 217).

Fortunately, there are abundant examples of deliberative democracy's various institutional elements that can be identified on the international environmental stage (Caldwell 1996). Much of the recent progress in international environmental governance (as well as progress on issues like children's rights, population control, and social development) has been due to the involvement in collective decision making of nongovernmental organizations (Camilleri, Malhota, and Tehranian 2000). Moreover, this activity has evolved from its earlier reactive form to seize the policy initiative in a number of areas (Snidal and Thompson 2003). For instance, throughout the 1970s, the International Whaling Commission was plagued by environmental protesters who would drench its members in faux whale blood at every opportunity. But by 1981, the Commission's meeting offered representation to fifty-two nongovernmental organizations (NGOs) ranging from species preservation and animal rights groups to religious organizations and groups representing indigenous peoples. In this more open and democratic environment, the Commission agreed to a zero quota for the 1985–1986 season (Birnie 1985). In fact, in this area it is the state actors who are the weak links. Setbacks in whaling regulation after the 1985 moratorium can be attributed to a lack of state follow-through in enforcement and accommodationist backsliding among state members (Vogler 2000; Andresen 2002).

Our experience with whaling suggests not that deliberative participation in international civil society is futile but, rather, that it must penetrate international governance more deeply to be fully effective. Environmental NGOs now routinely enjoy observer status in international organizations and conferences, sometimes even serving as members of state delegations (Porter, Brown, and Chasek 2000). Some deploy a level of environmental expertise matched only by the largest and most developed states. Many are able to mobilize consumer boycotts that make them key policy actors (Thomas 1992). This provision of observer status and the increase in NGO participation is one of the most significant trends in international environmental law in the last twenty years (Vogler 2000). But environmental interests in international civil society have not been satisfied with this.

By the time of the Earth Summit in 1992, international environmental NGOs had mobilized and coordinated sufficiently to stage a parallel Citizens' Forum that was, in many ways, more promising than the official meeting itself (Susskind 1994). In the absence of central monitoring agencies, much of the international environmental work is likely to fall to NGOs. As an example, the Arctic Treaty System has had to substantially modify its "working rule" of secrecy in response to pressure brought by NGOs. And NGO pressure seems to have been the determining factor in changes in the London Convention outlawing the disposal of low-level radioactive waste at sea (Vogler 2000; Miles 2002). These experiences have led to the call for a full-fledged advisory and monitoring role for nongovernmental interests in the environmental treaty process (Susskind 1994). A model for civil society's role in global environmental governance already exists in the EU's European Environmental Bureau, an umbrella organization for over 140 environmental organizations in both EU countries and neighboring states that monitors the performance of the EU's Environmental Directorate (Axelrod, Vig, and Schreurs 2005).

Whatever we may think about the relative merits of (or actual necessity for) some form of international sovereignty, relying on the spontaneous collaboration of individual nation-states seems inadvisable if we wish to move environmental matters in the right direction in the flawed world we now inhabit (Laslett 2003). From the environmental perspective, waiting for the creation of an ideal world order is allowing the perfect to become the enemy of the good. The main hope for democratizing global governance, across a wide range of issues, lies in cross-national partnerships among government, industry, and the popular forces of civil society (Camilleri, Malhota, and Tehranian 2000). We concur with John Dryzek that institutions of deliberative democracy should be more at home at the international level than liberal aggregative models of democracy precisely because "there are no constitutions worth speaking of in the international system" (Dryzek 2000, 115–116). Dryzek (ibid., 133) proposes the development of a "network" form of international discursive organization, based on exactly the existing institutional models we have been discussing. But whatever particular form they take, deliberative democratic institutions offer an approach to environmental challenges that, if applied internationally, offer an escape from "the trap of nationalism and crystallized community aggressiveness" that seems to dominate world affairs and threaten the global ecology (Laslett 2003, 220).

Encouraging examples can be found in recent experience. In circumstances requiring a consensus among all nations involved, Europeans have taken a step-by-step constitutional approach to environmental policy that in a few decades has become sweeping enough to boggle the minds of incrementalists. Precommitments to such principles as "the polluter pays" principle, the precautionary principle, sustainable development, subsidiarity, and local participation have been enshrined in foundational treaties and action programs of the European Union since 1987. Likewise, on a global basis, the nations of the world have adopted precommitments in framework conventions for such matters as the regulation of ozone-depleting chemicals and trade in endangered species that have made possible subsequent effective policymaking for these international problems. They do so knowing very little of what the future has to offer or the long-term significance of the commitments they undertake. In this respect, they might be compared to the deliberatively democratic actors in Rawls's original position. Deprived of sufficient knowledge to pursue their particular ends, they still have enough information to evaluate general alternatives. They know that they must try to protect the value of their liberties, widen their opportunities, and enlarge their means for promoting their aims whatever they turn out to be (Rawls 1999a, 123). The parallel to Rawls does not end there.

Rather than a single decision and its outcomes, this institutional reform as political architecture produces "future streams of valued outcomes" (Majone 1989, 96–97)—and, one might add, for those metapolicies that facilitate and require deliberative innovation, future streams of valued processes. This is suggestive of Rawls's discussion of the problem of justice between generations. According to Rawls, how the burden of raising the standard of civilization and culture should be distributed admits of no definite answer. But, from a moral point of view, there is no reason for discounting future wellbeing on the basis of a pure time preference (Rawls 1999a, 253). Thus a general principle of justice between generations would be the result of a deliberative process in which no participant adopted the point of view of any particular generation. Participants search for a principle that members of any generation would adopt as the one their generation would follow and that other generations (both before and after) would be required to follow (Rawls 1993, 274). While American, European, and global efforts to build ethical precommitments on general questions of resource conservation and limited global governance (Paehlke

2003) doubtless have far to go before they reach a principled position that would meet this standard, they can be recognized as a deliberative process of the appropriate type.

Conclusion

These multifarious institutional developments suggest that citizens ought to have, and must be able to fill, a complex array of participatory roles that will demand a great deal—both of them and for them. Citizens, of course, will need to navigate among these roles as they are actualized by other citizens.

For purposes of pure theorizing, it may initially have been useful to assume direct, unmediated deliberation by citizens in any possible institutional arrangements being tried or yet to be invented. It may also have been helpful to assume away the need for expertise and the political inequalities that differential expertise necessarily creates. Finally, there may have been some value to assuming away the distortions in deliberation that might be wrought by rhetorical bias and distraction. But expertise exists and will continue to be essential to reasonableness and rationality in the realm of environmental politics and elsewhere. Citizens unavoidably will need to interact directly with other citizens who will vary in the nature and degree of their expertise and many of whom will double as government agents in institutional contexts. Citizens also must contribute to, engage in, and be influenced by the social movements that energize civic politics—in modernity, a civic politics that usually interacts with government while simultaneously functioning autonomously. Rhetoric cannot, and indeed for good reasons should not, be prohibited, prevented, or ignored in these political interactions. All of these complications are evidence of democracy at its best, rather than some failure of deliberative theory or practice.

A practical deliberative politics must accommodate all this additional complexity, complexity that is a direct consequence of the inescapable scientific, technological, and social realities of modernity. Ultimately we must anchor our theories to this complexity as well.

8

Expertise, Adjudication, and the Redemption of Rhetoric

Rhetoric poses challenges to deliberative democracy, yet few theorists have grappled with it in ways that would be useful to the applied design of democratic institutions. Models of how expert rhetoric can be handled in deliberative democratic institutions can be educed from the practical political world of adjudication, with its need for both deliberative processes and expert contributions. Special masters and administrative law judges, judicial notice, and expert witnesses are all examples of how institutionalized deliberative adjudication grapples with the problems of the rhetoric of expertise. The existence in the law of successful procedures, arrangements, and principles for handling the deliberative problem of expert rhetoric suggests that a practical deliberative democratic politics can be adapted to accommodate both expert and nonexpert forms of rhetoric.

Deliberative democrats have a fundamental need to rescue and set free rhetoric, in spite of their almost instinctive distaste for it. Deliberative democracy's core proposition is that interpersonal democratic reasoning must be the overall guiding political procedure, with the giving, weighing, acceptance, and rejection of reasons as public acts (Parkinson 2003, 180). Many theorists, most notably Habermas but also others including Spragens (1990), Benhabib (1996), Chambers (1996), and, by implication, Rawls (1993), seek to define democratic deliberation as based solely on noncoercive reasonable argumentation, free from rhetoric and other forms of communication—in a phrase, democracy by "the unforced force of the better argument" (Habermas 1996, 541).[1] In the eyes of many, rhetoric is the negation of reasoning and can serve only to distort the deliberative process. By framing issues in misleading or distracting ways, rhetoric may threaten one's capacity to make informed and properly reflective democratic decisions. To allow rhetoric and other modes of communication into deliberative processes is to induce arbitrariness and create capricious-ness (Benhabib 1996, 83), thereby "opening the door to demagogues, ma-nipulators, deceivers, and flatterers" (Dryzek 2000, 67). The personal insights and inspirations of rhetorical persuasion may have the potential to transform the worldviews of individuals, but they require shared expe-riences and values that, almost by definition, are closed to many members of the polity.

Yet to elevate the exclusionary use of reason and rationality to be the sole demarcation criterion for what constitutes deliberative democracy is to give rise to a different bundle of theoretical, moral, and practical prob-lems. Requiring a dispassionate style of discourse disenfranchises many citizens and impoverishes public debate (Young 1996; 2000). The poten-tial of narrowly rational deliberative decision making is necessarily re-stricted to those situations entailing only limited political conflict since there must be shared premises among all the participants (Young 2000, 56). Moreover, wholly rational deliberative democracy may be generally incompatible with the values of widespread popular participation (Haupt-mann 2001; Fishkin 1995; Bessette 1994). The problem of rhetoric in de-liberative democracy, then, is more than simply a matter of artful deceivers carrying away the masses.

Several accommodationist claims for rhetoric and deliberative democ-racy have been advanced by democratic theorists, most forcefully by Young (who prefers the term "communicative democracy" for her more inclusive revisions). To privilege rational argument, she says, is to exclude the expression of "some needs, interests, and suffering of injustice" (Young 2000, 37). Gutmann and Thompson (1996, 136) argue for "matching reason to passion" in incorporating rhetoric into deliberation. Indeed, according to O'Neil, "Most of what we believe is founded on the testimony of others. Because we cannot confirm their claims themselves, we have to rely on judgments about the reliability of their sources. Such judgments are unavoidable . . ." (1998, 218). Rhetoric and rationality cannot be disentangled by complex human beings who are always simul-taneously rational and emotional. Rhetoric and rationality are compat-ible, and rhetorical theorists argue for the deliberative embrace of rhetoric: "There is more to the processes of rational deliberation than deductive argument" (O'Neil 1998, 219). That emotions themselves are open to rational persuasion is an old and well-established idea, originating with Aristotle's important contributions to the understanding of rhetoric:

"Rhetoric involves giving grounds for belief and can be appraised in virtue of doing so" (O'Neil 1998, 222). Since the emotions involve both evaluation and appraisal, they must be part of any deliberation to resolve moral debates (Gutmann and Thompson 1996; Rorty 1985). We are never better off when political or other decisions are made, even democratically and deliberately, by intellects lacking empathy (Nussbaum 1995), which is why that fear is such an enduring theme in fiction.

Remer notes that "though the question of when and how to appeal to the emotions can be morally troubling, it cannot be escaped in the realm of politics" (Remer 1999, 55). He accuses deliberative democrats, however, of closing their eyes and avoiding the hard questions that rhetoricians have faced (ibid., 56). An exception is William Rehg (1997, 359, 365), who acknowledges that a plausible account of argumentation and public reason must take rhetoric seriously, going beyond the rhetorical "shadow cast by dialectic." He proposes a substantive conception of rhetoric, one that plays an intrinsic role in argumentation (defined as "cooperative judgment formation") (ibid., 368). At least two traditional aspects of rhetoric may be positively required in many settings: proofs of the speaker's character (or *ethos*), and appeals to audience emotions (*pathos*). Properly employed, these devices do not circumvent or undermine *logos* or substantive arguments on their merits, but rather assist in the intersubjective judgment of such arguments (ibid., 369).

Rehg calls for development of rhetorical criteria and standards for deliberation, but he offers no specific proposals or suggestions. A few other prominent deliberative democrats have also acknowledged the appropriateness and the need for rhetoric in public deliberation (Dryzek 2000, 167; Bohman 1996, 7; Gutmann and Thompson 1996, 135; Young 1996; 2000), but while still leaving unanswered some of the hardest questions as well: How ought rhetoric be handled in deliberative processes? What political procedures, rules, or organizational principles might best accommodate rhetoric to deliberation while minimizing the dangers of manipulation and deceit? Can rhetoric be fit into the same rule-governed structure of language games involved in everyday practical problem solving (or the political problem solving of public policy and administration), without loss of its viewpoint-transformative qualities?

Practical models already exist for handling certain types of rhetoric, namely, expert rhetoric, in deliberative processes, and examination of these models from practice suggests how other types of rhetoric might be handled more generally. Ordinary language requires no special experiences or background, but rhetoric by its nature appeals to passions and levels of meaning that are not shared by all members of society and are fully meaningful only to specific groups (racial, ethnic, cultural, literary, scientific, etc.). Likewise, expertise expresses itself in languages, and in appeals to values, both of which are specialized—that is, also not fully public. If rhetoric can be accommodated in circumstances driven by special knowledge and specialist languages, including the languages of knowledge disciplines, then this begins to suggest ways to think about how it might be similarly accommodated at less sophisticated levels as well.

We explore these potentialities for reconciliation of reason, rhetoric, and democracy in the context of adjudication, a policy arena that exemplifies many principles of reasoned deliberation as well as a necessary dependence on outside expertise. The models that we examine are those that have evolved over decades through pragmatic experimentation by the courts to address the special problems posed for adjudication by highly specialized expertise and the rhetorical problems of this expertise. Collectively, models for accommodating expertise and expert rhetoric in adjudication processes are robust across multiple conceptions of deliberative democracy—such as ideal discourse, public reason, and full liberalism—making this area of pragmatic experimentalism fairly robust in speaking to deliberative theory.

Adjudicatory Deliberation and Democracy

There are several levels at which judicial decision making and deliberative democracy run parallel to one another. Habermas (1996, 260–261) observes that "an adjudication oriented by principles has to decide which claim and which action in a given conflict is right—and not how to balance interests or relate values." To the extent that deliberative democracy is about actually reconciling interests and perspectives, rather than merely compromising and balancing them, it is also about the testing of claims in a search for action that is in some sense correct. Furthermore, the legal validity of such judgments has the character of an authoritative command rather than a political compromise (Habermas 1996).

This explains why a number of theorists compare deliberative politics to judicial decision making. Michael Walzer (1999) offers juries as a prime example of deliberative interaction between individuals. James Fishkin (1991) takes the parallel one step further in his discussion of political decision making through deliberative citizen juries. Cass Sunstein (1999) offers the work of judges on multimember panels and the techniques they use to justify their decisions as an example of how deliberation can produce agreements that are defensible in spite of the fact that they are incompletely theorized. Furthermore, Sunstein (1985) argues that judicial review of legislation has evolved a "reasoned analysis requirement" geared to the deliberative character of the legislative process. Judges, in Sunstein's view, inspect the work of legislators to determine whether they have at least tried to act deliberatively. The standard of judgment is whether the legislative decision turned on reasons that can be publicly advocated or on private interests. One of the distinctive features of this approach is that the outcomes of the legislative process become secondary. What is important is that the decision process is deliberative, that it is undistorted by private power.

These clear parallels between judicial decision making and deliberative democracy offer us existing procedures from which we may draw inferences about the form that deliberative democracy might take. "By virtue of its comparatively high degree of rationality, judicial deliberation and decision making offer the most thoroughly analyzed case" of a system that institutionalizes rules of discourse without regulating or intervening in the argumentation as such (Habermas 1996, 178). So, by exploring the structure, rationale, and limitations of various approaches to the use of experts in judicial deliberation, it may be possible to derive comparable approaches to integrating scientific expertise into deliberation in participatory deliberation on issues of public policy.

Experts and Deliberative Democrats

With its emphasis on rational discourse, one might expect deliberative democratic theory to be especially open to the use of scientific expertise in policymaking. That expectation would, however, lead to significant disappointment. Many deliberative democrats worry that specialized science, and the knowledge it produces, is built on a rhetorical foundation that necessarily includes analogy, metaphor, and nondemonstrative reasoning from opinion. As O'Neil notes, "the very claim to truth seeking is itself a rhetorical device to produce conviction in an audience" (1998, 205). Despite the influence of some anti-intellectual and antirational tendencies in modernity, science and expertise still have an overall cachet and legitimacy that can be used to appeal to a lay audience, as readily to deceive as to enlighten. The rational recognition of an expert's authority involves taking his or her reasoning as proxy because we suppose that the expert knows more than we do and that, if we had access to what the expert knows, we would therefore arrive at the same conclusions (Friedman 1973). Understood in this way, there are at least three more basic reasons that deliberative democrats find expertise problematic. First, it is difficult to transfer claims of expertise, based as they often are on membership in a scientific discipline, to policy problems because most policy issues extend well beyond the boundaries of any particular discipline (MacRae and Whittington 1997). Second, because of the multidisciplinary character of most policy problems and the indeterminacy of most science, there may never be sufficient reason for thinking that any particular expert is in fact reasonably reliable (Estlund 1997). Finally, given the first two problems, if the qualifications of alleged experts will always be open to reasonable disagreement, so too will be any general list of qualifications alleged to be appropriate to a given policy problem (ibid., 1997).

The ambivalence of deliberative democrats toward science and expertise can be briefly illustrated by the work of Habermas. On the one hand, Habermas advocates a style of reasoning (the ideal speech situation) in which participants in collective decision making test each others' claims about the world (Baber and Bartlett 2001). In such a circumstance, science and technology can be regarded positively as instrumental methods for viewing the world that can effectively secure the preconditions for human survival (Habermas 1987a). On the other hand, science and technology can be seen as fundamental elements of administrative power, the nature of which conflicts with precisely the forms of communicative power Habermas advocates (Scheuerman 1999). This conflict has led some to complain that Habermas overly privileges a single, homogeneous public discourse engaged in the quest for a rational agreement approaching unanimity (Bohman 1994). Other accounts of communicative rationality seem to throw into question the centrality that Habermas gives to explicit and deliberative argumentation as the ultimate test and guarantee of rationality. In order to restore the communicative link between humanity and nature (an objective to which Habermas seems indifferent), it has been suggested that discursive democracy should draw on genres of communication that are able to evoke subtle understandings that typically prove illusive to the forceful, yet sometimes clumsy, literal-minded approach typical of scientific discourse and its expression through administrative power (Torgerson 1999). Habermas, however, has his defenders. Stephen White (1988) acknowledges that Habermas's theories allow for privileged parties (like experts) in the deliberative arena. But to enjoy their privilege, those parties are required to demonstrate the degree to which their inequality "can be discursively justified, of showing that it is in accordance with standards of procedural equity, participation, non-deception and non-manipulation" (White 1988, 76–77). If nothing else, this controversy surrounding Habermas's views demonstrates that deliberative democrats are ambivalent (and divided) about expertise.

In searching for a model or models for the appropriate role of either rhetoric or scientific expertise in a deliberative form of politics, we fortunately need not be limited to proposals emerging from the teased-out implications of existing theory. As has often been true in the history of democratic theory, "the practice of democracy has been ahead of its theory" (Lippmann 1922, 286). In judicial deliberation, a decision process with which deliberative democracy is often compared, at least three practical models—special masters, judicial notice, and expert witnesses—can be found for incorporating expertise and expert rhetoric into deliberation without compromising the rational integrity of collective deliberative reasoning.

Special Masters: Using Experts to Handle Expert Rhetoric

In the U.S. federal court system, special masters are appointed by district courts pursuant to Rule 53 of the Federal Rules of Civil Procedure. A special master is most often used by a district court in evaluating complex claims involving highly technical or scientific facts about which a judge or jury could not reasonably be expected to educate themselves (Brazil 1986). Special masters may possess wide-ranging authority. They may serve as an auditor, an examiner, and an assessor. They possess the power to regulate their own proceedings and take all actions necessary to the efficient performance of their duties. They may rule on the production and admissibility of evidence, may examine witnesses under oath, and are required to make a record of the evidence, both offered and excluded, for review by the appointing court. Rule 53 special masters may make findings of both fact and law (Fed. R. Civ. P. 53 a–e).

Special masters are also appointed from time to time by the U.S. Supreme Court in its cases of original jurisdiction, particularly those between the states over such issues as boundary disputes and water rights (Carstens 2002). The Supreme Court's special masters are generally senior judges from the circuit or district benches who are not scientific experts but have some significant experience with litigation involving claims similar to those presented to the Court. Supreme Court special masters perform many of the same functions as special masters in district court, but they operate under a less well defined system of rules, largely created by the Court itself on a case-by-case basis (ibid., 668).

As one might imagine, the use of special masters by U.S. federal courts has not escaped criticism. These criticisms fall into two general categories. First, the use of special masters poses an issue of legitimacy. Masters exercise considerable judicial power without having gone through the appointment and approval processes set forth in Article III of the U.S. Constitution. Other non–Article III actors (such as magistrates and administrative law judges) perform somewhat similar functions. But they do so in more substantively and procedurally constrained environments. Second, the relative absence of procedural constraints can lead to a lack of uniformity in results. This can manifest itself in the form of different decisions in factually similar cases, or inconsistent treatment of parties in a single case that extends over such a lengthy period of time that more than one master is involved (Carstens 2002). Either scenario casts doubt on the fundamental fairness of the work of special masters.

Problems of legitimacy and fairness would be no less serious were the special master approach for experts to be used in participatory deliberations on policy problems. Democratic legitimacy (as opposed to judicial legitimacy) requires that decision making be procedurally fair and that it can be held, in terms acceptable to all reasonable citizens, to be, epistemically, the best procedure among those procedures that are better than random (Estlund 1997). Although the work of a special master in deliberative decision making might improve the epistemic quality of the process, it might also reduce the ability of reasonable citizens to evaluate the quality of that process. Habermas goes even further, arguing that legitimacy signifies the uncoerced compliance of citizens out of respect for the law, born of an expectation that the laws altogether guarantee the autonomy of all persons equally (Michelman 1997). It is difficult to imagine how one maintains personal autonomy while deferring to the authority of a supposed expert, particularly when the issues in question involve significant threats to human health and environmental sustainability. If, as Joshua Cohen (1997) argues, democratic legitimacy relies on the free and reasoned agreement among equals, it may be hard to reconcile so expansive a role for the special master as is suggested by Habermas's notion of testing competing validity claims in an ideal speech situation.

Problems of fairness pose a somewhat different challenge for deliberative democrats who wish to sustain a special master role for policy experts. The possibility that similar cases might receive dissimilar treatment, or that the treatment parties receive might change during the course of a single deliberation, is no abstract matter. These threats to the interests of parties affected by public deliberation undermine the willingness of individuals to submit to collective decisions once they are made. After all, self-interested claims provide a significant portion of the normative scaffolding in terms of which the very concept of fairness is defined (Knight and Johnson 1997). Habermas argues that a requirement of procedural fairness can be inferred from our reflection on the presuppositions of a discussion by which a diverse set of participants seek to find rational and self-respecting norms to govern their social life (Michelman 1997). In fact, Habermas treats certain substantive constraints on political discourse (liberty and fair opportunity) as procedural preconditions for legitimate deliberation (Knight 1999). So it appears that the problems of legitimacy and fairness implicit in the use of special masters may, ultimately, exacerbate one another.

How could these problems be avoided without dismissing the special master approach to expert rhetoric altogether? There are at least two basic steps that might be taken. First, it is possible to delineate a body of procedures applicable to the special master in citizen deliberation that parallel the procedures that have developed in judicial deliberation. Second, it could be argued that special masters should be selected for their legal, rather than scientific or technical, background (Carstens 2002).

Happily enough, a significant body of law already exists that could be adapted to govern the work of special masters in deliberative decision-making arenas. Administrative law judges (ALJs) have, for over a century, performed functions that are largely similar to those of the special master. ALJs are appropriately seen as Article I adjudicators, vested with the authority of the executive rather than the judiciary. They engage in both quasi-legislative and quasi-judicial functions under the rules set forth in the Administrative Procedures Act. There are clear rules for ALJs to follow in procedural and evidentiary matters and a well-developed body of law to answer larger political questions. These include the standing requirements that parties must meet to appear before an ALJ, the deference to which ALJ decisions are entitled when they are reviewed by agency boards, and the circumstances under which judicial review of ALJ decisions may be conducted (Gifford 1997). In addition to answering the need for procedural fairness (or, at least, regularity), ALJs also bring an adjudicatory rather than a technological perspective to the integration of expertise and decision making. Although they certainly develop an understanding of the fields in which they hear cases, ALJs (like special masters in Supreme Court original jurisdiction cases) bring legal rather than scientific training to the deliberative arena (Wood 1997).

Ultimately, this style of special master may be more consistent with Habermas's general view of deliberation in the ideal speech situation than the special master approach taken by district courts. Habermas makes the point that scientists, if they wish to affect collective will-formation, will have to take on the lay perspective. They will have to communicate in the ordinary language of everyday existence in the lifeworld, no matter how specialized the knowledge they wish to deploy. The language of law will ultimately be the common dialect in which specialists and citizens communicate, with each other and with the civil servants who must ultimately carry out the discursively expressed public will (Habermas 1996).

Judicial Notice: Mutually Stipulated Rhetoric?

Judicial notice is best thought of as an exception to the general common-law rule that any party relying on a proposition for proof of a fact required by a case must prove that proposition to the satisfaction of the trier of fact. In the U.S. federal court system, the practice of judicial notice is governed by Federal Rule of Evidence (FRE) 201. In general terms, FRE 201 restricts judicial notice to facts that are not subject to reasonable dispute in that they are either (1) generally known within the territorial jurisdiction of the trial court, or (2) capable of accurate and ready determination by resort to sources whose accuracy cannot reasonably be questioned. In civil actions, the jury is to be instructed that they are to accept as conclusive any judicially noticed fact. In a criminal case, the court shall instruct the jury that it may, but is not required to, accept as conclusive any fact that has been judicially noticed. Parties to a case are entitled, upon timely request, to an opportunity to be heard as to the propriety of taking judicial notice and the tenor of the matter noticed.

A legislative fact would not be perceived as immediately threatening to either party and therefore would always be appropriate for judicial notice. An adjudicative fact is one that can be expected to have an immediate and direct impact on the case. For example, in a toxic tort case the fact that 30 percent of the workers in a defendant company's industry develop cancer would likely be regarded as a legislative fact. That the plaintiff employee in the case had developed cancer would clearly be an adjudicative fact (Davis 1942). Aside from the exceptions allowed for in FRE 201, adjudicative facts are not generally appropriate for judicial notice. One exception would be situations where there is a question of fact about which reasonably intelligent people might not have in mind the information at issue, but where they would agree that the facts are verifiable with certainty by consulting authoritative reference sources. Also subject to notice are facts generally known with certainty by all the reasonably intelligent people in the community.

Judicial notice is a much-discussed doctrine of law, and FRE 201 is not without its critics (Davis 1969b). As a general matter, courts seem to have ignored the restrictions imposed by FRE 201. Judicial notice is a significant time-saver for courts, and it can also operate, at the appellate level, to rescue otherwise sound verdicts that are plagued with evidentiary gaps of a technical nature. The adjudicatory–legislative fact distinction has, itself, proven difficult to work with in practical terms. Something more like a distinction between critical and noncritical facts has developed (Turner 1983). Furthermore, Davis (1969b) has argued that the rule is actually dissuading courts from employing judicial notice, depriving the judiciary of one of the key methods at its disposal for husbanding its limited resources.

The trend toward a more permissive form of judicial notice is consistent with the general principle that triers of fact, in both law and democratic theory, should not be deprived of relevant information without significant justification. For Rawls (1999c, 269), depriving deliberative participants of information can be justified only where (1) the failure to do so "would permit self- and group-interest to distort the parties deliberations," (2) where the information concerns "contingencies and accidents that should not influence the choice of moral principles," or (3) where the information "represents the very moral conceptions" that we seek to understand in light of more fundamental principles.

This three-part test leaves ample room for the introduction of general expert information about the state of the world. For our present purposes, that information could constitute the sort of background facts of science that Davis (1942; 1969b) characterizes as "legislative facts." Citizens deliberating the fundamental elements of some environmental problem would, for example, be entitled to take "deliberative notice" of the fact that ingestion of lead damages cognitive functions in humans, assuming that this fact represents a scientific understanding that no reasonable person could dispute. Such "generally known" facts about the environment would create a strong presumption, one that the trier of fact would accept in the absence of persuasive rebuttal. Such strong presumptions could, in turn, serve as the empirical grounding for regulations of a particularly Rawlsian sort.

Thus, in sharp contrast to Habermas, Rawls seeks to incorporate expertise but allows no special role for the individual expert in deliberative democracy. This view corresponds to the common idea that judges and juries are novices in the special fields of knowledge that appear before them and that this is appropriately so. All that the judge, or the deliberative citizen, needs is an appropriately dispassionate frame of mind and the appropriate principles of adjudication. At this level, it could be argued that science and expertise play no special role in the democratic process, at least when issues of fundamental rights or constitutional essentials are at stake.

This view, however, may overlook important questions. It should be remembered that Rawls's "veil of ignorance" is a veil rather than a curtain. It is not so opaque that decision makers in the original position know absolutely nothing of the world in which their principles will be applied. From its earliest appearance, Rawls's veil of ignorance allows deliberators the benefit of several kinds of information and beliefs that are the foundation for rhetorical persuasion. They know that goods in the society for which they plan will be moderately scarce and unequally distributed. They know that they will have interests and responsibilities that require them to protect their liberties. They know that they will live as part of a household and that they might possess religious duties and cultural interests. They are allowed to reason "from general beliefs shared by citizens generally, as part of their public knowledge. These beliefs are the general facts on which their selection of the principles of justice is based and . . . the veil of ignorance allows these beliefs as reasons" (Rawls 1993, 70).

In short, Rawlsian deliberation allows participants to know virtually every important feature of their society, at least in a general way. They are deprived only of specific information about their ultimate place in that structure (Rawls 1999c, 226; 2001, 81). In fact, general beliefs that are widely shared (precisely the sort of facts that are subject to judicial notice and to which rhetoric would appeal most powerfully) are the very foundation of the deliberative process. In the judicial arena, to which citizen deliberation is so often compared, such general and uncontested common knowledge—including expert rhetoric that all parties have mutually stipulated is not subject to reasonable dispute—finds its way into the decision process through the mechanism of judicial notice.

Expert Witnesses and the Marketplace of Expertise

Courts have been struggling with the rhetorical role of experts for at least seven centuries (Hand 1901). Rarely have courts taken a hands-off approach to the subject. Many jurists harbor a fear that the phrase "scientific expert" is so value-laden that juries will be overawed by an aura of invincibility that will impair their critical faculties (Lunney 1994). Alternatively, when faced with contradictory testimony from conflicting experts, triers of fact may be tempted to split the difference in intellectually indefensible (but entirely human) ways (Epstein 1992). Juries may also give undue credit to a reputed expert merely because he has generated a lengthy list of qualifications that others in the field would regard as less impressive (Osborne 1990). There is also evidence that scientific experts can so overawe a jury that the expert may actually usurp the fact finder's ultimate responsibility for deciding the facts of the case (Davis 1988). And there is also a broad suspicion that you can find someone to say anything for the right price (Lunney 1994). Add to all of this that much of what passes for scholarship in the courtroom may actually be "junk science" (Huber 1991), and the worry among legal scholars that their discipline is being hijacked is not difficult to understand.

This complex of rhetorical problems associated with expert witness testimony has generated a literature that can only be characterized as immense. Happily, a review of that material is not critical to, or even consistent with, our present purposes. A greater degree of focus is possible because the task at hand is to suggest how scientific experts should be involved in deliberative policymaking in a broadly participatory context. James Bohman (1996) provides us with several useful points of departure for that effort.

For Bohman, the concerns regarding experts that are central to jurists (admissibility, scope of testimony, the criterion of general acceptance, and so forth) are simply irrelevant. As noted earlier in chapter 3, an epistemic division of labor is, for Bohman, an unavoidable characteristic of deliberative institutions. A variety of deliberative roles must be filled, for neither innate capacities nor acquired knowledge will ever be evenly distributed in any society. But experts cannot assume that their special knowledge will have practical effects unless they can successfully take on the lay perspective. This observation is consistent with the argument of Kelly and Maynard-Moody (1993) that, to remain relevant in a postpositivist world, where the pervasiveness of the media and a growing cynicism tends to bring all authority figures low, the policy expert must establish a participatory relationship with the client—in this case, his or her fellow citizens. In fact, when this trend is combined with the growing extension of analytical capacities to the media and the population generally, the very boundaries of expertise are increasingly blurred (MacRae and Whittington 1997). In the deliberative democracy of full liberalism, then, experts play a needed specialist role but are constrained by ineffectiveness unless they can transcend the deliberation barriers between themselves and nonspecialists.

This form of deliberative democracy, which might be described as "full liberalism," demands neither the ideal speech situation of Habermas nor the Rawlsian veil of ignorance. Full liberalism, exemplified by the work of Bohman, requires equality of access and influence among participants in deliberation, good faith bargaining, and plurality rule with minority acquiescence. Participants look to their own motivation and look to experts to provide them with arguments to aid them in achieving the interests. In such a process, we might expect the expert to play a role similar to that of the expert witness in a court proceeding. In this approach, experts provide each side of the argument with contrasting views of the issue in question. Because this "proceeding" must by its nature result in a negotiated settlement, experts are reduced to little more than a source of bargaining chips. The difficulties that may arise in deciding what role technical experts may play in deliberative democracy can be inferred from the challenges faced by the judiciary in dealing with experts in the deliberative processes carried on in a courtroom.

Reason and Rhetoric in Deliberative Institutions

Each of three approaches to theorizing about deliberative democracy suggests a corresponding role for the expert in converting the genuine reasons for the positions adopted by citizens, as expressed in their personal rhetoric, into public reasons for collective decisions that can be offered in the dispassionate language of the deliberative process. The deliberative politics of Habermas envisions a style of reasoning that emphasizes the testing of competing validity claims in an ideal speech situation. Participants are in search of a general consensus based on reasons that are public in the sense that they can be accepted readily by all involved. Neither the pessimistic assumption that technology excludes democracy, nor the optimism that science and democracy must ultimately converge, is warranted (Habermas 1970). Expertise must be regarded as a necessary tool, but one of instrumental value only. Consultation between scientific experts and policymakers is an unavoidable necessity. Habermas recognizes that the development of new scientific and technical capacities is governed by social interests and political values. The limits of science and technology have the salutary effect of putting those public values and interests to the test of technical feasibility (ibid.).

Thus, Habermas suggests that the input of experts is vital to the testing of validity claims (both normative and empirical) put forward by the parties to a deliberation. In this sense, the expert functions for Habermas in somewhat the same way that a special master satisfies the need of the court that appoints him or her for a source of unbiased appraisals of the arguments advanced by the parties to litigation. The value of expertise is in isolating the empirical elements in the rhetoric of citizen participants and allowing them to come to a discursive clarification of their own perceptions and interests. It should be emphasized, however, that this principle of rational agreement does not entail any substantive policy commitments (Hayward 1998). Thus arises the complaint that Habermas's approach unduly privileges rational discourse at the expense of complex and pluralistic rhetoric (Bohman 1994).

If the approach advocated by Habermas is dry from a rhetorical point of view, the philosophy of Rawls is positively arid. Rawls envisions a deliberative process in which a virtually disembodied consciousness seeks unanimous agreement on basic principles with other similarly thin personalities. Their search is for binding precommitments that are in no way anchored in personal interest and that are free of the influence of policy experts. The academic disciplines provide only general background information necessary for this exercise in reason (Baber and Bartlett 2001). If decision makers can be isolated from the effects of interest, they can, using the precepts of common sense, arrive at a position that all can support for the same reasons. No information concerning the world may enter except that which is beyond reasonable dispute. Deliberative (judicial) notice allows room for rhetoric, but only mutually agreed upon rhetoric.

Bohman, in contrast to both Rawls and Habermas, holds out an explicit and expansive place for rhetoric in deliberation. Bohman's work can be interpreted as an attempt to synthesize the theories of Habermas and Rawls in a way that reconciles their divergent approaches to deliberative democracy, where that is possible, and provides new insights where it is not. It is where he diverges from both Rawls and Habermas that Bohman's work is most intriguing. As mentioned earlier, his abandonment of impartiality in public discourse, his elevation of diversity to the level of a primary deliberative value, and his treatment of preferences as (to some extent) cultural givens are problematic. But Bohman's (1996) insistence on the protection of cultural pluralism in all its rhetorical richness answers those who complain that the relentlessly rational approach that dominates deliberative democracy must inevitably disarm disadvantaged groups who require the recourse to rhetoric if they are to successfully place their concerns on table (Dryzek 2000).

Perhaps the strongest advocate of a free flow of rhetoric in deliberative democracy is Iris Young. Young's primary concern is that the assumption that reason, disengaged from culturally specific interests, should be the basis of the deliberative process is inherently exclusionary (Young 1990a,b). It will produce a cultural hegemony of privileged groups that will dominate deliberative process, systematically disenfranchising racial and ethnic minorities as well as women. To counter this trend, Young advocates a principle of deliberative inclusion, which states that "a deliberative procedure is legitimate only if all interests, opinions, and perspectives present in the polity are included in the deliberation, provided they are compatible with the reciprocity principle" (Young 1999, 155). For this inclusionary principle to be satisfied, the deliberative process must be open to forms of rhetoric and storytelling that engage others at an affective level and demonstrate what culturally specific values mean to those who hold them (Young 1995). This level of inclusion is vital to deliberative democracy because it expands the meaning of reciprocity and ensures that every potentially affected agent has the opportunity to influence deliberative outcomes (Young 1999).

It would be hard to argue that Young's principle of inclusion could fail to make deliberative outcomes more just. Inclusion and diversity should also render deliberation less error-prone and more socially productive. The inclusion of groups from outside the cultural mainstream sets up a "rhetorical competition" with the dominant social paradigm by rendering problematic elements of social reality previously taken for granted (Brulle 2000). This "experimental spirit" is a necessity not only for the essential legitimacy it confers, but because a diversity of ideas, wisdom, and experience is a needed social good in an uncertain world (Menand 2001).

For his part, Habermas agrees that deliberative inclusion is vital: "The pursuit of political freedom through law depends on our constant reach for inclusion of the other, of the hitherto excluded—which in practice means bringing to legal doctrinal presence the hitherto absent voices of emergently self-conscious social groups" (Habermas 1996, 275). But notice the "in practice" qualification. It recapitulates Habermas's earlier (1973a) observation that although dialectics as a form of rhetoric is an effective discourse of instruction, finally, it is merely a prologomenon to rigorous analysis. The rhetorical content of culturally specific discourse must, eventually, be translated into the public vocabulary of legal norms and procedures if it is to have substantive effect. The rhetoric of cultural groups, no less than the jargon of science, comprises specialized discourses not fully open to all. If there is to be true dialogue across discourses, the mutually comprehensible language of legislation (law) must come into play. Only when competing discourses express themselves in fully public terms can dominant social groups see them as potential sources of solutions for problems with which the dominant paradigm alone cannot cope (MacIntyre 1988).

This insight helps explain Habermas's curiously ambivalent attitude toward rhetoric, as well as the fact that it has been such a contentious issue among deliberative democrats. Despite his openness to rhetoric (especially in the form of dialectics), Habermas (1996, 282) concludes that discourses aimed at the working out of group identities cannot be allowed to overwhelm the essential objective of deliberative self-legislation, the deciding of matters "in the equal interest of all." It is true that initiatives, issues, contributions, problems, and proposals come "more from the margins than from the established center of the spectrum of opinions" (ibid., 275). But it is also true that transposing radical discourse into the domain of rhetoric "dulls the sword of the critique of reason" (Habermas 1998b, 210). When critique is relieved of the duty of problem solving and shifted to rhetorical functions, it is robbed of both its seriousness and its capacity to be productive (Habermas 1998b).

So how do we reconcile the necessity for rhetoric and the danger it presents to deliberative self-legislation? One possibility is again suggested by the deliberative process of the judiciary. Direct testimony in court is about accumulating a factual record on the basis of which judicial decision makers may deliberate. And yet, rhetorical material abounds in adjudication. Witnesses describe feelings, victim impact statements inflame passions, and closing arguments provoke tears of sympathy and outrage. These rhetorical elements of deliberation play carefully circumscribed roles. They are limited in their impact by procedural rules regarding when and how they may be used and what supporting evidence must accompany them.

A parallel experience in environmental deliberations might be the efforts of environmental justice advocates in administrative and judicial adjudications. The environmental justice movement is one of the most significant developments in environmentalism in the last two decades. It is a flourishing element of the environmental movement, but not because its proponents are held to a lower standard of reasoning than other citizens. Rather, it has earned a role in environmental deliberation because it has been able to combine the rhetoric of local activists with the rigor of ecology to present a perspective on environmental risk that is both scientifically valid and culturally significant (Hajer 1995). Here is an example of an aggregation of local groups into a larger political community of identity and difference that can maintain its radical and culturally pluralistic character without sacrificing the rationality and publicity valued by Habermas and Rawls. Its practical successes result from its ability to provide participants in deliberation with significant legislative and adjudicatory facts as well as the ethnic and cultural context in which those facts have meaning. In this sense, the environmental justice movement, through the interventions of its adherents, functions in much the same way as expert witnesses. Their status as experts is not based on membership in a learned profession or the ability to deploy specialized skills of analysis. Their expertise is, rather, of an interpretive sort. To recall Young's (1996) description of rhetoric and storytelling, environmental justice advocates provide their audience with reflective insight and show them what the values of cultural minorities mean to those who hold them. By entering into explicitly political dialogue, the distinctive character of the critique advanced by environmental justice advocates is also protected. There is reason to believe that political disagreement is more easily tolerated and accommodated than disagreement expressed in other terms. Where disagreement is sustained by both the particular structures of political interaction and the inherently subjective nature of democratic politics, the pressure toward conformity that would disadvantage poor and minority groups is reduced (Huckfeldt, Johnson, and Sprague 2002). Furthermore, narratives offered in the public sphere by actors from the periphery of the opinion spectrum can constitute valuable empirical evidence in support of historical models (Buthe 2002), models such as those that have been used to explain the disproportionate exposure of minorities and the poor to environmental hazards.

That some form of "interpretive expertise" plays an essential role in deliberation holds out the hope that scientists and other scholars can make a uniquely valuable rhetorical contribution the democratic experience generally without sacrificing their critical stance toward the social status quo. It suggests, however, that they can do so most effectively in concert with citizen activists who populate the nongovernmental public sphere described in such detail by Habermas. It is also clear that additional thought must be given to the procedural rules that might appropriately govern expertise as it is transposed from the well-theorized environment of judicial deliberation into the relatively sparse experience of deliberative democracy and self-legislation: "Only by insisting that problems shall not come up to him until they have passed through a procedure, can the busy citizen of a modern state hope to deal with them in a form that is intelligible" (Lippmann 1922, 303).

Conclusion

Rhetoric poses difficult challenges to deliberative democracy, yet any successful realization of deliberative democratic ideals in a practical world mandates that somehow it be redeemed in several senses of the word—as recovered, rescued, fulfilled, saved, set free. Few theorists have yet grappled with those challenges in ways that would be useful to the applied design of democratic institutions. We argue that, for deliberative democratic theory, particularly useful is the special case of expert rhetoric. Expert and non-expert rhetoric are problematic for the same reasons—both present specialized perspectives that, not being available to all either rationally or experientially, are not automatically accessible and acceptable as public reasons. In many ways, accommodating expert-based rhetoric to deliberation is more difficult than challenges posed by other rhetorical problems. But it is nevertheless not as difficult a problem as the traditional distaste or general avoidance of democratic theorists would suggest. The practical political world of adjudication, with its need for both deliberative processes and expert contributions, has, through evolutionary practice and derivation of principles therefrom, worked out several models that can inform deliberative theory and further practical democratic experimentation. Special masters and administrative law judges, judicial notice, and expert witnesses all present instances in which institutionalized deliberative adjudication has long grappled with the problems of accommodating—redeeming, if you will—expertise for the public reason demands of a deliberative judicial process. (Legal language, of course, is just as much rhetorical as that of any other discipline and is accommodated as readily.)

The evolution in the law of successful procedures, arrangements, and principles for handling the deliberative problem of expertise suggests reasons for optimism in constructing a practical deliberative democratic politics that can redeem both expert and personal rhetoric and, thereby, redeem the ideal of deliberative democracy itself.

Expert rhetoric, then, has already been redeemed by a practical politics of deliberative democracy. The task remains of transposing this experience and the principles derived therefrom to nonjudicial forums for political deliberation.

9

Environmental Citizenship in a Deliberative Democracy

Humankind has always found the natural world an inspiration for fantasies, mythology, culture, and religion. In the hands of eighteenth-century Europeans, however, nature came to be viewed as a tool, one that could be exploited to improve the material condition of humankind. Purged of the superstition and ignorance that confounded it, human reason would be able to discover a "form of knowledge which copes most proficiently with the facts and supports the individual most effectively in the mastery of nature" (Horkheimer and Adorno 1972, 83). Not only that, the Enlightenment carried with it the promise that, through the use of reason, humankind could discover the good. Instead of remaining the province of priests and philosophers, ethics could be rendered a matter of discovery, open to anyone capable of the careful observation of cause and effect (Elliot 1994). Thus the Enlightenment promised a world not only more comfortable in material terms, but also more just and democratic.

Now, it would appear, all bets are off. The scarcity and environmental degradation that confront humankind are so severe that they have been characterized as a form of revenge taken by Nature against Science for centuries of social oppression and for the evils of industrialization (Alford 1985). Furthermore, ethics seems to have become little more than a code to which people obligate themselves rather than an affective commitment to support social solidarity (Bennett 2001). For their part, political liberals appear to have lost their faith in the distinction between power and legitimate authority, leaving them cynical and their democracies moribund (Chaloupka 1999). Worst of all, these problems seem to be mutually reinforcing. Scarcity and environmental degradation, it has been argued, are so severe that politics-as-usual is unable to deal with them. Modern democracies have been rendered so ineffectual that they are unable to confront the necessity for strong action (Ophuls 1977). The physical and social milieus in which the democracies exist are so large and complex that today's citizens find their lives isolating and confusing. Having become passive consumers of a politics that offers only biennial or quadrennial ratification of marketing campaigns, and having been rendered a mere audience by an "artificial, commercial, self-referential, mesmerizing and specious media environment" (Ophuls 1997, 77–78), today's citizens are unable to critically examine the course of their own collective future. So when confronted by ethical choices in a circumstance of environmental scarcity, they give themselves up to a "lifeboat ethics" (Hardin 1974) that constitutes the final betrayal of the Enlightenment promise.

In the face of such a grim diagnosis, many have argued that we have no choice but to forgo democracy in favor of precipitate action, that only authoritarian government will suffice (Heilbroner 1996; Stravrianos 1976; Ophuls 1977; 1997; Ponting 1991). Others have taken the opposite approach. Deliberative democrats argue that there is nothing wrong with democracy that a little (or a lot) more democracy would not cure. Some have even argued that this is particularly true with respect to the knotty problems of environmental scarcity and degradation (Gundersen 1995; Hajer 1995; Dobson 1996; Dryzek 1997; 2000; Eckersley 2000). A few point out that although scientism may be the root of many evils, more and better science will be necessary if economic institutions are to be changed to reflect what some regard as the ecological truth (Brown 2001). Furthermore, it has been suggested that environmentalism as a movement represents a potentially powerful reunion of science and reason (Ehrlich and Ehrlich 1996).

Such a political-scientific movement has the potential to provide a new ground for ethical commitments that will encourage the development of a society that is both more sustainable and more just (Valadez 2001). Success in such an endeavor would constitute a powerful reminder that, in a pluralistic and normatively fragmented society, positive law derives its legitimacy solely from democratic procedures in which the convictions and commitments of citizens find representation (Gregg 1997). So even though the political, epistemological, and ethical problems presented by the ecological problematique may be mutually reinforcing, it is at least possible that their solutions might be synergistic as well.

There is an enormous literature that discusses the role of citizens in conventional policy processes. Much of this literature is anchored in participatory theories of democracy developed in the 1960s and 1970s (Walker 1966; Kaufman 1968; 1969; Pateman 1970; Bachrach 1975; Barber 1984). Most deliberative democrats see their conceptions of democracy as "continuations of the theoretical project participatory theorists began" (Hauptmann 2001, 399). Both participatory and deliberative theorists "believe most citizens can contribute intelligently and reasonably to politics, especially when they know their contributions matter. And most believe that citizens should be able to contribute to more areas of decision-making than they can now" (ibid., 398). The participatory roles that citizens might play in deliberative democracy have just begun to be theorized (Dobson 2003). How does citizen participation frame deliberative responses to the ecological challenges confronted by developed democracies? Each of three versions of deliberative democracy—public reason, ideal discourse, and full liberalism—implies not only a particular role for citizens, but also a pattern of relationships between the three categories. Understanding this pattern will, ultimately, allow theorists of deliberative democracy to suggest the range of situations in which each of these three general conceptions can be appropriately deployed.

The roles of citizens in a deliberative democracy raise many questions, most of which fall into three major categories. The character of citizen participation ultimately depends on how one defines the *individual,* on how one conceives of *interactions* among individuals, and on how the *institutions* that host those interactions are designed.

Individuals

Critical theorists and some liberal theorists view government and business as two sides of the same elite dominance coin without seriously questioning whether it *has* to be that way. Yet if we can't use the power of government to counter the power of money, then we really are as doomed as Ophuls says. What is needed is simultaneous embrace of both the "public sphere" (which critical theorists imagine to be nongovernmental) and the public institution (where actual policy change can be made). This explains the necessity of anchoring our analysis with discussions of environmental statutes and policy design. These matters will ultimately determine the role played by citizens in the process of environmental decision making. Will they continue to be spectators only? Or will their interests play a different role, that of primary motivator for action (Bohman) or source of competing validity claims in the deliberative process (Habermas)? Or will citizens play a different role altogether? Might they become (as Rawls imagined) the disinterested judges of public issues?

The conception of individual citizens advanced by Rawls's theory of public reason is a most difficult approach because it diverges the most dramatically from our everyday experience. Rawls's well-ordered society is populated by people who are "equal . . . autonomous . . . reasonable" and possessed of the "capacity for social cooperation" (Rawls 1993, 306). Furthermore, they view society as "a fair system of cooperation over time, from one generation to the next" (ibid., 15). This imposes on them an ecologically useful responsibility to preserve (and even enhance) natural resources over time so as to meet their obligations to their successors. Also, they aspire to be both rational in a technical sense and reasonable in a broader political sense. This is because "merely reasonable agents would have no ends of their own they would want to advance through fair cooperation; merely rational agents lack a sense of justice and fail to recognize the independent validity of the claims of others" (ibid., 52). Because they share these characteristics, the citizens of a well-ordered society would readily commit themselves to abide by the principles of justice flowing from a discourse in which they (or their representatives) were guided by the regulative concept of the veil of ignorance. This concept would deprive decision makers of virtually all information about their positions in society, their individual interests, and even which generation they represent (Rawls 1999a).

The approach taken by Rawls has both advantages and difficulties. Some critics of deliberative democracy have complained that deliberation has a sedative effect that curbs the behavior (and thus the influence) of the historically disadvantaged. They also argue that some citizens are better at articulating their arguments than others, so much so that well-educated white males are destined to prevail in the deliberative environment (Sanders 1997). The Rawlsian approach, however, sedates all participants with the same dosage of the same drug. Although Rawls acknowledges that we all have a right to products of our own abilities, they can justly provide us only what we become entitled to "by taking part in a fair social process" (Rawls 1993, 284). Presumably, fine debating skills, whether innate or acquired, are covered by that injunction.

Others have suggested that Rawls's conception of public reason is too narrow because it is based on the assumption that people's preferences are determined prior to political interaction and do not change as a result of such interaction (Offe 1997). But this is true only to the extent that Rawls's theory embodies an attempt to justify collective decisions by appealing to reasons that can be adopted by people simply by virtue of their common citizenship and the shared interests implied by that common status (Evans 1999). Indeed, the greatest problem with Rawls's approach to public reason may be that, rather than counting too little on change, it counts on change far more than is reasonable. Deliberative democracy of the kind he advocates would require a radical equality of access for individuals, groups, and interests that historically have been excluded from decision making. If actually achieved, such a circumstance would unsettle, if not subvert, existing understandings about the dimensions and boundaries of political conflict (Knight and Johnson 1994).

The view of citizens in the ideal discourse situation adopted by Habermas shares much with that of Rawls, but it also differs in some important ways. Recall that Habermas speaks of personally autonomous participants in deliberative discourse who are "free and equal," each of whom is "required to take the perspective of everyone else" and who thus projects him- or herself "into the understandings of self and the world of all others" (Habermas 1995, 117). But these citizens do not adopt this attitude out of any commitment to abstract principles of justice produced in a reflective equilibrium free of ideology and interest. They are committed to advancing their normative validity claims in forms that can be treated like truth claims; that is, in forms that can be subjected to empirical evaluation (Habermas 1990). There is no mechanism of impartiality at work. Indeed, Habermas criticizes Rawls for his willingness to purchase the neutrality of his conception of justice at the cost of forsaking its cognitive validity claim (Habermas 1995). It is as if Habermas is invoking the second clause of Rawls's own maxim that "justice is the first virtue of social institutions just as truth is of systems of thought" (Rawls 1999a, 3).

The reasonableness Habermas seeks is born of a social and cultural commitment to an inclusive and rational discourse (Habermas 1995) based on "the justified supposition of a legitimate order" (Habermas 1996, 68). It is true that the processes of internalization that structure the normative foundations of the values espoused by citizens are not free of repressive and reactionary tendencies (Habermas 1996). It is also true that those who constitute the politically interested and informed class of the public may be disinclined to submit their views to discussion (Habermas 1998b). Ultimately, however, the consciousness of their own autonomy gives rise to an "authority of conscience" that becomes an integral part of the politically informed and active citizen's motivational foundation (Habermas 1996, 67). This commitment to intellectual honesty would seem to be an essential element of the ideal discourse situation, conceived of as a rational and noncoercive discourse designed to test empirically the truth-value of competing normative claims.

The theory of full liberalism as advanced by Bohman and others is less demanding than either public reason or ideal discourse. Bohman assumes that citizens in a democracy are unavoidably divided by deep-seated normative differences he describes as attributable to cultural pluralism (Bohman 1994). He also doubts the possibility that any form of public reason or any view of the common good can ever command a consensus in communities as complex as the modern democracies. "Community biases" and the exclusion of many from "effective political participation" are, in his view, unavoidable to at least some extent (Bohman 1996, 238). Finally, Bohman argues that knowledge and information are always scarce resources in a complex society, and that neither innate capacities nor acquired knowledge can ever be evenly or widely distributed. Consequently, citizens in pluralistic democracies will inevitably "surrender their autonomy to experts, delegates, and other forms of the division of labor" (Bohman 1996, 168).

This does not necessarily require or even suggest a surrender to all the injustices currently observable in democratic life. Bohman supports an equalization of deliberative resources and capacities as far as that is possible, as do other deliberative democrats (Cohen 1997; Gutmann and Thompson 1996). But as Dryzek has pointed out, some degree of inequality not only may be unavoidable, it may actually serve as grist for the deliberative contest (Dryzek 2000, 172–173). The point of providing support to the disadvantaged in the context of public deliberation is not to equalize their position with "the other interest groups jostling for influence" but, rather, to make "effective use of their political liberties" (Gutmann and Thompson 1996, 305, 277). Strict equality is neither necessary nor desirable from the point of view of maintaining the critical edge brought to deliberation by the disadvantaged. After all, it is not as if deliberation is a search for one correct solution.

Having rejected the notion of a singular form of public reason, it is not surprising that full liberalism theorists should find themselves in the company of the majority of representative theorists who, from Burke's time, have regarded political questions as "inevitably controversial ones without a right answer" (Pitkin 1967). The objects of deliberation, in their view, are the interests of specific persons who have a right to help define them. Politics is recognizably democratic when it gives them that right. These deliberative democrats do not try to specify a single form of citizenship. They search for "models of representation that support the give-and-take of serious and sustained moral argument within legislative bodies, between legislators and citizens, and among citizens themselves" (Gutmann and Thompson 1996, 131). In this way, deliberative democracy is not so much a search for ethically or empirically defensible solutions as it is a process of personal development for citizens. Dryzek may have captured the thought most felicitously: in the face of ideologies and structural forces that perpetuate distorted views of the political world, we should seek "the competence of citizens themselves to recognize and oppose such forces, which can be promoted through participation in authentically democratic politics" (Dryzek 2000, 21). Thus, one might argue that the most important product of deliberative democracy is neither just principles nor rational policies but, rather, the critical capacities of the citizens themselves. To the extent that permanent solutions to the ecological crisis require significant changes of collective consciousness, preserving our species and its environment may be possible only through such an act of social evolution.

Interactions

Having described in some detail the varying conceptions of the citizen in alternative conceptions of deliberative democracy, we may now more usefully discuss the nature of the interactions these citizens might be expected to have.

The deliberative interactions envisioned by Rawls, like his theory of the deliberative citizen, diverge more from our everyday experience than those implied by the accounts of most other democratic theorists. For one thing, Rawls views the well-ordered society as a "fair system of cooperation over time, from one generation to the next" (Rawls 1993, 15). Even leaving aside his very specific and demanding definition of fairness, Rawls has parted company with most liberals by characterizing society as a system of cooperation. Liberal theorists generally would be more likely to hope that society could become a fair system of competition than one of cooperation. But even among deliberative democrats, who might at least share his preference for cooperation over competition, Rawls stands out by insisting that a particular form of public reason be employed.

In developing his theory of public reason, Rawls seeks the highest level of impartiality one could imagine. For Rawls, it is an all-or-nothing affair. Without a stringent veil of ignorance, the bargaining problems facing citizens in their choice of their fundamental institutions would be hopelessly complicated. But with the veil, it is possible to arrive at "a unanimous choice of a particular conception of justice" (Rawls 1993, 121). Such a conception is essential, in his view, because "a purely procedural theory that contained no structural principles for a just social order would be of no use in our world . . ." (ibid., 285). That is because the central task of our cooperative social order is to secure to each citizen the "primary goods" that each of us wants (whatever else we want) simply by virtue of the fact that we are all rational agents (Rawls 1999a, 223). Not only would we all insist on these goods, we would not agree to any arrangement that did not provide them to each of us "in the same amount" (ibid., 235).

To meet these criteria, it is clear that "arranging for and financing public goods must be taken over by the state" (Rawls 1999a, 236) and that this process will always be one of the central issues confronting the political order in any society. Furthermore, this conception of public goods opens a clear path to the arena of environmental decision making. For an adherent to the Rawlsian approach, it is but a small additional step to argue that environmental goods should be regarded as public goods (Miller 1999). And it seems clear that a decision rule as robust as the veil of ignorance would yield so strong an obligation to secure intergenerational equity that a commitment to environmental protection would result in spite of the anthropocentrism of Rawls's underlying theory (Norton 1989).

The deliberative interactions imagined by Habermas are less the search for first principles described by Rawls than a form of communicative action. Habermas defines communicative action as conversation that is "governed by binding consensual norms which define reciprocal expectations about behavior" that allow the participants to understand their relationship and their mutual obligations (Habermas 1970, 92). Such conversation is the foundation of a free society, one in which as many people as possible may meaningfully participate in the public sphere. This is an arena in which various interests may engage in a free and open discussion about society's normative agenda (Habermas 1974). Habermas later described such discussion as "discourse ethics," which is grounded on the assumption that normative claims have cognitive meaning that can be treated like competing truth claims (Habermas 1990). Discourse ethics further assumes that the competition among conflicting truth claims is to be carried on without coercion, with participants yielding only to the force of the better argument (Habermas 1998b). Anything less than the unforced agreement of all discussants would fail to provide legitimacy to the democratic process of self-legislation. It would fail bridge the gap between *fact* and *norm,* to unite in our collective decisions the deontological character of a command with the teleological character of a desirable collective good (Habermas 1996).

Habermas recognizes that the prospects for such a critical discourse in the public sphere are undermined by a number of social trends. In modern societies, the critical public ceases to be a collection of literate generalists. It declines into minorities of specialists, on the one hand, who use their intellectual abilities to dominate the political process, and a mass public, on the other hand, that shows an uncritical receptiveness to the demands of capital and state (Habermas 1998b, 175–188). The press abandons its role in mediating the public reasoning process in favor of the more lucrative task of simply reinforcing mass consumption. Electoral processes are debilitated as small numbers of party activists isolate themselves from the public. They cease trying to lead public opinion as a source of critical judgment and begin to manipulate it as a social-psychological variable in their efforts to advance narrow group interests (ibid., 230–244). To correct these problems, several things would have to happen. The broad mass of citizens would have to become repoliticized. Secrecy and economic competition would have to be eliminated to the extent that they impede the free flow of politically relevant information. And the isolation of specialists from each other and from the population as a whole would have to be eliminated (Habermas 1970, 75–76). It would seem that ideal discourse, the inclusive and noncoercive rational conversation in which everyone is required to take the perspective of everyone else (Habermas 1995), is a very distant goal indeed.

As if Habermas were not tough enough on his own theories, other critics have raised further problems. It is claimed that discourse ethics sometimes seems like little more than a regulative principle for our personal moral judgments, indicating that we should bear in mind what we think an ideal communicative community *would* say on a given subject (Benhabib 1990, 343–346). It can also be argued that discourse ethics is neither fish nor fowl, falling as it does in the gap between the Kantian notion of universalizability and the communitarian notion that ethical commitments must be embedded in cultures and ways of life (Outhwaite 1994). Moreover, others have suggested that Habermas's project of closing the gap between legitimacy and rationality through inclusive reason toward rational consensus is largely an exercise of the imagination (Mouffe 1999). From the environmentalist perspective, it has been claimed that Habermas is so preoccupied with rational discourse that he is willing to accept the devastating estrangement of humans from nature as simply part of the price we pay for modernity (Hayim 1992).

But perhaps most serious is the argument that Habermas (like Rawls) has made a mistake by insisting that citizens converge on the same reasons rather than agreeing on a course of action each for his own reasons. This convergence, it has been suggested, is merely an ideal of democratic citizenship rather than an actual requirement of public reason (Bohman 1996). Worse yet, his preoccupation with this convergence has led Habermas to the strong principle of unanimity that ultimately renders his theories impractical in a world characterized by social complexity and moral pluralism (Bohman 1994). In fact, Dryzek has concluded that Habermas "long ago realized the practical difficulties that precluded the realization of consensus in practice" (Dryzek 2000, 72). Habermas, however, may also have done something rather more subtle.

In his recent work, Habermas (1996) maintains a strong emphasis on reasoned consensus while showing a willingness to discuss majority rule in certain circumstances. Some have concluded that he has abandoned his earlier commitment to unanimity in the face of moral complexity and now regards consensus as merely a "regulative ideal" (Gaus 1997). In this view, consensus is merely "a model for real world discourse in concrete, historical conditions" (Postema 1995, 359). But before we reduce consensus forever to the status of a hopeless aspiration, it might be worth looking at Habermas's view more closely.

Habermas describes a form of majority rule that suggests a certain practical priority for consensus. Consensus and majority rule are compatible, in his view, "only if the latter has an internal relation to the search for truth" (Habermas 1997, 47). Public reason must "mediate between reason and will, between the opinion-formation of all and the majoritarian will-formation of the representatives" (ibid.). A decision arrived at in the political realm through majority rule is legitimate only if "its content is regarded as the rationally motivated but fallible result of an attempt to determine what is right through a discussion that has been brought to a *provisional* close under the pressure to decide" (ibid., emphasis in the original). Habermas is careful to indicate that such a decision does not require the minority to concede that it is in error or to give up its aims. It requires only that they forgo the implementation of their view until they better establish their reasons and gain the necessary support (ibid.). Ideally, then, a vote is only "the concluding act of a continuous controversy" carried out publicly between argument and counterargument (Habermas 1998b, 212). If the idea of a concluding act fits poorly with the concept of a continuous controversy, we can better understand why many have found Habermas to be elusive on this subject.

What are the practical implications of this view of majority rule? First, it should be apparent that accepting something less than consensus is justified where the pressure to decide precludes further deliberation. Listing a species as endangered when its population is in decline would be one example. Acting on budget proposals where spending authorization is about to lapse might be another. Dispatching aid to a disaster scene without full knowledge of the need would be a third. In the first case, action must be taken if an opportunity is not to be lost. In the second, an institutional imperative requires that something be done in a circumstance where the perfect may have become the enemy of the good. In the third, the prospect of immediate and irreparable harm to human interests justifies action in the face of what may be significant uncertainty about the facts. Other examples, capturing other principles of immediacy, are certainly conceivable. But the concepts of lost opportunity, institutional imperative, and imminent harm are clearly major categories of the pressure to decide.

Second, accepting something less than consensus may also be justified where no action, or continuation of the status quo, is an option that may be strategically sought through extension of discussion or commissioning of further research (a strategy sometimes known as "paralysis by analysis"). In other words, neither the time it takes to deliberate, nor a failure to act because of lack of consensus, is politically neutral. A nondecision is a choice, however inadvertent or inconspicuous. To delay deciding is to delay acting; to fail to decide is a decision not to act. All are options that are always value-laden and inherently biased. Ophuls, for example, would criticize a consensus requirement as in fact creating a bias toward doing nothing or maintaining the status quo even while continuing on a costly path, including even a path toward eventual disaster (Ophuls 1977; 1997). To fail to curb pollution, global warming, or whatever until everyone is of the same mind is to accept holding society hostage to a few who, for reasons of self-interest or ideology or diminished capacity, may be resistant to public reason. Any deliberative political system is likely to face the problem of what to do absent a consensus, or pending a consensus, because the do-nothing option is never neutral and it may be more or less costly. But some sort of provisional majoritarian rule can reduce the opportunity costs of deliberation or at least keep them from rising above a certain threshold.

An implication of this view is that public reason, which is a product of the ideal discourse situation, must be the tool used to determine when the need to decide is sufficient to justify majority rule. In this way the political process of majoritarian will-formation is disciplined by the social process of the opinion-formation of all. In effect, the minority maintains a veto on collective action but chooses not to exercise it immediately in the expectation that the discourse will continue and any intermediate action will be regarded as a provisional decision based on only a weak consensus that prompt action is required. So majority rule will always be available, but it will be legitimate only where members of the minority are satisfied that the discourse will continue and they will not ultimately be required to yield to the force of numbers.

Where lost opportunities and immediate harms are major concerns, and where many (if not most) decisions will be regarded as legitimate only if they are provisional, there must be a strong bias against any action with irreversible consequences as well as against any inaction with similarly weighty irreversible consequences. Providing protection for an endangered species is a positive manifestation of this negative bias. Decisions forced by fiscal deadlines can be accepted because a budget passed in haste can be amended at leisure. Emergency aid can flow freely because aid erroneously given can be recouped at a later date. But an old growth forest that is logged, or a wetland that is paved over, is a permanent loss that later regrets cannot recover. These are actions that a majority could not justify as provisional decisions. So, if our description of Habermas's theory is sound, neither he nor other deliberative democrats who accept his reasoning should ever tolerate such decisions absent a genuine consensus among all those choosing to debate the issues in the ideal discourse situation.

The full liberalism view of what constitutes acceptable interaction between deliberative citizens is less philosophically taxing than that of Rawls or Habermas and may, for that reason, be more representative of deliberative democrats generally. For advocates of full liberalism, the goal of political deliberation is to solve a problem together with others who have distinctly different perspectives and interests. The process does not have to begin with a shared commitment to impartiality, or even a shared set of rules for the discourse. All that is required is that participants have a "shared definition of the problem" and "something to say about the conditions under which they deliberate" (Bohman 1996, 55, 198). Political deliberation succeeds not when it has achieved unanimity, but rather when it produces "a shared intention that is acceptable to a *plurality* of the agents who participate in the activity of forming it" (ibid., 56, emphasis added). This intention is neither a set of principles that represent what any impartial citizen would choose, nor a truth claim that has been tested against the available information and found reliable. For advocates of full liberalism, a Rawlsian form of impartial precommitment depends on the dubious assumption that "all citizens have the same desire for the same object" (ibid., 48). Bohman, for example, is more sympathetic to the approach of Habermas, which he characterizes as "open to input from a vibrant and informal public sphere" and "structured to support the rationality of the relevant types of discourse" (ibid., 177). But Bohman does not require that agreement be supported by shared reasons or that the agreement be complete. In his view, consensus is precluded by the practicalities of a pluralistic society. The solution is to think of public reason as itself being plural, such that a plurality of the participants in deliberation can come to an agreement with one another for reasons that are different but mutually comprehensible (ibid., 83–85).

The plurality rule advocated by advocates of full liberalism is, in a variety of ways, more compatible with the approaches of other deliberative democrats than with the work of either Habermas or Rawls. It escapes the criticism leveled at Rawls that his original position is overly cautious because it is designed merely to make as good as possible the worst that can happen (Wenz 1988). Neither can it be argued that full liberalism, like Rawls, erroneously assumes the existence of a common unit of measure for evaluating the relative position of citizens or commits itself to an abstract individualism that is blind to the importance of social relations between deliberative participants (Benton 1999). And full liberalism, unlike Rawls, is open to free-ranging moral argument about the substance of political controversy by citizens fully aware of their own stake in the matter at hand (Gutmann and Thompson 1996). This is especially important for deliberative environmentalists, who have taken Rawls to task for excluding the obligation to animals that such moral reasoning would promote (Pritchard and Robison 1981; Wenz 1988; Kelch 1999).

To the extent that full liberalism has distanced itself from Habermas, it has escaped another set of criticisms. For one thing, "Habermas's theory of the state insists that citizens identify with the norms that govern them" and that "the products of public discourse are to be internalized as the subjective will of individuals" (Bennett 1987, 106). By allowing for agreement on the basis of diverse reasons, full liberalism avoids this apparent intrusion on the autonomy of the individual. This insulation of the citizen from the discourse also carves out greater room for representation instead of direct participation, something that some deliberative democrats have found both necessary and desirable (Gutmann and Thompson 1996). Full liberalism's abandonment of consensus also allows for a less ambivalent attitude toward voting, something most deliberative democrats acknowledge to be a necessity (Cohen 1989). Its less stringent approach to the reasons that may be offered in public discourse is more open to "the power of ideas, metaphors, images, and stories" (Healey 1993, 244). This openness is important to many deliberative democrats, particularly those whose focus is environmental. It allows for the possibility of a world of reason that is not entirely disenchanted, where humans can share in a free and indeterminate accord between understanding and imagination (Bennett 1997). Only in such a world can deliberative citizens escape the inherent anthropocentrism of contemporary liberalism (Matthews 1991) by discovering the compelling independent reasons for adopting an ecological perspective (Valadez 2001). This would appear to be an essential step in overcoming the complaint that whereas "to advocate democracy is to advocate procedure . . . to advocate environmentalism is to advocate substantive outcomes" (Goodin 1992, 168).

Institutions

It is unfortunate for purposes of critically examining environmental citizenship in deliberative democracy, and for other reasons as well, that institutional structure is not a subject on which deliberative democrats have spent much time. Any effort to institutionalize deliberative democracy will necessarily involve the provision of modern constitutional rights, all of which are necessary both to induce citizens to agree to participate and to establish the necessary conditions for successful outcomes. Moreover, the main rights and liberties that are central to political liberalism can be derived as substantive outcomes of free and open public discourse among equals carried out in terms of consideration that all have reason to accept (Cohen 1996, 100–107). But rights in themselves may only make deliberation possible. They tell us nothing about what deliberation is or about how it is best conducted under any prevailing set of conditions (Bohman 1996, 23–25). Other institutional conditions are clearly necessary. For instance, in structuring deliberative institutions it is essential to overcome the effects of economic inequity as well as the dominance of local or sectional power issue arenas (Cohen 1997). Either of these phenomena can lead to deliberation that is inequitable or insufficiently general and open. Furthermore, in designing deliberative institutions it is important to avoid isolating the exercise of reason from the exercise of power or confining deliberation to government institutions alone. We must also avoid separating issues of institutional structure from those of institutional culture or dividing deliberative labor such that representatives give reasons and citizens merely receive them (Gutmann and Thompson 1996, 358–360). Fortunately, deliberative democrats have developed possible responses for these problems.

A number of theorists have tackled the problem of economic inequality and the deliberative disadvantages it causes. In general, their answers involve creating a more open public sphere by organizing those who would challenge the dominant order into collectives, perhaps supported through public funding. There have also been several procedural innovations suggested, including new voting rights legislation, more aggressive campaign finance reform, new equal time provisions, and other methods for expanding public discourse (Bohman 1996). Other participatory mechanisms have been suggested that are relatively insensitive to the influence of wealth. Fishkin (1991; 1995) has experimented with "deliberative polling" in which a random sample of citizens is brought together for deliberation in order to model what the population would want upon sober reflection. A similar technique has been found to be useful in encouraging citizens to deliberate environmental issues. Gundersen (1995) found in a series of "deliberative interviews" that forty-six subjects who did not initially identify themselves as environmentalists became more committed to environmental values as a result of the interview process. Neither of these procedures would likely be distorted by the effects of wealth. The challenge, however, would be to integrate such procedures into governmental processes in order to provide a "legitimation filter" for administration agencies "still oriented as much as ever toward efficiency" (Habermas 1996, 441). Since the legitimacy of law depends on self-legislation, the informal discursive sources of democracy must be linked with the formal decision-making processes of government (Avio 1999).

Moving from informal institutional arrangements into the realm of government confronts us with the problem of local and regional power elites and their ability to distort deliberative discourse to their own advantage. Local and regional organizing presents significant opportunities to enhance the deliberative quality of democratic practice, especially where environmental issues are concerned. Watershed partnerships have been used to good effect in bringing together the wide variety of citizens who share a concern with the policies adopted for federal water projects in the West (Levine 2000, 195–199). Ecological awareness has been promoted by bioregional organizations like the Northwest Power Planning Council, which has engaged in the ecological restoration of the Columbia River Basin while relying for its information on both biological scientists and structured opportunities for participation in a variety of forums organized by the council (Lee 1993). These examples of local and regional deliberation, however, do not eliminate the problem of the narrowing and distortion of democratic discourse that can result from local concentrations of political power.

The devolution of power from central government agencies to local and regional arenas is one way that the constitutional state protects the variety of interests and outlooks present in the citizenry as a whole. Decentralization places functional limits on the influence of hierarchy and establishes mechanisms for the dispersal of democratic power (Bohman 1996). But public discourse is effective only to the extent that it is widely diffused, and thus only under conditions of a broad and active participation (Habermas 1996). For deliberative discourse to flourish, participatory organizations, formally organized mass political parties, and state bureaucracies must be organized and coordinated so as to bring a greater degree of procedural equality (and therefore social rationality) and an increased orientation toward consensus at the local level (Ingram 1993). Examples of participatory problem-solving arrangements from which ideas might fruitfully be borrowed are various forms of adjudication.

According to Habermas, "by virtue of its comparatively high degree of rationality, judicial deliberation and decision making offer the most thoroughly analyzed case" of a system that institutionalizes rule of discourse without regulating or intervening in the substance of arguments as such (Habermas 1996, 178). At its best, adjudication is a substantively neutral and consensus-oriented procedure designed to decide "which claim and which action in a given conflict is right—and not how to balance interests or relate values" (ibid., 260–261). Walzer (1999) has suggested that juries provide a particularly useful example of the deliberative interaction of citizens within a governmental framework. Fishkin (1991) has called for the use of deliberative citizens juries in areas beyond the criminal and civil cases of traditional jurisprudence. So how might adjudication, limited at the trial level to resolving particular disputes and at the appellate level by the small role of citizens and restricted scope of the institution, serve as a model for a wider form of self-legislation in deliberative environmental democracy?

There is little doubt that courts have a profound effect on environmental policy in the United States and elsewhere. But average citizens play only a limited role in these processes as they currently exist. The impact of citizens is limited by several fundamental characteristics of our jurisprudence. Important among these are the reactive character of litigation and the relatively undemanding standard of review typically used in evaluating the actions of regulatory agencies. An example of these problems, and their potential solutions, can be provided through a brief discussion of the U.S. National Environmental Policy Act (NEPA).

NEPA creates an important opportunity for citizens to become involved in environmental policymaking and implementation. Used in conjunction with the Administrative Procedures Act, NEPA has provided a legal ground for citizen suits if the environmental impact statement (EIS) and other procedural requirements of the act are not properly followed by federal agencies (Lindstrom and Smith 2001, 50). NEPA requires that federal projects with significant potential to affect the human environment should be considered under conditions of full disclosure after extensive public hearings and opportunities for public comment (ibid., 94). It further requires that the EIS documents produced to satisfy the requirements of the act should be written in language that is accessible to the general public (ibid., 95). This process of open debate and evaluation has preempted many questionable projects since the passage of NEPA and has spread the concept of impact assessment into other areas of policy analysis (Bartlett 1989; Bartlett and Kurian 1999).

Like many other environmental laws, however, the impact of NEPA has been limited by the fact that the act can bring environmental issues into the policy arena only in the form of specific development proposals and can address them only in the terms posed by the case at hand. Moreover, review of administrative actions under the act has been less stringent that it might otherwise have been because of the judiciary's use of the "hard look" standard of review, requiring only that an agency show it has examined the alternatives and (in its sound discretion) adopted the proposed solution. As limiting as circumstances such as these have been, the literature is not entirely without possible solutions.

In discussing reviews of the legislative process, Sunstein has proposed a "reasoned analysis requirement" (1985, 58). This standard would require that the decision maker show that it has acted deliberatively. This standard requires a judgment to be made whether the decision in question turned on reasons that can be publicly advocated or on private interests that cannot be declared within the framework of a free and open deliberation among equals. In essence, the standard requires both that the deliberative procedure be appropriate and that its substantive outcome be undistorted by private power. Davis (1969a) has advanced a possible solution for the narrow scope and reactive character of litigation processes generally, recommending that hypothetical cases, carefully designed to present critical policy issues in the clearest factual context, be litigated as if they were actual disputes. Representatives of interests potentially affected by such "cases" could play the role of both parties, witnesses, and amicus curiae. The judgments produced could serve as persuasive authority in the same way that restatements of the law and model codes currently do. Opportunities for public involvement in establishing the precedential background for the development of real-world environmental law would be increased. And the deliberative scope and reach of adjudicatory processes could be extended from the arena of resolving particular disputes into the realm of self-legislation through the development of common law.

Such an expansion of public involvement in the adjudicatory processes of policymaking, and the extension of adjudicatory practice into civil society beyond the boundaries of government, would provide several potential advantages to deliberative theory. As noted earlier, Habermas calls for procedural law "to build a legitimation filter into the decisional processes of administration still oriented as much as ever toward efficiency" (Habermas 1996, 441). A stronger and broader regime of judicial review would certainly answer that need. Bohman calls for differentiation within deliberative institutions to meet the challenges of complexity in modern democracies (Bohman 1996, 162). Establishing a more deliberative approach across the diverse and highly specialized collection of federal agencies with rule-making and adjudicatory authority fits that prescription. It is even possible that public enthusiasm for direct involvement in government might be enhanced. In discussing the current literature on the disenchantment of modern culture, Bennett has cautioned us not to underestimate the "enchanting potential of material complexity, especially in its manmade forms" (Bennett 2001, 110). It is worth pointing out that, according to Bennett, bureaucracy is one of the major sources of this institutional form of enchantment.

Conclusion

As individuals, citizens in a deliberative democracy are to be regarded as both rational and reasonable. It should be assumed that their interests lie in developing a fair system of cooperation that, over time, will provide to each an equal system of fundamental liberties and basic goods such that all are capable of the fullest development and enjoyment of their own potential. A continuing supply of essential natural resources as well as protection against the inequitable imposition of environmental risks clearly falls within these parameters. Interactions among these citizens should be governed by norms of discourse that encourage the giving and receiving of reasons that are acceptable (or at least potentially acceptable) to all regardless of their particular interests or the comprehensive systems of thought to which they subscribe. Although there is considerable disagreement on the subject, there is strong justification for a norm of consensus to govern these interactions, and there is considerable reason to suppose that the benefits of such a norm would outweigh the costs it would impose on the decision-making process. Deliberative institutions will comprise both governmental and nongovernmental organizations designed to give citizens the opportunity to influence collective decisions through an open and equal discourse. A broad and settled collection of modern constitutional rights will need to exist, as will a basic equality in the value of the citizen's right to participate. Governmental institutions will tend toward decentralization, both in the choice among alternative courses of action and in the implementation of favored alternatives. Deliberative institutions will constantly experiment with various participatory arrangements, borrowing liberally from other areas of human activity and collective problem solving, such as existing adjudicatory processes.

10

Problematic Participants: Experts and Social Movements

Of political actors whose place in the democratic order is more open to question, the most important are those who advance a claim to expertise based on some specialized training and those who represent broad social movements with ideological commitments that bear on issues of public policy. The theory of deliberative democracy is especially focused on individuals as participants, with particular conceptions of the autonomy, rationality, and equality of individuals determining the appropriate institutionalization of democratic governance. This individualistic focus renders certain types of political participation always illegitimate—coercive participation of elites based on physical, economic, or organizational power, for example. Other political actors who traditionally have been among the engines of interest-group democracy, notably experts and social movements, are also highly suspect in deliberative theory. To the extent that those who advance a claim to expertise based on some specialized training, and those who represent broad social movements with ideological commitments bearing on issues of public policy, might attempt to achieve their aims coercively, their participation would of course be illegitimate on the same grounds as that of power elites. But experts or social movements exercise influence not primarily or even at all based on traditional sources of power but rather from their potential contributions of reason to the deliberative political process, giving them a potentially "special" status in deliberative theory. Should their status as repositories of needed specialized knowledge allow them to exercise extra weight in deliberative democratic processes? Unlike power elites, then, experts and social movements are problematic but still desirable deliberative participants. If we could successfully figure out how to integrate their reasons and forms of reasoning into deliberative democratic processes, we could immeasurably improve the quality of deliberation by enhancing its knowledge base.

As with citizens, there is an enormous literature that discusses the role of scientific experts and social movements in conventional policy processes, but scarcely theorized at all are the roles that these problematic participants might play in deliberative democracy. Does the deliberative process require (or even allow) empirical inputs that would justify a role for experts that differs from the role played by others? Do ideologies enter into deliberative politics in such a way that social movements can be appropriate parties to deliberation? In seeking answers to these questions, we frame our analysis herein in terms of the ability of deliberative democracy to cope with environmental politics, a political realm that poses particularly challenging demands on both experts and social movements as well as common citizens. How do environmentalism as a social movement and scientific expertise frame deliberative responses to the ecological challenges confronted by developed democracies?

Experts in the Policy Process: Questions of Long Standing

The role played by science and expertise in the policy process has long been problematic. It has been observed that there are three fundamental ways to organize human activities: markets, expert analysis, and political choice (Munger 2000). Markets and politics have been widely explored in two vast literatures. But even defining expertise has been a challenge. According to one view, expertness refers to a claim by a specially trained group that they can contribute uniquely valuable knowledge or advice. This group claim of intellectual authority can be based both on collectively organized and sanctioned training and on group members' quality control of one another's work through peer review (MacRae and Whittington 1997). Alternatively, expert judgment has been seen as a form of tacit knowledge, something that people know without being able to put it into words, much less formulate as rules (Stone 2002). This disagreement is about more than the source of expertise, training, and group understandings in the first instance and individual insight in the second. These conflicting definitions suggest different roles for the expert in the policy process. In the "group expertise" model, one might argue that the most appropriate role for an expert is as a discipline representative. The expert provides policymakers with his or her assessment of a discipline's general consensus on a matter of empirical interest. In the "tacit knowledge" model, on the other hand, the expert's role is personally authoritative. He or she is required to puzzle out the underlying reality of a problematic circumstance, using both professional training and individual instincts to provide a unique perspective that is not fully explained but is accepted on the basis of the expert's authority.

Each of these views suggests its own reasons why expert influence in the policy process is (and, perhaps, should be) resisted. "Representational" expertise is critically dependent on the peer review process, supposed by its proponents to enhance objectivity. But the actual function of peer review may be to enforce orthodoxy, making a new or revolutionary idea difficult to establish. As a result, the academic perspective may be suspect for its "inherently cautious and conservative" character (Munger 2000, 149). Tacit knowledge, on the other hand, even when it appears to be objective and factual, may be subject to resistance because of the personal perspective it legitimates. Citizens, policymakers, and scientists alike may reject expert authority because of their attitudes about its source or because of the challenge it presents to their own tacit knowledge (Stone 2002).

Both forms of expert knowledge face additional challenges. The conventional separation between normative premises in decision making (supplied by citizens or their representatives) and empirical facts (potentially supplied by experts) seems increasingly untenable (Kelly and Maynard-Moody 1993). What we regard as facts, true statements about the state of the world, are actually the products of specific social institutions and processes. They come not from direct observation, but from socially constructed knowledge, from the accumulation and presentation of both observations and beliefs in social discourse (Stone 2002). Yet, as noted in chapter 8, at the same time that this postbehaviorist critique is problematizing expertise, the demand for expertise is increasing. In the last half-century, Americans have experienced a transition from an administrative to a scientific state with an agenda heavily loaded with difficult scientific issues. Scientific and technological thoughtways permeate the language, culture, and conceptual premises of citizens, administrators, and elected officials alike (Schmandt and Katz 1986). As Walter Lippmann noted long ago, the quantity and necessity of expertise in the modern world imposes unavoidable constraints on rational participatory democracy: "The amount of attention available is far too small for any scheme in which it was assumed that all the citizens of the nation would, after devoting themselves to the publications of all the intelligence bureaus, become alert, informed, and eager on the multitude of real questions that never do fit very well into any broad principle" (1922, 301).

Even when the issue at hand is not obviously scientific or technological, we now look for expert input. For example, by commissioning studies into the effects of segregation on children and society and by drawing on previous studies of those subjects, the Warren Court in *Brown v. Board of Education* (347 U.S. 483) appeared to accept the notion that social science should form the empirical foundation of public policy. It would seem that now is not the time for experts to go missing in action. And, as if these challenges were not sufficient, deliberative democrats have their own grounds for resisting the influence of science and expertise.

Many deliberative democrats have had surprisingly little to say on the subject of experts and their role in the process of collective decision making. For example, as discussed in chapter 8, behind a Rawlsian veil of ignorance one might not be expected to know enough about anything to make a claim to expertise. In fact, Rawls has described the reasoning process he advocates by likening it to the ideal discourse situation advanced by Habermas, calling it "an omnilogue" in which "there are no experts" (Rawls 1995, 140). Furthermore, he characterizes his theory of justice as a conception that "can no more be voted on than can the axioms, principles, and rules of inference of mathematics or logic" (ibid., 144, fn. 22). This would seem to leave the approach advocated by Rawls empty of the empirical matters that form the basis of scientific inquiry and, thus, out of the reach of experts as policy theorists understand it. But elsewhere Rawls describes reasoning behind the veil of ignorance in a slightly different way: in using public reason, "we do not look at the social order from our situation but take up a point of view that everyone can adopt on an equal footing. In this sense, we look at our society and our place in it *objectively*" (Rawls 1999a, 453, emphasis added). In discussing what he characterizes as the "circumstances" of justice, Rawls characterizes "objective circumstances" as the "normal conditions under which human cooperation is both possible and necessary" (ibid., 109). Finally, in discussing the justifications that people may reasonably offer in defense of their political positions, Rawls has said that "we are to appeal only to presently accepted general beliefs and forms of reasoning found in common sense, and *the methods and conclusions of science where these are not controversial*" (Rawls 1993, 224, emphasis added).

What are we to make of this opening for science to enter into the original position? For Rawls, depriving deliberative participants of information can be justified only where (1) the failure to do so "would permit self- and group-interest to distort the parties deliberations"; (2) the information concerns "contingencies and accidents that should not influence the choice of moral principles"; or (3) the information "represents the very moral conceptions" that we seek to understand in the light of more fundamental principles (Rawls 1999c, 269). So the idea of public reason advanced by Rawls is not nearly so closed to scientific experts as it might first appear. But if we are looking for guidance about how to integrate experts into collective deliberation, we will have to look beyond the work of Rawls, for it simply was not one of his concerns.

Habermas offers a view of science and expertise in collective decision making that is both more fully developed and more useful than that of Rawls. As discussed in chapter 8, Habermas views consultation between scientific experts and policymakers as an unavoidable necessity. He recognizes that the development of new scientific and technical capacities is governed by social interests and political values. Expert knowledge is needed from the "first stage of opinion and will formation" and it is "naturally fallible and rarely value-neutral" (Habermas 1996, 164). Moreover, "as soon as specialized knowledge is brought to politically relevant problems, its unavoidably normative character becomes apparent, setting off controversies that polarize the experts themselves" (ibid., 351). But the limits imposed on collective will-formation by science and technology have the salutary effect of putting those public values and interests to the test of technical feasibility (Habermas 1970). This is vitally important, not only because it aids in testing the validity claims put forward by citizens in deliberative discourse, but also because it shows that "problems of functional coordination . . . are intertwined with the moral and ethical dimensions of social integration" (Habermas 1996, 351).

So, the problem for Habermas is to determine how the power of technical control can be "brought within the range of consensus of acting and transacting citizens" (Habermas 1970, 57). Given the need in complex democracies for functional coordination and factually sound decision making, "the simpler model of a division of labor between experts and lay persons no longer suffices" (Habermas 1996, 320). A reciprocal form of communication is necessary in which scientific experts advise decision makers who consult scientists as their practical needs dictate. Thus, the development of new techniques and scientific insights is "governed by a horizon of needs and historically determined interpretations of those needs, in other words, of value systems" (Habermas 1970, 67). Particularly in the environmental arena, this process simply cannot be dispensed with. The modern "risk society" makes such high demands on the "analytical and prognostic abilities of experts" and the "reaction time of precautionary administration" that the challenges to the regulatory state are dramatically exacerbated (Habermas 1996, 432).

For these reasons, Habermas (1996) suggests that the input of experts is vital to the testing of validity claims (both normative and empirical) put forward by the parties to a deliberation. In this sense, as noted in chapter 8, the expert functions for Habermas in somewhat the same way that a special master satisfies the need of the court that appoints him for a source of unbiased appraisals of the arguments advanced by the parties to litigation.

Habermas is well aware that there is a danger that "cognitive" problems of functional coordination may displace moral and ethical reasoning and "overburden the problem solving capacity of democratic procedures" (Habermas 1996, 320). After all, science and technology can be seen as fundamental elements of administrative power, the nature of which conflicts with precisely the forms of communicative power Habermas advocates (Scheuerman 1999). But Habermas gives us reason to hope that the domination of collective decision making by intellectuals can be avoided. He argues that the articulation of any shared will in accordance with technical knowledge "can be ratified exclusively in the consciousness of the political actors themselves," a fact that experts must anticipate when considering their role (Habermas 1970, 75). Thus "the influence of intellectuals could coalesce into communicative power only under conditions that exclude a concentration of power" (Habermas 1996, 490).

Furthermore, experts face significant constraints resulting from the means through which they must exercise their influence. In the first instance, experts must recognize the inherent superiority of ordinary language, which, with its "grammatical complexity, prepositional structure, and reflexivity," possesses a "multifunctionality" that special codes lack (Habermas 1996, 55). Moreover, given the high degree of division of labor in the sciences, the lay public and its ordinary language "often provides the shortest path of internal understanding between mutually estranged specialists" and serves the "necessity for the translation of scientific information which grows out of the needs of the research process itself" (Habermas 1970, 77). Thus, the use of ordinary language by aspiring scientific experts not only benefits the communication between experts and the public, it benefits communication within the research process while it empowers the citizen in the public sphere.

For still other deliberative democrats, as we have seen, an epistemic division of labor is an unavoidable characteristic of deliberative institutions. In fact, Bohman (1996, 64) has urged experts to take on the lay perspective and for citizens to take on the perspective of technical experts by becoming far better informed. This would create the foundation for "an epistemic division of labor based on public trust," which would increase through successful use rather than deplete over time (ibid., 169).

Regardless of the division of labor between science and citizenship, then, those who hold themselves out to be experts must offer public reasons in support of their arguments, reasons that are accessible to "a general and unrestricted audience, rather than a specialized and restricted collective" (Bohman 1996, 46). But engagement across divergent forms of discourse is likely only where one discourse encounters a crisis that its adherents recognize but cannot solve within the limits of their own tradition (MacIntyre 1988). It is here that deliberative democracy and environmental preservation may have the most to contribute to each other. Many environmental problems cannot even be perceived as such without a great deal of scientific and technological sophistication (Kirkman 2002). Furthermore, to believe that environmentalism can exile scientists is to ignore the fact that there has been a transition from the administrative to the scientific state. Our public agenda is now heavily loaded with difficult scientific issues. Technological thoughtways permeate our language, our culture, and the conceptual processes of both the middle and upper levels of our political leadership (Schmandt and Katz 1986). In a culture such as ours, "the authority of science needs to be brought to bear in the service

of ecological literacy if a perspective on the environment is to have sufficient credibility to create general agreement that environmentally sound
policies should be adopted" (Valadez 2001, 363).

For its part, science needs the perspectives offered by a deliberative
environmental politics as much as environmentalism needs scientific
insight. Even the most mainstream policy theorists have observed that
science (especially scientism) has characteristics that are problematic
from an ecological perspective. One need not believe that science is racist
or sexist, or that Mother Nature won't love us if we play with test tubes,
to recognize that the "facts" of science come from "social knowledge,
from the accumulation and presentation of observations and beliefs"
rather than from unmediated observation (Stone 2002, 310). The empiri-
cal-analytic sciences are governed by a technical interest in the prediction
and control of both material and social processes (Habermas 1971). As
citizens become more aware of this, they feel freer to resist even the most
apparently objective and factual knowledge because of its source, its implications, or the challenge it presents to their tacit knowledge (Stone
2002, 312–314). Moreover, "the rationality of a specialized and competent fulfillment of tasks by experts is no protection against a *paternalistic*
self-empowerment" on the part of agencies that employ them (Habermas
1996, 188). The scientific society is, therefore, always in danger of becoming "ecologically irrational . . . when its forms of epistemic authority and
institutional practice threaten the eco-systemic relations on which it relies" (Dryzek 1987, 245). Subjecting the practice of empirical science and
its claims of policy expertise to the rigors of democratic deliberation is,
therefore, as much about the survival of modern science and the conditions that support it as it is about popular government.

Social Movements

Also not explored extensively by deliberative democrats is the role of social movements and the organizations they spawn in collective decision
making. It might seem that there is little room in a theory like that advanced by John Rawls for social movements to participate directly in
public deliberations. In his words, "a liberal society with a constitutional
regime does not, as a liberal society, have a comprehensive conception of
the good" (1999b, 34). But Rawls's theory is not one of isolated individu-

alism, as some have complained. Rawls recognizes that "we are by ourselves but parts of what we might be" (1999a, 464). His view that we achieve more when we work in groups than when we isolate ourselves is particularly evident in his discussion of the basic liberties. Holding office and having an influence on the outcome of political decisions are liberties that all enlightened citizens would want regardless of what else they wanted. Furthermore, these liberties must be of equal worth or usefulness to all citizens regardless of their social or economic position (Rawls 1993, 326–327).

But if this level of equality is a prerequisite for effective public reasoning toward collective decisions, how can public reason bring about these conditions where they do not already exist? An answer lies in Rawls's discussion of the civil rights movement. Civil rights organizations, as Rawls recognizes, have always advanced arguments and employed tactics that are alien to his concept of public reason. Their appeals have often been highly emotional and driven by "comprehensive views" based on experiences so distinctive that the broader polity could not possibly have shared the same perspective. Yet Rawls defends the civil rights movement and its tactics even though they were grounded in reasons that were far from public. The comprehensive views appealed to in this historical case were "required to give sufficient strength to the political conception to be realized," and, given the circumstances, "it was not unreasonable of them to act as they did *for the sake of the ideal of public reason itself*" (ibid., 251, emphasis added). So here is a situation in which the ideal of public reason allows for less than fully public reasoning in order to establish the necessary conditions for the exercise of fully public reason.

The potential of social movements is even greater in other approaches to deliberative democracy. Recall, for instance, that communicative power of the sort generated in Habermas's ideal discourse situation acts in the manner of a siege: "It influences the premises of judgment and decision making in the political system without intending to conquer the system itself" (Habermas 1996, 486–487). The activities of social movements are experiential lifeworld practices that can "put together—and also put right"—the cultural systems that have been divided by the disintegration of metaphysical and religious worldviews (Habermas 1992, 51). The protests of social movements are a "continuation of politics by extra parliamentary means," by which democracy can establish limits to the power of dominant interests by showing them what might happen if they are unresponsive to demands made through conventional means (Fisk 1989, 178–179). In addition, once a new social movement has established its identity, it enters into a "rhetorical competition" with the dominant social paradigm by rendering problematic elements of social reality that were previously taken for granted (Brulle 2000). Thus, the involvement of social movements in public deliberation serves both as a political constraint on parties that otherwise might dominate the discourse and as a critical force that broadens the range of the conversation.

The importance of a vibrant, unconstrained, and undistorted public discourse is well recognized among deliberative democrats. Michael Walzer (1991) has, for example, located the deliberative function of the U.S. Constitution not in the opportunities for deliberation that it creates within government but rather in the existence of a broad public realm that it protects. Moreover, progress on environmental issues depends heavily on the vitality of this civic arena. Habermas argues that "only if men could communicate without compulsion and each could recognize himself in the other, could mankind possibly recognize nature as another subject. . . . Instead of treating nature as the object of possible technical control, we can encounter her as an opposing partner in a possible interaction" (1970, 88). This happy outcome, however, could be threatened by risks inherent in both the concept of deliberative democracy and the practical necessities of environmental activism. These risks arise from at least three different, but not unrelated, sources—decentralization, co-optation, and resource inequality.

Both deliberative democracy and environmentalism strongly suggest that a smaller scale and more locally focused politics is in order. In the first instance, the notion of a single movement is practically useless in describing the vast array of organizations and efforts dedicated to protecting or repairing some part of the environment (Bosso 1991). Furthermore, it has been argued that the key to representing nature in politics is the idea of an "encapsulated interest," in which an ecological value is internalized and represented by sympathetic individuals (Goodin 1996). Finally, the vitality of deliberative communication depends on its variety. Only in a decentralized discourse is there room for forms of communication that facilitate diversity by showing explicit mutual recognition, reflexive attention to the audience, and the various levels of meaning attached to political values by those who hold them (Young 1996).

But decentralized political jurisdictions have long been recognized to be problematic, from both a democratic and an environmental point of view. In *The Federalist no. 10*, Madison observed that smaller political units are no protection against the mischief of faction, allowing as they do local elites to exert themselves in ways they never could at higher levels of government. Environmentalists have long observed that states and localities are perfectly willing and able to export their environmental problems to other jurisdictions (Gormley 1987). These problems come together in the realization that not every element in oppositional civil society represents discursive democratic vitality. Some participants will represent Astroturf organizations—synthetic creations having no organic link to the community—rather than grassroots environmental organizing.[1] They will take on the guise of a popular movement when, in fact, they are organized and bankrolled by interests pursuing the exploitation of nature for narrowly distributed financial gain that shifts environmental costs to the general population. Other participants may represent movements that seek to use democratic discourse to undermine democracy's discursive vitality, such as groups of the far right who are not committed to the fulfillment of modernity's potential but who will use a highly selective radicalization of modern values to resurrect premodern forms of political oppression (Offe 1985).

As real as the dangers of decentralization may be, the search for a deliberative form of environmental democracy cannot avoid them. Political decentralization is consistent with the core environmental value of making decisions at the local level and the development of small-scale institutions (Kriz 1995). And decentralization is a strong trend within environmentalism as a movement, as reflected in the structure of mainstream environmental organizations (Graham 1990). There is at least some reason to hope that the risks of decentralization can be minimized. Civic environmentalism has always showed its greatest strength at the local level. It has allowed numerous state and local stakeholders to take creative collective actions that are independent of, and sometimes more demanding than, parallel federal policies (Weber 2003; John 1994). The success of the environmental justice movement is an especially hopeful example. Environmental justice is not a centrally organized discourse but one that arises from multiple local struggles (Hajer 1995). The emergence of this network form of organization and its associated discourse has coalesced around a common story line about the inequitable generation and distribution of environmental risks. But the ultimate strength of the environmental justice movement is that it is a paradigmatic case of deliberation across difference (Schlosberg 1998). This insight strongly suggests that a powerful antidote to the dysfunctional characteristics of decentralization is ready at hand. It is the inherent diversity of genuinely open and equal public discourse, which can be promoted most readily by the rule of consensus advanced by Habermas and (more strongly) by Rawls.

A second danger facing social movements like environmentalism, one not unrelated to decentralization, is the problem of co-optation. The goals of the environmental movement, related as they are to ecology and equity, ultimately require that both local organizations and national groups operating in a decentralized manner band together to pursue democratic decision making with binding national and international authority (Wainright 1994). This is just one example of the quandary faced by groups and movements that enjoy initial successes in the public sphere. In an effort to cash in on the momentum generated in their take-off and consolidation phases, social movements are tempted to enter into the state process in order to achieve greater power over decisions that are central to their concerns (Offe 1990). Success at this level can lead to accusations of "corporate environmentalism" as pressures mount on environmental groups to manage their budgets wisely and maintain a public image of respectability. The result is often an efficiency orientation and an emphasis on rational decision making that elevates organizational concerns above the core values of both deliberative democracy and environmentalism (Bosso 2000). This tendency of decentralized social movements to transform themselves into centralized national agents cannot be avoided, at least not in the case of environmentalism. Politics generally is increasingly organized around risk allocation. The targets of risk are so numerous, and so capable of political mobilization, that the legitimacy of the socioeconomic order faces a growing crisis of legitimacy that can be ameliorated only by the broadest public participation in risk allocation (Beck 1992). Social movements like environmentalism will be challenged to maintain simultaneous and sustained action both within the confines of the state and in the wider civil society if they intend to be both politically effective and genuinely democratic (Rucht 1990). A firm commitment to the conceptual underpinnings of deliberative democracy is required. Also required is a firm foundation of political resources, the shortage of which is a third challenge both to environmentalism and deliberative democracy.

Throughout the history of modern democracy, there have been groups and organizations that have successfully pursued moralistic, good government, and public interest agendas (Berry 1997). Nevertheless, social movements impose a high demand on their members for constant participation. They also tend to lack the financial and organizational resources that give other organizations (like corporations and political parties) political staying power (Alario 1994). As a result, environmental organizations often find themselves outspent and outgunned (Dowie 1995). So the green lobby generally finds itself strong enough only to repulse legislative efforts it opposes, but it enjoys little success in building wide support for its own reform proposals (McCloskey 1993). Also, there is little evidence that a green voting block has emerged that would provide a political foundation for the environmental movement to exercise significant influence at the ballot box (Dunlap 1991). But overall public concern for the environment endures to the point that support for environmental protection as a general matter can be regarded as a consensual issue that generates little open opposition (Dunlap 1995). This explains, at least in part, why the movement has greater success in blocking initiatives to which it objects than it does in advancing a positive agenda.

How might the resource problem confronting environmentalism, as well as other social movements, be dealt with in order to improve the likelihood that a genuinely deliberative democracy can be developed? At one level, growth in the size and vitality of the environmental movement probably requires that populations not normally associated with these organizations be integrated into their membership. The environmental justice movement has already shown the potential for the economically disadvantaged to bring new vitality to environmentalism. Other groups to whom environmentalists have rarely appealed, like farmers and loggers, should not be considered out of reach (Gottleib 1993). Moreover, fiscal conservatives might help in the elimination of subsidies for resource extraction, and religious conservatives might support protection of an endangered species based on the notion of stewardship and their love of all God's creations (Kelly 1997). All of these "nontraditional" environmental groups should be targeted as potential allies at the state and local levels, where their national organizations can be more effectively circumvented and direct discourse may achieve a local consensus.

Addressing the inequality of material resources between social movements and institutions of capital and the state is also imperative. In a deliberative democracy, inequality of opportunity to define problematic situations and advance possible solutions must be dealt with at more than one level. Procedural reforms, such as public meetings laws, hearing requirements, and campaign finance reforms are sensible first steps. A further step would be for courts and/or the legislature to interpret the First Amendment as prohibiting not only government infringements on speech but also political and administrative practices that imposed deliberative disadvantages on citizens and citizen organizations (Bohman 1996, 139–141). A final step would be far more controversial, precisely because it would be the most effective approach to eliminating deliberative inequality. Any democracy that is serious about full and open citizen participation will eventually have to deal with the inequality of representation by state promotion of organizations to represent the disenfranchised (Cohen and Rogers 1992). Not only would this step serve to equalize discursive resources, it would serve as an antidote to the rampant individualism of contemporary culture that threatens both the environmental agenda and the realization of public deliberation's full promise (Walzer 1994).

Imagining the particulars of such a system is a challenge. Joan Aron (1980) has suggested the use of nonpartisan and nonideological independent boards that would be empowered to offer support to individuals and organizations after a showing of need and the public interest rationale for their activities. The likelihood of ideological disputes arising from such a process is clear. Litigation, at least occasionally, would be unavoidable. But the existence of government programs, both national and local, supporting scientific research, the humanities and arts, and other social goods suggests that the support for public deliberation is not out of the question. And if the process was carried out in an open and inclusive manner, using the rule of consensus advanced by many deliberative theorists, the results could advance democratic inclusion in significant ways and might well prove to be both politically and legally sustainable over the long run.

A Conclusion (of Sorts)

In developing a full account of the role of citizens, experts, and social movements in deliberative environmental politics, most important is a description of the background social conditions and political culture necessary to sustain this approach to collective will-formation. The general outlines of an answer to the question we set for ourselves have emerged.

As *individuals,* citizens in a deliberative democracy are to be regarded as both rational and reasonable. It should be assumed that their interests lie in developing a fair system of cooperation that, over the course of time, will provide to each an equal system of fundamental liberties and basic goods such that all are capable of the fullest development and enjoyment of their own potential. A continuing supply of essential natural resources as well as protection against the inequitable imposition of environmental risks clearly falls within these parameters. The *interactions* among these citizens should be governed by norms of discourse that encourage the giving and receiving of reasons that are acceptable (or at least potentially acceptable) to all regardless of their particular interests or the comprehensive systems of thought to which they subscribe. Although there is considerable disagreement on the subject, there is strong justification for a norm of consensus to govern these interactions and there is considerable reason to suppose that the benefits of such a norm would outweigh the costs that it would impose on the decision-making process. Deliberative *institutions* will comprise both governmental and nongovernmental organizations designed to give citizens the opportunity to influence collective decisions through open and equal discourse. A broad and settled collection of modern constitutional rights will exist, as will a basic equality in the value of citizens' right to participate. Governmental institutions will tend toward decentralization, both in the choice among alternative courses of action and in the implementation of favored alternatives. And deliberative institutions will constantly experiment with various participatory arrangements, borrowing liberally from other areas of human activity and collective problem solving, most especially from existing adjudicatory processes.

As for the role of "problematic participants" in deliberative discourse, *experts* will play an important role in deliberative environmental politics. They will provide both the methods and conclusions of science, as those establish the background conditions of our deliberations. They will lend their skills and insights to the process of testing competing validity claims advanced by other deliberative participants. The will also act as advocates for their own interests, as representatives of the professions and disciplines to which they belong. They will, however, be constrained in these activities by several important features of the deliberative process. First, experts must understand that their inputs to the deliberative process are not self-sufficient; they require political ratification to have any effect. For this reason, experts will find it necessary to adopt the lay perspective when engaged in collective decision making. They will be required to express themselves in ordinary language, in recognition of the practical, problem-solving character of public deliberation. Finally, they will be required to offer public reasons in support of their recommendations, reasons that are accessible (or potentially accessible) to all citizens. From all of this we can conclude that it is the facilitative potential, rather than any authoritative quality, that justifies any deliberative influence that experts might enjoy beyond that of the general public.

Social movements will also play an important role in deliberative democracy. The voluntary organizations that make up social movements will be acknowledged to represent democratic citizenship at its best. Social movements will be recognized as important in establishing the essential preconditions for deliberative democracy (i.e., equality, justice) even if they themselves do not always employ public reason as our theories of discourse would dictate. They will also serve to problematize existing structures of power and control in ways that open a wider range of issues to democratic deliberation. They will operate as an ongoing restraint on those who would use positions of power and privilege to distort the public discourse to their own advantage. To achieve these ends, social movements will have to overcome limits on their effectiveness resulting from the unavoidable decentralization they bring to politics, the danger of co-optation they face when their influence grows, and the inequity of political resources they will always confront in the early stages of their development and sometimes beyond.

The risks of decentralization can be dealt with if the organizations that make up social movements will use loose networks to translate their influence to the national level instead of consolidating into larger organizations. The tendency of decentralized decision making to empower those who enjoy privileged positions in local communities can be overcome if the requirement for consensus is reinforced both normatively and through administrative and adjudicatory procedures that afford participants mutual veto power. Problems resulting from the inequitable distribution of deliberative resources can be addressed both by participants in social movements and by government agencies. Movement activists can expand their resource bases, both material and human, by seeking growth opportunities among previously unrepresented populations. Governments can facilitate deliberative equity by strenuously enforcing political and administrative reforms and by providing material support to organizations pursuing public interest agendas. Numerous examples could be offered of isolated examples of each of the innovations we have described. All that is lacking is a concerted effort to integrate these approaches and to elevate the goal of reforming politics in a deliberative direction to the necessary level of salience.

11

Reconciliation by Enlightenment: The Idols of the Mind

Professed optimism, however necessary for the electoral success of the modern politician, is nevertheless unfashionable among environmentalists, political theorists, and social critics. Such readers of the preceding chapters might be inclined to the conclusion that we have demonstrated an embarrassing degree of optimism. However hopefully we have actually presented our claims, arguments, and evidence about deliberative democracy and environmental politics, we decline the dubious honor of being labeled optimists. John Dryzek is undoubtedly right in his sobering caution that "any piecemeal introduction of innovative forms of social choice into a world of ecologically irrational mechanisms is perilous" (Dryzek 1987, 245). Markets, legal systems, bureaucracies, and other political institutions of all kinds have imperialistic tendencies, resist deliberative innovation, and are vested in the status quo. Evidence of the appearance of incipient discursive designs (Dryzek 1990b; 1996) is far from being evidence that these designs will inevitably dominate the demography of politics, even with a high birth rate and a great deal of nurturing. Moreover, reasons for caution and even pessimism extend beyond those of political realism.

The history of the human relationship to the environment is, in many ways, a reflection of humanity's relationship to humanity. Transformative events in one relationship have often been associated with transformations in the other. The Enlightenment is a case in point. Both the advent of industrialism, with its devastating ecological consequences, and the development of a dominating attitude toward nature have been attributed to Enlightenment thinking (Horkheimer and Adorno 1972). The Enlightenment challenge to hierarchy and teleology has been blamed for contemporary philosophy's apparent inability to ground the relationship among humans in the making of moral and political judgments in anything beyond "individual desire and will" (MacIntyre 1984, 62). One approach to resolving these issues is contained in the utilitarianism of Bentham. Another is the attempt to follow Kant in grounding moral and political judgments in some form of practical reason. This, we would argue, is a fair characterization of the work of the major theorists of deliberative democracy, which represents yet another transformation in humanity's relationship to itself as well as (potentially) humanity's relationship to nature.

For ordinary citizens to play the role of critical auditor of the social and political meaning of scientific and technological advances would seem to be a tall order. But a hopeful attitude toward the problem is not wholly unreasonable. Enlightenment values may have penetrated mass culture sufficiently to give rise to a "cognitive populism" that makes citizens willing to perform this function (Gunderson 2000, 144–145). In his discussion of the relationship between experts and citizens in the deliberative process, Bohman optimistically argues that "the layperson can take on the perspective of the expert by becoming a well informed citizen" (1996, 64). If all of this is so, it would seem to sustain the belief advanced by Aristotle (Politics, book III, ch. 11) that when average citizens meet together, their perceptions, combined with those of the "better classes," are quite sufficient to the public purpose. On the other hand, we have the apparently inescapable logic of collective action; that because individual citizens cannot affect the course of political events, they lack any rational justification for political participation and have even less reason to become politically informed (Hardin 2003). Of course, the logic of collective action assumes that citizens do not share the Enlightenment philosophers' interest in the intrinsic rewards of expanding their understanding of the world or their normative commitment to the value of democratic self-determination. Here we come to the real irony of the environmentalists' attack on the Enlightenment: it may turn out that the way forward to a more sustainable future is blocked not by the Enlightenment's conceptual shortcomings or internal contradictions, but by the fact that its insights and attitudes never spread to humankind at large. The Enlightenment may not be seized in dialectical contradiction so much as it is simply incomplete.

The Limits of the Enlightenment

In order to understand more fully why the Enlightenment remains incomplete, even in the most technologically advanced and wealthy countries, it may be useful to explore some of the limits of enlightenment as a process of human intellectual growth rather than a historical epoch. We might do this, of course, through an exhaustive historical review and critique of the Enlightenment, its manifestations, and its consequences. Such a critique would likely duplicate, for example, Beck's (1992; 1995; 1999) critique of industrial society as only "semi-modern." Industrial society is not fully modern (and thus not a full realization of the Enlightenment) because by putting economic organization and technological change off-limits to conscious human control, it has only partially realized modernity's promise of rational social development. In Beck's view, an emerging "risk society" confronts, indeed must confront, these issues of risk to arrive at true modernity—reflexive modernity by way of ecological enlightenment through public deliberation. This process of critical self-awareness Hajer (1995) labels "reflexive ecological modernization."

Much more simply, but possibly just as insightfully, we might achieve the reflexive enlightenment needed for full realization of a deliberative environmental politics by confronting the caveats actually offered by those who gave birth to the Enlightenment. Indeed, perhaps the most incisive and sagacious warnings about the insidiousness of obstacles to human understanding were offered by the philosopher many think of as the father of the Enlightenment, Francis Bacon.

The personality of Francis Bacon is puzzling indeed. The nobility and power of his intellectual pursuits seemed often to have been blended with an unscrupulous and sometimes foolish pattern of personal behavior. Moreover, Bacon conducted no experiments, made no discoveries. His singularly important contribution was to lay down a recognizably modern pattern for the conduct of empirical science (*The Great Instauration*) and to infuse the philosophy of his time with a sufficiently critical attitude toward traditional authority that the Enlightenment could flower. In *Advancement of Learning* he cataloged the failings of traditional scholarship that made its adherents useless for contemporary purposes. In *Novum Organum* he argued that "as the present sciences are useless for the discovery of effects, so the present system of logic is useless for the discovery of science" (book 1, sec. 11).[1] It may be surprising to discover that the philosopher most widely credited with (or blamed for) laying down the Enlightenment pattern for the domination of humans over nature ("Knowledge is power" and "Nature, to be commanded, must be obeyed") regarded the subtlety of nature as so far beyond human understanding that the "theories of mankind are but a kind of insanity, only there is no one to stand by and observe it" (book 1, sec. 10). It was, in fact, the cognitive limitations of humankind that Bacon's scientific method was intended to conquer, not nature per se.

In *Novum Organum* (book 1, secs. 38–68), Bacon details the human failings that must be overcome in the pursuit of enlightenment. Unlike the failings of the scholarship of his time, these defects are general tendencies of the human mind that must be corrected if knowledge is to be advanced. From our vantage point, they appear as obstacles to the completion of the Enlightenment as a sociohistorical process. Bacon characterized these obstacles as illusions or "idols," false notions that have "preoccupied the human understanding, and are deeply rooted in it" (38). These idols are so deeply embedded in our minds that they are difficult to access and resistant to change even when access to them is gained. The idols are of four types.

The *Idols of the Tribe* are "inherent in human nature and the very tribe or race of men" (41). These idols owe their existence to the assumption that human senses give us direct knowledge of the world. We forget that our sense perceptions are at least partially dependent on our own minds and that, therefore, all of our impressions are necessarily contingent. It is we who structure our perceptions, giving rise to all manner of superstitions that are reinforced as we subsequently apply them to new events. We do this because the human understanding "is active and cannot rest or halt, but even, though without effect, still presses forward" (48). We must have an explanation for our perceptions, even if it means imposing an imagined pattern on reality where none truly exists. Once these patterns are formed, we are highly reluctant to surrender our belief in the reality of them.

The *Idols of the Den* are particular to each individual, reflecting processes of individual and collective socialization. We all live in our own den, or cavern, that "intercepts and corrupts the light of nature" (42). This tendency arises in each person from "his own peculiar and singular disposition, or from his education and intercourse with others" (42). As we become attached to "particular sciences and contemplations," we become habituated to their worldview. This led Bacon to warn that man should "suspect whatever takes and fixes his understanding" (58). Our tendency to see the whole in light of the particular part in which we are especially interested means that our most strongly held convictions are also those most likely to be in need of critical examination.

The *Idols of the Market* are "formed by the reciprocal intercourse and society of man with man" (43). These idols trace their origin to our dependence on language. Since the time of Babel, humans have depended on diverse languages to communicate with fellow humans. This dependence means that our ideas can be no clearer than our use of words. In Bacon's view, because "words are formed at the will of the generality . . . there arises from a bad and unapt formation of words a wonderful obstruction to the mind" (43). Thus two persons may use the same words to express different meanings and find themselves in agreement when they do not really agree and later will be disappointed to discover that they differ where they thought they were in accord.

Finally, the *Idols of the Theater* have "crept into men's minds from the various dogmas of peculiar systems of philosophy" and from their "perverted rules of demonstration" (44). These are inventions out of whole cloth, like plays on a stage. Most persons "take for the groundwork of their philosophy either too much from a few topics, or too little from many" (62). The *sophist* philosophy is based on too many elements of reality examined in too little depth. The sophist "seizes upon various common circumstances . . . without reducing them to certainty" and relies for the rest on "the activity of his wit" (62). *Empirics* diligently and accurately attend to a few elements of reality and, having mastered them, "presume to deduce a system of thought that conforms everything else to them" (62). The *superstitious* seek to derive their view of reality from their faith and religious veneration. Whereas the sophists and empirics lead perception like a captive to their particular fascinations, the superstitious abandon experience altogether.

The first task of the Enlightenment, for Bacon, was to see that the human understanding was "freed and cleared" of these idols, which must be "abjured and renounced with firm and solemn resolution" (68). His project is obviously a collective one rather than a matter of individual self-improvement, because its objective is a "kingdom of man, which is founded on the sciences" (68). This kingdom is a realm into which "no admission is conceded except to children" (68). One's very membership in Bacon's enlightened society (beyond the years of childhood) would, therefore, depend on one's ability to engage in reasoning free of these idols of the mind. The implications of this view are as relevant now as they were in the early seventeenth century. The persistence of these idols in our time imposes the limits on human understanding that prevent the attitudes and commitments of the Enlightenment from reaching all of humankind. And, if our argument to this point is valid, they also prevent the development of a more enlightened attitude toward nature. In fact, whereas many environmentalists have focused on the internal contradictions of the Enlightenment, it might be well for us to look more closely at how the idols of the mind manifest themselves in our politics.

Idols and Environmental Politics

What can the idols of the mind tell us about contemporary democratic politics and environmentalism? More, perhaps, than we might want to hear. Bacon's idols of the mind manifest themselves in the politics of the developed democracies in ways that frustrate the objective of environmental protection. More perversely still, these idols often creep into the internal logic of environmentalism itself.

Contemporary Idols of the Tribe

Many of today's idols of the tribe conspire to frustrate the goals of environmentalists. These consist largely of hasty and doubtful generalizations that prevent ordinary citizens from adopting an appropriately critical attitude toward both the actions of industry and government and toward the content of their own beliefs. One of these generalizations, based on the everyday experiences of citizens in developed democracies, is that market mechanisms efficiently allocate scarce resources and produce socially desirable outcomes. Full grocery shelves and affordable durable goods argue every day that laissez-faire economics is an unproblematic approach to organizing society's institutions of labor and production. This view, of course, ignores the argument (and its supporting empirical evidence) that unregulated market economies foster accelerated ecological degradation and resource depletion through ever rising levels of production and consumption (Ophuls and Boyan 1992).

Another problematic generalization with which environmentalism must contend is that environmental protection raises the cost of products to consumers and diminishes overall economic growth. It is easy for consumers to grasp the additional cost that regulatory policies add to the price of, for example, a new automobile. It is more difficult to appreciate that only one of those policies (the corporate average fleet economy standards) may save a driver enough through fuel economy that, over the life of the car, it pays for itself and the other regulatory requirements as well—or that application of the principles of industrial ecology and clean production (ecological modernization) can lead to products with both fewer external costs and lower direct costs to consumers. The connection between general economic growth and environmental protection is even more troublesome and tenuous. It is exceedingly difficult to determine what percentage of the job losses in extractive and manufacturing industries in recent decades is due to environmental regulation. Discussions of the subject rarely include a careful enumeration of the jobs created by the development of the environmental services industry. But the negative relationship between economic growth and the environment is so widely assumed that it structures our thinking to the point that the implied tradeoff is used by polling organizations to gauge the public's support for environmental policies.

Moreover, environmentalists themselves are not immune to the idols of the tribe. Their generalizations are no less prone to error and are, perhaps, more resistant to challenge than those of average citizens. Habermas has suggested that those who constitute the "politically interested, informed and active core strata of the public are themselves the least inclined to seriously submit their views to discussion" (1998b, 213). So it is especially important that we subject our own perceptions of environmental reality to the same critical analysis that we impose on the reasoning and rationalizations of businessmen and bureaucrats. As an example, the environmental justice movement may be the most vibrant and promising element of contemporary environmentalism. Its indictment of risk allocations that appear to have a disproportionate impact on women and racial minorities carries a political and legal power for which environmental activists have often longed.

But the empirical evidence to support the position that race and gender are the critical variables, rather than class or a general political disenfranchisement, is far from clear (Rosenbaum 2002). In the wake of Marxism's demise, the lack of adequate theories of social stratification (Cohen 1982) make race and gender attractive categories of analysis. Add to this the sense that advocates of deliberative democracy sometimes overly privilege a single, homogeneous public sphere dedicated to rational unanimity, ignoring cultural specificity in favor of social hegemony (Bohman 1994; Young 1990b), and we have a powerful mandate for a politics of "deliberative inclusion" (Young 1999, 155). This version of inclusiveness requires not only that all interests, opinions, and perspectives be present in deliberation (Young 1999) but also that disadvantaged groups have a veto power over policies that affect them (Young 1989). This robust environmental inclusiveness would be part of a larger politics of identity and difference that would contest any attempt to impose universal identities that are rational or neutral, as some have accused deliberative theorists of trying to do (Mouffe 1996).

But are the underlying generalizations of the environmental justice movement valid, and are the prescriptions that flow from it reasonable? The relative importance of race, ethnicity, gender, income, and political organization and influence are difficult to specify. A definitive analysis of the question lies in the perhaps distant future. Yet critics of deliberative democracy have simply assumed that its orientation toward rational consensus is inherently repressive. In its place, they have advocated various antimajoritarian voting mechanisms and decision rules designed to tip the political balance in favor of the historically disadvantaged. This intellectual shortcut is entirely human, and something that Bacon would have recognized instantly. But it may be unnecessary and even counterproductive.

A different approach to protecting the disenfranchised and disadvantaged is found in the work of Rawls, one of the deliberative democrats of whom advocates of the politics of difference have been most critical. Rawls has argued for a society the basic structure of which "is to be arranged to maximize the worth to the least advantaged of the complete scheme of equal liberty shared by all" (Rawls 1999a, 179). This element of Rawls's theory offers an equity-oriented approach to resource conservation and allocation through its application to his just savings principle (Rawls 1999a, 251–267). It would suggest a similarly progressive approach to environmental hazards affecting human health once health is understood as a primary social good to be controlled by the principles of distributive justice (Manning 1981). Note that this preference for the disadvantaged is not an a priori requirement motivated by any lack of confidence in the deliberative process. It is, rather, one of the fundamental principles that Rawls expects rational deliberation among free and equal citizens to produce. No thumb on the scales is required to provide a just outcome. All that is required is a confidence in the ability of ordinary citizens to arrive at fair and impartial arrangements through deliberation under conditions of reflective equilibrium (Rawls 1999a).

In addition to being unnecessary, a privileged position in deliberation for the disadvantaged may also be counterproductive in a number of ways. For example, while sharing with many of the difference democrats a commitment to preserving cultural differences, Habermas has remained mindful of threats to individual autonomy (and, thus, to the legitimacy of deliberative outcomes) that are implicit in much of the contemporary discourse of collective identity and recognition. For Habermas, inclusive politics is a straightforward application of individual equality rights that cannot provide survival guarantees to particular identity communities (Fairfield 1999). To do so would both deprive individual members of those communities of the right to interpret their cultural heritage in personally meaningful ways and erode the generalizable interests and universal human rights that underlie the free and unforced deliberation among equals.

Furthermore, the consensus building that is required for progress toward community-accepted solutions to ecological problems will survive outside the carefully constructed environment of the deliberative group only if both the process and its product eschew polarizing language and entrenched viewpoints (Plevin 1997). Discourses aimed at the "working out of group identities" cannot be allowed to overwhelm "the essential objective in deliberative self-government—deciding a matter in the equal interest of all" (Habermas 1996, 282). To have its greatest effect, environmental deliberation must progress toward an "ecological community vision" that will contribute to the development of intercultural solidarity in multicultural societies (Valadez 2001, 52). The growing environmental consciousness thereby produced can be "a useful vehicle for developing the moral, cognitive, and affective character traits conducive to social solidarity . . ." (ibid., 352). Environmental deliberation cannot serve this function if it is weighed down with culturally specific elements not shared by citizens at large. Yet a process of environmental deliberation constituted along the lines of Habermas's discourse ethics would actually create the counterflows of knowledge that would empower traditionally subordinated social groups (Simon 1994).

So, from the perspective of the deliberative democrat, it is no more acceptable to make assumptions about the nature of political and social disenfranchisement than it would be to assume without proof that environmental protection and economic growth are inherently inimical. Both kinds of assumptions extrapolate from evidence that is anecdotal at best to reach conclusions that threaten our ability to arrive at a deliberative consensus about how we should deal with the ecological challenges that confront us. They are both idols of the mind that confound our understanding, frustrate our efforts at rational self-governance, and threaten the ecological foundations of our survival.

Contemporary Idols of the Den
In Bacon's view, the essential quality of idols of the den is that they arise from what we have come to value based on our personal interests and individual experiences. Each of us is prone to view the whole of reality in light of that part with which we are most familiar and to which we are most firmly attached. A more human failing, and one more difficult to avoid in practical terms, would be hard to imagine. But political thought in the developed democracies evidences considerable awareness of the dangers in such partial vision. A strong theme in democratic theory has been that diverse interests should be represented in the political process, generally in the form we have come to know as interest groups. So dominant has the association of multiple interests and democracy become that we often now refer to our present form of government as interest-group liberalism.

Interest-group liberalism is, however, problematic for deliberation and the environment in ways that relate to both the internal dynamics of liberalism and the external conditions in which it exists. First, as Lowi (1967) has pointed out, interest-group liberalism has spawned its own public philosophy, according to which public officials take account only of *organized* interests and produce policies that cater to those interests so far as possible. If all interests in society were represented fully and equally in the process, less complaint would be possible. But we cannot simply assume that all social needs are transformed into organized interests. Those needs that are organized into interest groups often enjoy unequal success in attracting the attention of government and the application of collective resources, for reasons having nothing to do with the merits of their claims. Citizens in the interest-group liberal democracy are, therefore, never more than "semi-sovereign" (Schattschneider 1960). This outcome is not random, but rather, structurally determined. It is a result, in large part, of business organizations using financial and political advantages to command a privileged position in the political system (Lindblom 1977). The potential for deliberative disadvantage to noncorporate interests, and to environmental interests in particular, arising from these internal limits on group representation in liberal democracy is clear.

Second, the problems of mobilizing interests into effective political groups do not fall evenly across different sorts of social needs. If organizing a group around an interest was equally demanding in all cases, the fact that some interests remain unrepresented in the political process might be less troubling. The successful organizing experiences citizens do have might be assumed to distribute themselves across the diversity of interests such that a roughly fair representation could be assumed. There are, however, powerful reasons not to make that assumption. Environmental interests, for example, will generally manifest themselves in the form of regulatory policy issues that face a political dynamic different from interests that are distributive or redistributive in character (Lowi 1964). Moreover, environmental protection is usually characterized by a concentration of costs on a small number of political actors for the sake of benefits that are widely diffused throughout the society. This pattern of impacts imposes a much more difficult situation on the organizers of environmental groups than it does on the interests to be regulated (Wilson 1980). Beyond this guarantee that resistance to environmental protection will always be easier to mobilize than will support for it, the diffused and collective character of the environmental goods at stake imposes a free-rider problem. The organizing efforts of environmentalists are undermined because individuals who value environmental goods will enjoy them to the same degree as others whether or not they participate in securing them (Olson 1965). So, as with the internal limits on group representation, these external limits also work to the disadvantage of noncorporate interests trying to gain attention for their needs in the interest-group liberalism environment.

How should environmentalists who are also deliberative democrats respond to these obstacles? One approach is active political partisanship. All across Europe and, more recently, in the United States, the growth of Green parties has given hope to many that environmentalism would one day fight and win electoral battles that would give nature its due. Beginning in 1981, European Green parties enjoyed some success in electing members of European parliaments. A survey of electoral results in thirteen European countries shows that during the 1980s Green parties received from 1 percent to nearly 7 percent of the popular vote in national elections. But the growth since then in Green electoral support has been weak. During the 1990s, only two of these same thirteen countries saw Green support in national elections exceed 8 percent (Carter 2001). In the United States, Green party success has been even more limited.

Although public concern over the environment is evident in opinion polling in the United States, and although Green candidates have competed successfully in some municipal elections, only about 5 to 6 percent of the American electorate include environmental considerations in deciding how to vote. As a consequence, the environment has generally been insignificant in national elections (Tatalovich and Wattier 1999; Guber 2003). The obvious (and somewhat perverse) exception is, of course, the presidential election of 2000. Ralph Nader's performance may have highlighted the political weakness of the environmental movement in the United States (Rothenberg 2002). His candidacy seems to indicate that the prospects for the Green party in the United States are not bright. Even in Europe, where Green partisanship has been somewhat more successful, there is considerable evidence that Green parties moderate their strategies and compromise their positions in pursuit of parliamentary success (Carter 2001). So what is a deliberative environmentalist to do? The way forward may become clearer if we examine the plight of a Green party as a manifestation of Bacon's idol of the den. The essence of political partisanship is, after all, the tendency to see the whole of reality in the light of that part of our experience to which we are most attached. But the demands of both parliamentary politics and national elections in a presidential system require the aggregation and accommodation of partial viewpoints and particular interests in a minimum winning coalition. Furthermore, the very heart of the concept of public reason in deliberative democracy is that citizens offer each other reasons for their positions that do not depend on perspectives that cannot (at least in principle) be shared by all.

By concentrating primarily on electing public officials, adherents of Green parties have fixated on what the environmental movement does poorly and turned their backs on what it does (or might do) well. Much of the recent success of environmentalism is due to its efforts to redress the political imbalance between corporate and environmental interests through direct political action. Although it is too soon to claim parity with organized business, environmental lobbyists no longer wear comfortably "the rags of the politically disadvantaged and the establishment outsider" (Rosenbaum 2002, 55). Moreover, environmentalists acting individually and in small groups have achieved significant results through the mobilization and exploitation of legal resources to restrain both corporate and government behavior. This emphasis on litigation and involvement in administrative rule-making and adjudication provides a uniquely democratic mechanism for citizens to invoke public authority to protect the environment without the necessity for large-scale institutional support or access to the public consciousness (Zemans 1983). And it helps to redress the political imbalance between business and environmentalism as environmental activists become repeat players in the legal system rather than "one-shotters" at a perpetual disadvantage (Galanter 1974).

Even when electing environmentalists to public office is desirable, as it usually is, a narrow focus on that goal is likely to become self-defeating. The experience of the civil rights movement may be instructive in this regard. In 1965, there were only seventy black elected officials at all levels of government in the United States. By 1981, the United States had over five thousand black elected officials, including one hundred and seventy mayors. This electoral success did not result from the creation of a black political party. Rather, it can be traced to the development of black social and political leadership in the parallel institutions of community action programs (Morone 1990) and to the importance of the African-American vote in the Democratic party.

The lesson for environmentalists should be clear. Political influence cannot be associated with the possession of particular offices or the creation of single institutions. Political power is the by-product of whole lives lived in the public sphere. Political parties may manifest themselves at the national level and may attract the most attention there. But they are ultimately no more than aggregations of social and economic resources rooted in local political action. This fact explains why Green parties in both Europe and the United States have enjoyed greater success at the subnational level than they have nationally, and it suggests that the "greening" of major political parties (Carter 2001) may make more sense than the perpetuation of a separate Green party.

Idols of the Marketplace—Then and Now

Bacon observed that much confusion in human understanding results from the fact that the words and names we use arise from social practice and are "formed in a popular sense" rather than by rigorous definition. Even our efforts to arrive at definitions do not solve the problem, because such definitions "consist themselves of words, and these words produce others" (*Novum Organum*, bk. I, sec. 59). At one level, this is an unremarkable observation. Humans have long appreciated the difficulty of communicating across language boundaries. What is important, however, is Bacon's insight that overcoming these difficulties may require more than a tourist's phrase book. The perplexity of language is not merely a technical problem of ambiguous definition but, rather, a function of the complex and diverse nature of human experience. When we leave our own culture to visit another, it is often more than words we fail to understand. It is the lived experiences underlying those words that eludes us.

The cultural disconnection inherent in differences of language is a particularly troubling aspect of at least one idol of the marketplace—nationalism. Some concept of national identity is essential to both environmental protection and democratic self-government. One of government's most important roles is to be the "effective agent of a people as they take responsibility for their territory and the size of their population, as well as for maintaining the land's environmental integrity" (Rawls 1999b, 39). But the concept of nationality is often devoid of any connection to meaningful social reality. It can obscure the differences between diverse cultures that may share only one characteristic (language, for instance). It can also blind us to the fact that social and economic inequities often do not heed political boundaries (Stone 2002). Nationalism often gives rise to a climate of public opinion that is an obstacle to the development of a "transboundary environmental politics" that is essential in this era of globalization (Rosenbaum 2002).

There is some hope, however, that the politically and environmentally problematic aspects of nationalism can be overcome. A common concern for survival can unify a multipolar community despite the divergent values of its members. This common concern for survival can be reinforced by the knowledge that the world's ecosystems are closely interconnected (Valadez 2001). Thus the political and ecological imperatives of survival are mutually reinforcing. These background features of the global ecological challenge may support a trend toward internationalism in environmental decision making. But they are no argument for world government.

Progressive political reform is based to a considerable degree on social trust, on the confidence groups have in one another to support each other's just demands. This trust, a form of social capital, requires solidarity both within groups and across them. This solidarity, in turn, depends on a common identification of the kind that nationality can provide (Miller 1995). By the same token, the national identities of existing states normally contain elements that are repugnant to the self-understanding of at least some of their own component groups as well as to the members of other societies. These offensive cultural elements must be stripped from the structure of national identities insofar as possible, and members of offended groups must become more willing embrace an "inclusive nationality" and to set aside elements of their own values that are at odds with its principles (ibid., 142). These same national groups must be willing to embrace a concept of global citizenship that acknowledges our common interest in environmental protection and our mutual responsibility for its promotion.

National groups must recognize that the exportation of their environmental problems to other countries by immigration, economic domination, or conquest is unjust and unacceptable (Rawls 1999b). Nation-states can no longer claim a right to unlimited sovereignty based on the traditional notions of international law, which have failed to secure either human rights (Habermas 1996) or environmental sustainability (Weiss 1999). A liberalization of the global polity is required to secure both fundamental political rights and social justice (Rustin 1999). Moreover, effective environmental protection will require the dispersion of sovereignty across nested territorial units at levels from the local to the global (Pogge 1992). Fortunately, the role of nationalism in determining the fate of both political rights and environmental protection is open to amendment once one understands its linguistic nature.

Nations do not have intrinsic and unalterable characters but are, rather, imagined communities. They rely for their existence on symbols, historical narratives, and customs that create and reinforce a sense of national identity (Anderson 1983). Grounded as they are in the words and names that give rise to the idols of the marketplace, national identities are subject to change through innovation in the use of language. This is an area in which environmental activists have proven themselves to be especially adept (Brulle 2000). The language innovations of environmentalism are not, however, universally useful, either on their own terms or in wider cultural and political contexts. Environmentalism is not immune from its own form of idols of the marketplace. A case in point might be the ecofeminist movement.

Women have played a prominent role in the environmental movement throughout its history (Wolf 1994). The Federation of Women's Clubs, the Daughters of the American Revolution, the General Federation of Women's Clubs, and the Woman's National Rivers and Harbors Congress were all early and active supporters of forest conservation (Brulle 2000). The California Federation of Women's Clubs fought the damming of the Hetch Hetchy Valley and women nationwide contributed to the cause of wildlife conservation by promoting the elimination of feathers from hats (Merchant 1996). Women took the lead in developing the consumer-environment movement. Jane Addams at the Hull House in Chicago and Ellen Richards at MIT, each in their own way, promoted an approach to environmentalism that grew directly from women's management of the home environment and their responsibility for the health and safety of their families (Brulle 2000).

Ecofeminism builds on this historical foundation a critique of environmental politics, which it alleges has ignored issues of gender. The breadth of the literature that has resulted is genuinely impressive (Caldecott and Leland 1983; Collard 1988; Plant 1989; Warren 1994). One strand of ecofeminism promotes the inclusion of women and their environmental perceptions in the design and implementation of environmental policies as well as the development of a network of women activists in environmental and natural resource protection (Kelber 1994; Kurian 2000; Kurian and Bartlett 2003). Were ecofeminism to limit itself to this, it would be merely an important component in the structure of environmentalism as a social movement. But ecofeminism contains another strand that is more problematic.

The growth of ecofeminism's influence in the environmental movement has been limited by a number of factors. First, as in the environmental justice movement, many of ecofeminism's initiatives have been local in character. Clearly, a broader and more inclusive ecofeminist discourse would offer women a larger role in the environmental movement (Brulle 2000). Second, ecofeminism has yet to integrate feminist theoretical perspective into the practical concerns of environmental protection. Because it offers "no coherent vision of a green society and no clear strategy for feminist environmental action" (Carter 2001), cofeminism has made only limited contributions to ecologism. These shortcomings can be traced to ecofeminism's most problematic quality: its dependency on the politics of difference.

Rather than working within existing social structures for environmental progress, many ecofeminists choose to emphasize the virtues of female attributes, such as being nurturing and kind, that they regard as specifically feminine (Collard 1988). Besides alienating many male environmentalists, this celebration of stereotypical female traits causes many feminists to shudder (Carter 2001). Not only is it problematic to identify particular human traits as specifically feminine, it is not clear that feminine traits will always be desirable or that masculine traits are always bad (Dobson 2000). Some ecofeminists have backed away from the nature-female discourse, arguing that gender roles are socially constructed rather than biologically determined (Plumwood 1993), and arguing that environmentalism needs a module of a degendered human consisting of traits chosen for their ecological sustainability rather than inherited genetically. This would seem to be an admission that difference based ecofeminism is not only conceptually flawed, but also politically impractical. This would be especially true in a system of deliberative democracy, where citizens are required to give reasons for their positions that are potentially acceptable to all rather than based on the special understandings of a limited discourse. The existence of such limited discourses betrays the fact that environmentalism has spawned its own idols of the marketplace, grounded in language forms that inhibit the search for common understandings rather than advance it.

Theater Idols: Ideology, Scientism, and Dogmatic Religion

Recall that, according to Bacon, idols of the theater are of three basic types. There are idols that result from our tendency to deduce too much from many things examined in too little detail. There are idols that grow from our study in depth of so narrow a range of topics that we mistake part of reality for the whole. And there are idols that can be traced to our renunciation of reason altogether, relying instead on our faith in religious authority. In our modern era, we might relate these three idols to the impact on society of *political ideologies* that explain all of our shared experience in terms of simplistic formulae, to the technological worldview that sees all reality through a narrow prism of *scientism,* and to *religious doctrine* that replaces reason with dogmatic authority. Rawls employs a concept that encompasses all of these idols. He describes these as "comprehensive doctrines" that are part of the background culture of civil society (Rawls 1993, 14). These doctrines include conceptions of what is of value in human life, ideals of personal character, ideals of familial and associational relationships, and much else that informs and limits our conduct in society. Such a conception is fully comprehensive when it covers all recognized values and virtues in one precisely articulated system.

Comprehensive doctrines are assumed to exist in every civil society and it is further assumed that nearly all citizens affirm at least one such doctrine. These are not merely conceptual abstractions, like the perfectly competitive market or Rawls' own original position.[2] But even absent the discipline imposed by intellectual pluralism, comprehensive doctrines may remain politically benign. They become problematic for democracy only when they take on substantive elements that "cannot support a reasonable balance of political values" (Rawls 1993, 243). It is then, and only then, that comprehensive doctrines undermine the effectiveness of public reason and make themselves the enemies of deliberative democracy. This opposition manifests itself powerfully in the impact of political ideology, scientism, and dogmatic religion on the formation of public opinion and public policy on environmental questions.

The politics of left and right give most environmentalists the distinct feeling that their concerns are nowhere represented in the spectrum of conventional politics. The necessity of political authority to back up any system of rules that might protect the environment is well understood (Doyal and Gough 1999). But conventional politics are increasingly suspect in the environmental community. Traditional liberalism seems largely discredited, as the moral intensity it commanded in the 1960s has given way to "a managerial politics that seeks shallow, bureaucratic solutions to deeplying social problems" (Tokar 1999, 114). Most of the traditional left is now focused on enhanced productivity, growth, and international competitiveness. There is little interest in defending policies that might be identified as economic austerity in pursuit of environmental protection (O'Connor 1999). For their part, conservatives use the international dimension of ecological challenges to dismiss them as a result of Third World problems in which America has no stake and over which the industrialized nations have no control (d'Eaubonne 1999). The reason for this attitude is easily discovered. A peek below the surface of modern conservatism reveals a subservience to corporate power and a profound disrespect for individual rights and community interests (Tokar 1999). This moral vacuum allows for no commitment to even the most fundamental values associated with the survival of humanity.

Scientism, for its part, has been critiqued in equally harsh terms. Environmentalists have complained that modern science is a mechanistic viewpoint that allows for the exploitation of natural resources without due regard for the dynamic and long-term consequences (Bookchin 1981). Thus, scientism is the foundation for an entirely instrumental form of rationality that sets humans apart from nature, the domination of which becomes humanity's only intelligible goal (Leiss 1972). Science has also been taken to task by political theorists for reasons that go well beyond its environmental impacts. The early Frankfurt School theorists regarded the rationalization process brought about by modern science as a negative dialectics that was an inherently oppressive development in the human experience (Jay 1973). Marcuse (1964) observed that the principles of modern science were a priori structured in such a way that they could serve as conceptual instruments for a universe of self-propelling, productive control that reinforced the domination *of* humankind *by* humankind through the domination of nature. This led him to call for a new science, a liberatory science inaugurated by a liberatory society. In Marcuse's view, a free society would have different a priori principles and an entirely different objective that would lead to the development of scientific concepts grounded in an experience of nature as a total life-system that required protection and cultivation rather than exploitation (Marcuse 1972). That this development appears no closer today than it did thirty years ago is merely part of the reason that environmentalists have become frustrated with what they regard as the failed promise of critical theory (Eckersley 1999a).

Finally, dogmatic religion is an idol of the mind that, like ideology and science, is problematic from both an ecological and a political perspective. From the time that God gave humans dominion over the fish of the sea, and over the fowl of the air, and over the cattle, and over all the earth, and over "every creeping thing that creepeth upon the earth" (Genesis 1:26), the destiny of humankind to dominate and exploit nature carried a sacred imprimatur for those of Judaic or Christian faith. Other religions also have anthropocentric mandates. Given the reach these mandates have had, no intellectual or cultural historian can be unaware of the difficulties that stand in the way of the emergence of a religious belief system that might be adapted by concerned individuals worldwide to support just and effective environmental action (Laslett 2003). "Religious history has, always and everywhere, but perhaps particularly in the West, been marked by fierce ideological prejudices" (ibid., 222), prejudices that make an environmentally friendly global synthesis unlikely in the extreme. From the view of democratic theorists, dogmatic religion presents a different set of problems. Religious organizations tend to strengthen group members' religious convictions, simply through an association with like-minded others. Religious groups thus amplify the religious impulse that divides citizens from each other in a pluralistic society (Sunstein 2003). This is especially problematic for deliberative democracy with its uniquely discursive character because it complicates problems of "street-level epistemology" (Hardin 2003). People with strong religious convictions commonly claim to know the truth of the things they believe religiously far more confidently than the truth of many simple, objective things that they also claim to know. This may well make citizens whose deliberative behaviors are grounded in religious conviction less likely to accommodate, or even comprehend, the views of others.

Confronted with all the difficulties arising from ideology, scientism, and dogmatic religion, one might expect that environmentalists would steer clear of these dangerous shoals. One would, of course, be disappointed in that expectation. Environmentalists have jumped headfirst into the ideologies of ecofeminism, deep ecology, and socialist ecology. Many have embraced the dubious science of the Gaia hypothesis. Process theology, spiritualism, and the search for the Goddess preoccupy others. The difficulty with these excursions is not that they are irrational (though many certainly are) but rather that they are every bit as metaphysical as the traditions against which they rise. Habermas has observed that the antithesis to Christianity that substitutes "nature" for "God" has merely readjusted traditional religious concepts while remaining a part of "the metaphysical framework of world views" (Habermas 2002, 98). To borrow the language of Rawls, one set of comprehensive doctrines is bidding to replace another.

Environmentalism has long searched for its ideological, conceptual, and spiritual center. Perhaps its closest approximation is Murray Bookchin's (1982) advocacy of a mutualistic and cooperative view of nature to which human social, economic, and political life should be assimilated. We might be forgiven for hoping that a close enough examination of nature could reveal a master plan for the organization of human activity. But perhaps it is time to admit to ourselves that nature has no political lessons to teach us and that we should stop searching for them (Saward 1993). A common element in the work of deliberative democrats is the idea that the democratic enterprise is a limited one. Bohman has argued that "public reasons in a pluralistic society will not presuppose some particular conception of the good, or some comprehensive moral doctrine" (1996, 79) since it is reasonable to assume that they lack public scope. Rawls has defined his deliberative enterprise as the search for "a political conception of justice that we hope can gain the support of an overlapping consensus of reasonable religious, philosophical and moral doctrines in a society regulated by it" (1993, 10). If we look at the presentation of Rawls's conception of public reason and its products we see that it uses "no particular metaphysical doctrines" and that none appears among its premises or seem to be required by its arguments (ibid., 29). For his part, Habermas sees a rational society as one in which "traditional world views" lose their power and validity as public religion, customary ritual, and justifying metaphysic and are reshaped into entirely "subjective belief systems and ethics" that allow for more cogent and modern value orientations (Habermas 1970, 98–99).

The message seems clear that a deliberative democracy, indeed any fully modern society, cannot be founded on "a conception of the good as given by common religious faith or philosophical doctrine" (Rawls 1993, 304). Instead, it must be based on "a shared public conception of political justice appropriate to the conception of citizens in a democratic state as free and equal persons" (ibid.). This is also the way forward for environmentalists. Their goals can be achieved only by consensus-building between lifeworlds, and a breaking down of polarized and polarizing language that reflects entrenched ideologies, which is essential for progress toward broadly acceptable solutions that will survive outside the carefully constructed community of environmental groups (Plevin 1997).

We have begun to recognize that the pluralism of ideological and religious forces requires of us a reflective relationship to the particularity of our own beliefs. No segment of the lifeworld can immunize itself against the demands for argumentative justification. Yet, understanding who we are and what we desire requires a thick concept of the good. Thus each party must bring into the public sphere his or her own conceptions of the good and preferable life in order to find out what other parties might desire and agree to. But since a belief system that "has become self-critical does not trust itself any longer to offer universal assertions about the concrete whole of exemplary forms of life, it must refer those affected to discourses in which they answer their substantial questions themselves" (Habermas 2002, 70). Thus, viewed in this way, the true shortcoming of the Enlightenment may not be that it is torn by internal contradiction but, rather, that it is fundamentally incomplete. In a world full of learned societies, what we most significantly lack is the infrastructure of a learning society.

12

Prolegomena (To Any Future Politics That Will Be Able to Come Forward as Postmetaphysical)

In the previous chapter we employed Francis Bacon's "idols of the mind" as a construct for discussing many of the intellectual traps into which contemporary political thought can fall. We have not exempted from that discussion many traditions of environmental discourse with which we are entirely in sympathy. Our intention was neither to ensnare environmentalism and deliberative democracy in archaic disputes nor to force them into mental categories that are alien to their genuine nature. Rather, we have taken this approach because, as Sheldon Wolin has pointed out, political philosophy is so dependent on its conceptual origins that its entire history can be viewed as "essentially a series of commentaries, sometimes favorable, often hostile, upon its beginnings" (Wolin 2004, 27). That tradition of commentary has run aground on numerous shoals along its way. But it has documented those hazards for anyone who would consult its charts. So the role we have chosen is, as Wolin describes it, to raise warning flags in support of an evolving intellectual tradition that we value but which may wander off course. And our central concern, our foremost flag of warning, concerns precisely the kind of problem that interested Bacon, namely, the problem of bringing the promise of the Enlightenment to fruition in the arena of democratic politics.

There is a certain irony in our view that, at least with respect to the conjunction of environmentalism and democracy, the project of the Enlightenment is incomplete. A diverse group of philosophers, who might agree on little else, have adopted the view that the Enlightenment has actually been too successful, often to the detriment of both democracy and the natural environment. Max Horkheimer and Theodore Adorno (1972), for example, have argued that the Enlightenment's focus on instrumental rationality has become a domineering value system that oppresses both humans and nature. At the other end of the spectrum, Alasdair MacIntyre (1984) contends that the radical individualism and moral relativism of the Enlightenment have prevailed to such an extent that humankind has been left without any value system whatever. How, in light of these widely varied diagnoses, are we able to argue that what ails the Enlightenment can best be cured by more enlightenment? The difficulties inherent in our position, as well as its promise, can best be illustrated through the use of a few brief case studies.

Three Cases in Point

Pakistan—September 12

New York Times columnist Thomas Friedman (2002) tells the story of a Pakistani friend whose children came home from their Islamabad private school repeating an incredible rumor. The tale (widely heard and believed in the Islamic world) was that four thousand Jews were warned not to go to work at the World Trade Center on September 11, 2001. The implication, of course, was that Israel was behind the plot to destroy the World Trade Center. This Pakistani father patiently explained to his children all of the practical reasons why this simply could not be true. His conclusion was that such a plot would be impossible to create, carry out, or keep secret until the fateful day, while also warning four thousand individuals. It simply made no sense to believe such an implausible rumor. His children, so the story goes, were convinced by this line of reasoning and returned the next day to school determined to share their new understanding of events.

Careful and critical reasoning of the sort practiced by this Pakistani father with his children is precisely the kind of discourse that deliberative democracy would attempt to foster. It is worth noting, however, that even the teller of this story, an exceptionally skilled and perceptive chronicler of current affairs, has missed its most salient point. Friedman himself calls for Americans to confront radical Islam and its fevered imaginings with our own Western ideology rather than with rigorous critical discourse of the kind practiced by his Pakistani friend. In Friedman's case, the preferred ideological response is composed of equal parts individual rights, free enterprise, and globalization. Friedman's approach is likely to appeal to us because it reinforces our conviction that we have a view of the issues at

hand that is, at least fundamentally, the correct view. But Friedman's response is, of course, precisely the combination of concepts and commitments that promotes a blind fury among radical Islamists around the
world.

Perhaps Friedman's reluctance to follow his Pakistani friend's lead is evidence of an unbridgeable cultural gap, an inability to appreciate the importance of what Sheldon Wolin (2004) characterizes as issues of "politics
and vision." Or perhaps the difference in approach results simply from the
fact that the myth being deconstructed is initially more plausible to a Pakistani Muslim than it is to an American Jew. Or perhaps Friedman's sterner
approach results from the depressing fact that the children in his story
were sent home the following day with a warning from their teacher that
they would be ostracized if they continued to challenge what everyone else
knew to be true. In either case, Friedman's story (and his own response to
it) is anecdotal evidence that the development of a truly deliberative democracy will not come easily. The process will be slow because people will
ignore the fact that deliberation's distinctive focus is less on giving reasons
for one's own views and more on soliciting reasons from others for theirs.
Only through such a real meeting of the minds can the act of deliberation
provide genuine legitimation for collective action (Shapiro 2003).

But is a genuine meeting of the minds really possible in today's modern
societies, torn by cultural and ideological differences and awash in polarizing messages borne by an omnipresent mass media? To gain some insight
into this question, another case study may prove useful.

The Pacific Northwest—Now

All across the western United States, a quiet revolution in land-use planning has been taking place. Voluntary coalitions of citizens representing
widely varying political views have assembled to develop plans for natural
resource conservation in definable ecological regions. Characterized by
Edward Weber (2003) as "grassroots ecosystem management," this innovative approach has taken on a distinctive character, sufficiently well defined that we can place these institutions in the conceptual construct of
deliberative environmental politics that we have discussed thus far.

Weber describes three grassroots ecosystem management efforts in three
environmentally distinctive communities—the Henry's Fork Watershed

Council in Idaho's Snake River Valley, the Applegate Partnership in southwestern Oregon, and the Willapa Alliance of Washington's Columbia River area. In each of these areas, residents had been involved in a prolonged confrontation between developers and environmentalists over seemingly irreconcilable values. At a critical point in each community, representatives of the contending parties were able to recognize that they had become imprisoned in their own positions and that the way forward was blocked by the mutual veto power that they held over one another. In each case, the participants were able to step back from their own positions sufficiently that they could begin the task of political coalition-building that eventually produced conservation plans that could be presented to public officials as the products of a community consensus.

In order to advance these newly developing forms of community consensus, Weber recognizes that fundamental innovations in democratic theory are necessary. As an example, he observes that the conventional view of democratic accountability as a relationship between superior and subordinate institutions and individuals is ill suited to a process of policy-formation carried out in a decentralized arena by actors who are almost exclusively private citizens. In place of the older concept of accountability, Weber describes a "compact of mutual, collective responsibility wherein participating individuals are accountable to everyone else" (2003, 87) for the content and quality of policy outcomes.

This new concept of accountability suggests its own criteria for assessing the products of the policy process. Rather than comparing outcomes to ideologically defined policy alternatives, we should ask about the diversity of representation in the process of collective will-formation and the benefits accruing to a broad range of interests represented by the participants. And rather than asking whether the process was authorized in some official manner, we should examine the specific effects of its policy outcomes on individuals and groups within the community and the relationship of these outcomes to existing laws and regulations.

It is true that policy outcomes for which these criteria are appropriate may not be explicitly grounded in widely shared political values and may fail conventional tests of democratic accountability. But they are more likely to be accepted by the citizens who are most affected by them than are solutions imposed on the community from outside. Successful implementation in a fragmented political system fraught with veto points and opportunities is ultimately more likely on the part of those in government who are authorized to see that agreements reached in such deliberation are in fact carried out. To that extent at least, such deliberative outcomes are both more democratic and more likely to achieve some additional level of environmental protection than more conventionally adopted public policies. It could be asked at this point, however, whether there are deliberative democratic approaches that can be deployed beyond the rather particular circumstances that surround watershed partnerships and other examples of grassroots ecosystem management.

New Haven, Connecticut—and the Future

Some theorists of deliberative democracy have ventured outside of their philosophical laboratories in order to conduct political experiments. Of these, perhaps the most widely discussed is the practice of deliberative polling as conducted by James Fishkin and his associates (Fishkin 1991; 1995; 1999; Fishkin and Luskin 1999; Leib 2004). As a general matter, deliberative polling is a procedure that brings together a stratified random sample of citizens within a given jurisdiction to hear presentations about various policy proposals and to discuss their relative merits with one another. The objective is to try to arrive at a consensus that approximates what the general public would think if it had a chance to inform itself and consider the options more adequately than it actually does (Fishkin 1991).

In one recent example, Fishkin and his associates conducted a deliberative poll in New Haven, Connecticut on a weekend in March 2002. A self-selected group of approximately five hundred people from across the state gathered to hear a carefully balanced set of presentations about two policy issues: a regional tax-sharing plan and a proposal relating to a regional airport (Leib 2004). Participants were then broken into jury-sized groups moderated by a representative of the League of Women Voters. Participants were also given the opportunity to share their views with local elected officials in town-hall meetings after the final meeting of the deliberative assembly.

Observations by Fishkin's experimenters during the poll, as well as research after the fact, indicated that many of the purported advantages of deliberative polling previously advanced in the literature (Fishkin and Luskin 1999) had, in fact, been realized. Participants made an effort to prepare for the session by familiarizing themselves with the issues to be discussed. A large percentage of participants spoke at some point, note-taking was common, and incivility was rare. Also, participants in the New Haven assembly, as is generally the case with deliberative polls, indicated an interest in repeating the experience. And, perhaps most significantly, the New Haven session replicated earlier experiences with deliberative polls in producing measurable changes in citizens' attitudes and preferences (Fishkin 1995).

It remains, however, to extrapolate from the New Haven experience (and other instances of deliberative polling) an approach to deliberative democracy that can be deployed more widely across a large and complex society. Fishkin himself has seemed content to continue refining his approach (1995) and to suggest that deliberative polling replace conventional polling as our standard measure of public opinion (1999). Others, however, have ventured further. As an example, Peter deLeon (1997) has proposed that a similar approach be used to conscript a random sample of citizens who might plausibly be affected by a particular policy to participate in what he refers to as "participatory policy analysis." The object is to meet with policy experts and bureaucrats (thus the necessity for conscription) to provide popular input on regulatory and administrative matters. Another proposal, offered by John Gastil (2000), suggests that policy juries be charged to produce "special verdicts" on carefully structured policy questions under instructions to aim for consensus. Expert witnesses would be qualified to testify before these juries and all testimony would be subject to cross-examination. Gastil suggests that this process be repeated for all candidates and issues appearing on election ballots and that the jury verdicts be provided to voters in their preelection voter's guides.

Most ambitious of all is the proposal by Ethan Leib (2004) for an entirely new "popular" branch of government to replace the current system of initiative and referendum. Not content to nibble around democracy's edges, Leib proposes constitutional amendments at both the state and national level to create deliberative assemblies composed of 525 eligible (though not necessarily registered) voters. These assemblies would have the power to adopt laws that could be repealed (by supermajority) by the relevant legislative body, vetoed by the executive authority, or overturned by the judicial branch. The policy jury system would be employed by breaking up the assembly into working groups of approximately fifteen members to proceed as has generally been described by deLeon and Gastil.

Leib describes his populist branch of government as a "realist utopian vision" (2004, 134), suggesting that it is no more than a logical extension of the deliberative polling process already described.

Whatever our assessment of the realism of Leib's utopian vision, it is clearly unreasonable to suggest that deliberative democrats have failed to put potentially useful instantiations of their theories on the table. It remains only to indicate how these institutional alternatives offer possible solutions to the problems suggested by our argument that the Enlightenment project has not proceeded too far but, rather, remains to be completed.

Some Implications: Getting beyond Political Metaphysics

What can we conclude about the future of deliberative democracy from the cases just discussed and from how they reflect on the preceding discussions? If the conceptual structure we have tried to develop throughout this volume is clear and coherent, anecdotal evidence cannot much improve it. If it is seriously flawed, bedtime stories will not save it. What these cases can do, however, is highlight some of the major theoretical challenges that we have encountered and suggest why our treatment of them has been generally optimistic in tone.

As we argued in chapter 1, deliberative democracy is fundamentally an expression of the Enlightenment devotion to reason as an arbiter of disagreement. But environmentalists have seen an inherent tension between Enlightenment reason and ecological sustainability. Some emphasize the source of the demise of reason (broadly understood) as the twin forces of capital and bureaucracy building the modern world on a precarious foundation of instrumental rationality. Others hold out hope that this tension can be resolved positively and that science can free itself from technological imperatives to become a genuine partner in the preservation of nature. Our collective experiences with watershed partnerships and other forms of grassroots ecosystem management offer some evidence that the more hopeful view of science is not unreasonably optimistic. They suggest that the discursive approach to politics advanced by deliberative democrats is neither utopian nor inherently hostile to the environment. In fact, the evidence suggests that decision making that is more inclusive and contemplative is more eco-friendly than conventional interest-group liberalism has been. This reinforces the view that rationality may not be inherently reasonable (from either a general or specifically environmentalist viewpoint), but no environmentally reasonable policy is possible without it. Putting competing validity claims to the test and implementing policies designed to protect the environment requires a rationality that is at once reasonable and instrumental (chapter 2).

Another challenge that deliberative democrats have faced is to show that durable institutions of collective will-formation can actually be constructed on a foundation of popular participation that is intensive and widespread. The deliberative polling literature, as we have seen, is replete with suggestions about how many thousands of citizens might be involved in the formation of public policy regarding even the most complex issues. The broad use of policy juries and deliberative assemblies would instantiate a number of the institutional strategies advanced in chapter 7. These mechanisms of participation would be far more representative than the current electoral process. Samples of the population could be stratified in such a way as to represent popular opinion in ways that elections, with their low and skewed turnouts, never could. The problem of decentralization is addressed by the "scalability" of deliberative polling techniques. The deliberative policymaking variant also allows for administrative reform by extending the resources of government agencies, legitimating policy expertise, and adapting general understandings of policy issues to local circumstances. In fact, the joint involvement of citizens with policy experts, from both within and outside government, offers an opportunity to redeem the rhetoric of activists of all sorts and channel their contending views in ways that are moderated by the necessity to command broad attention and assent (chapter 8).

Finally, deliberative polling and grassroots ecosystem management tell us much about what a more environmentally friendly (and democratic) political culture would look like. The concept of environmental citizenship that these deliberative practices instantiate is grounded in norms of discourse that encourage the giving and receiving of reasons that are (at least potentially) acceptable to all participants regardless of their particular interests or comprehensive viewpoints (chapter 9). Democracy's problematic participants are able to more positively channel their political power in an environment where rationality and reason are reconciled, a broad and well-settled system of rights prevails in both government and civil society, and a norm of consensual decision making prevails (Chapter 10). This last point, the importance of consensus, has been much debated among deliberative democrats and is a matter to which we now turn.

Personal Observations in Lieu of a Conclusion

As we indicated in the middle chapters of this volume, John Rawls and Jürgen Habermas have both been associated with the idea that deliberative democracy should be governed by a norm of consensus. Consensus can play any number of roles. It can be a practical necessity that provides the basic motivation for a more deliberative approach to political life. As an example, watershed partnerships work well (when they do) in part because development interests and conservationists are able to frustrate each other's intentions through the use of mutual vetoes. Developers derive their veto power from the power of wealth and political influence, supplemented by property interests protected by common law. Environmentalists rely on the enthusiasm of their adherents as well as systems of planning and regulatory control found in statutory schemes that afford citizen activists access to judicial remedies on a number of grounds. Recognition of the resulting stalemate has the potential to loosen participants from their tightly held positions so that they can explore policy alternatives that might command broader support than either side of a dichotomous argument could command.

Consensus can also serve as a regulative norm. As an example, in chapter 9 we advanced a standard by which one might judge whether a decision based on majority rule is acceptable as a substitute for consensus in a given set of circumstances. Broadly speaking, we argued that a majority decision is acceptable if the minority side of the argument recognizes the existence of, and accepts the significance of, imperatives for timely decision that make continued discourse impractical. We also suggested that all decisions of this nature be regarded as provisional and that no irreversible actions be involved in carrying out the decision. In effect, this standard for majoritarianism requires that anything less than consensus be sustained by a separate decision (consensually arrived at) that an interim decision by the majority is necessary and desirable. This approach to the problem does more than offer a resolution of one troubling aspect of deliberative democracy. It suggests a broader perspective on the deliberative project that can focus our attention on political values we generally ignore. To see how this might be the case, we return briefly to Pakistan.

As the anecdote provided by Thomas Friedman suggests, getting people to submit their metaphysical views (whether religious or ideological) to critical examination is not an easy matter. It may not be easy even for those who are thoroughly familiar with the worst effects that religion and ideology can work in the world. Friedman's determination to counter Islamic ideology with Western ideology stands in stark contrast to the Pakistani father's desire to clarify (even purify) his children's patterns of thought. Friedman is concerned primarily with winning an argument. His Pakistani friend's concern is primarily to improve the thinking, and thus the life prospects, of his children. The difference in their approaches certainly cannot be due to any greater sophistication on the part of the father. The difference is clearly traceable to the different relationship in which the father stands to the children. To Friedman, the children are vessels for a viewpoint. This, of course, is how interest-group liberalism encourages all of us to regard each other. To a father, however, children are the living embodiment of the best of his own past and the brightest filament of his future. To improve their life prospects is his own truest interest.

Before it is objected that paternalism is neither a possible nor desirable foundation for political relationships, we should hasten to add that paternity is not the relevant feature of the relationship for our purposes. The closeness of identity we have in mind is more akin to Wilson Carey McWilliams's (1973) idea of fraternity. McWilliams describes fraternity as a bond that is based on interpersonal affection among a limited number of persons in a defined social space. It involves shared values and goals that go beyond mere existence as well as the recognition of the inevitability of failure in the ultimate achievement of those goals. But it provides an assurance of identity that makes it possible to pursue ultimately unattainable goals in a way that reconciles that tension as well as the tension between the fraternal relationship itself and one's commitments to society at large. Though fraternity may be the neglected third in the revolutionary triumvirate of liberty, equality, and fraternity, McWilliams sees it as an essential precondition of and an indispensable means to true freedom and equality. "With all of its difficulties," he argues, "fraternity is vital for anyone who would find himself and who knows that no one can do so alone" (McWilliams 1973, 18).

A fraternal attitude toward political discourse is clearly suggested by the idea that, in a deliberative democracy, no policy would ever be imposed on all without the consent of all. This would seem to be an obvious conclusion to be drawn from the work of both Habermas and Rawls. But post-Habermasians (like Bohman) and post-Rawlsians (like Gutmann and Thompson) have both shied away from the concept of consensus (chapter 6). Bohman has argued that there are political differences so deep and so grounded in cultural imperatives that it is unreasonable to expect people to surrender them, even in the face of overwhelming contradictory evidence. For their part, Gutmann and Thompson have viewed such immovable elements of the political landscape as fundamental threats to democracy itself. People who hold to bigoted or otherwise undemocratic views simply surrender their place in the deliberative arena. Thus, in what must surely be one of the greater ironies of the deliberative democratic tradition, some followers of Habermas wall off certain political claims from validity testing and some followers of Rawls argue that certain attitudes are so politically troubling that they merit less than equal treatment of those who hold them.

On the other hand, an approach to deliberation grounded in fraternity would suggest that those who hold antidemocratic attitudes must be central to discursive political practice. That they are so far from the mainstream indicates that they should be the primary focus of our attention. They are the members of the fraternal order most in the greatest need of identity affirmation because they have lost track of who they are and of what the fraternity they belong to really is.

Our ability to adopt this attitude toward those with antidemocratic attitutes has been made more difficult by some of our assumptions about how people get to be liberal democrats. In particular, we have always assumed that with education "the truth of liberal democratic ideas (or perhaps more fashionably, their relatively lesser untruth) becomes apparent" (McWilliams 1973, 567). Indeed, it is clear that a major difference between active citizens and inactive ones is education. But it is rarely suggested that the kind of education one receives is critical to this process. There is a persistent if often unspoken belief that with sufficient education the liberal values—including the humanistic assumptions of human dignity and fraternity—will simply emerge of their own accord. Whereas this assumption is obviously doubtful as a general matter, our specific experiences with deliberative democratic procedures and institutions suggest that the discursive practices they involve have the capacity to promote intellectual growth and to enhance commitment to popular government among those who participate. The educative function of deliberative democracy is especially important in the environmental context.

From our earliest collective experience, American political theorists have turned to the environment as a source for the American identity and sense of fraternity. The environment, after all, had been the basis for the "messianic hopes" that European visionaries held for America. And, by the nineteenth century Americans had come to regard nature as "a place of unambiguous virtue" and the "brotherhood of place" (McWilliams 1973, 178).

Historical warrant, therefore, exists for the proposition that environmental politics is related at the deepest level with the development of the shared attitudes and values that will make it possible to venture beyond the limits of interest-group liberalism. That we must deny antidemocratic (as well as antienvironmental) minorities their desires in the near term should offend our sense of justice only if we adopt the dubious proposition that the kind of equality that should concern us is the equality of welfare, wherein everyone is entitled to the same satisfaction of the preferences as everyone else (Dworkin 2000). A more sensible position to adopt, and one that is more consistent with a deliberative democratic emphasis on discursive political processes, is the view of John Rawls (see chapter 4) that the "fair value" of equal opportunity should be our central concern. If that view of democratic equality can win broad acceptance (no small order), we will be able to put to the test our central argument that deliberative political practices can produce collective decisions, at both the local and national levels, that are more democratic and more environmentally sustainable than those of interest-group liberalism.

Notes

Chapter 2

1. Many post-Weberian critiques of administrative processes focus on the pathologies or dysfunctions deriving from their flawed social logic (Merton 1957; Baber 1983).

2. According to Mannheim, functional rationality exists when "a series of actions is organized in such a way that it leads to a previously defined goal, every element in this series of actions receiving a functional position and role. Such a functional organization of a series of actions will, moreover, be at its best when, in order to attain the given goal, it coordinates the means most efficiently. It is by no means characteristic, however, of functional organization in our sense that this optimum be attained or even that the goal itself be considered rational as measured by a certain standard . . ." (Mannheim 1948, 52–53). Weber referred to a similar concept as formal rationality, focusing on the degree to which systems or institutions are organized by rationally calculable principles—principles that need not be known (Weber 1978; Gerth and Mills 1946; Henderson and Parsons 1947).

3. The rationality of individual acts or choices is called substantial rationality by Mannheim (1948) and Diesing (1962).

4. An illustrative example of the complexity of these linkages is provided by the "tragedy of the commons," in which purely economic rationality on the parts of individuals (each herder responds makes substantively rational decisions to add additional animals to graze the commons) will result in an economically and ecologically irrational system (the commons is overgrazed and all suffer) (Hardin 1968).

5. Diesing did, however, anticipate ecological rationality as a prerequisite of social rationality: "Characteristic of a rational social system is its compatibility with the nonsocial environment . . . , to which it must be adapted if it is to continue in existence" (1962, 88).

6. Environmental rationality might be thought of as the reasoned integration of all forms of rationality, including ecological, political, social, and economic.

7. The Gaia hypothesis is the proposition that the earth's biosphere behaves as though it constituted a single living entity (Lovelock 1979; Zoeteman 1991).

8. A more nuanced discussion of these points is possible, but beyond the point of this book. A simple warning of tribal and fascist dangers suffices to justify our reconsideration of rationality and reasonableness.

9. The modern concept of rationality is scarcely new. It originated several hundred years ago with Descartes.

10. This is a necessary step toward the reintegration of reasonableness and rationality, but it would not *inevitably* lead there. Another path might be subordination to the goals of authoritarian organizations.

11. Neither Habermas nor we are arguing that such an outcome can be prescribed by structure; rather, it is a value to which people must subscribe as a condition for critical discourse.

Chapter 3

1. The current environmental situation is more than a problem. It is a problematique: "an interrelated group of problems that cannot be effectively addressed apart from one another" (Soroos 1993, 318); "an ensemble of problems and their interactions" (Ophuls and Boyan 1992, 43).

2. Of course, the postmodern point of view is that these imperatives are socially constructed and thus many of them may be far from unyielding (Luke 1997; Darier 1999).

3. An overlapping consensus of reasonable comprehensive doctrines describes a diverse group of people with differing fundamental perspectives (religions and so forth) who are able to agree to certain fundamental political principles (constituting a shared political conception) not because the principles are consistent with their own perspectives but because they have recognized the reasonableness of those political principles as derivatives from certain first principles of justice. In contrast, citizens united by their comprehensive doctrines are the factions of Madison and Hamilton. They seek their own preferences rather than justice because their agreement is religious or ideological, rather than the product of a shared political conception.

4. Habermas contends that "because Rawls situates the 'question of stability' in the foreground, the overlapping consensus merely expresses the functional contribution that the theory of justice can make to the peaceful institutionalization of social cooperation; but in this the intrinsic value of a *justified* theory must already be presupposed" (Habermas 1995, 121). In effect, Habermas argues that the overlapping consensus on just decisions is a result of the legitimation process rather than its underlying cause. In exploring this issue, Habermas poses the question of why Rawls does not think that his theory admits of truth and in what sense Rawls has substituted the word "reasonable" for "true." Habermas's answer is that Rawls wants "to secure for normative statements—and for the theory of justice as a whole—a form of rational obligatoriness founded on justified intersubjective recognition, but without according them an epistemic meaning" (ibid.,

123). Rawls explains the meaning of practical reason by reference to the deontological dimensions of normative validity (its independence of any person's ends) and the pragmatic dimension of a public sphere and the process of public reasoning, which is the final court of appeal for the validity of normative statements. In other words, Rawls's political conception of justice is reasonable in the sense that it can afford a kind of tolerance toward worldviews that are not unreasonable. All that remains is a single act of faith in reason—a "reasonable faith in the real possibility of a just constitutional regime" (ibid., 125).

5. "Skeptical" in the sense of adopting a critical stance toward metaphysical assumptions and traditions; "not defeatist" in still embracing the core assumption of the modernist project, namely, the possibility of transcendent rational understanding; and "postmetaphysical" in the sense of being salvaged from shaky metaphysical foundations concerning the nature, structure, and constitution of reality. Habermas seeks an alternative that avoids both a return to discredited metaphysical traditions and a radical rejection of the possibility of rational critique. As such, postmetaphysical reason would not need what Rawls would call a comprehensive doctrine in order to make sense of the world and to say, for example, in something other than an arbitrary way that Bach is better than Chuck Berry.

6. But, for Habermas, that faith is as richly normative (and open to dispute) as any of the comprehensive doctrines Rawls attempts to evade (ibid., 122–125).

Chapter 4

1. Until the publication by Rawls of *Law of Peoples* (1999b), the same could have been said about the relationship of a just society with other societies (just and otherwise).

2. Considerable debate has surrounded this condition. Several commentators have argued for a stronger veil of ignorance than Rawls seems to demand, allowing no information about generational membership of any sort into the original position (see Manning 1981, Singer 1988, and Wenz 1988). Rawls's (1999a) recently updated discussion of this issue may have resolved the matter in a way agreeable to these writers.

3. Rawls has defined the concept of the *well-ordered society* number of times. In *A Theory of Justice* he wrote that the members of a well-ordered society have the common aim of cooperating together to realize their own and one another's nature in ways allowed by the principle of justice. This collective intention is the consequence of everyone's having an effective sense of justice (1999a, 462). In *Political Liberalism* he defined a well-ordered society as one in which: everyone accepts, and knows that everyone else accepts, the same principles of justice; the basic structure is publicly known, or reasonably believed, to satisfy these principles; and its citizens generally comply with these principles out of an effective sense of justice (1993, 35). By the publication of *Law of Peoples,* Rawls was referring to well-ordered societies as being either reasonable liberal societies or decent but not liberal societies (1999b, 4).

Chapter 5

1. Habermas's discourse is formal for the same reason that Rawls uses the veil of ignorance. To have a substantive dialogue you need substance. With substance comes bias. If you do not at least start at a more formal level and lay down some kind of criteia there, you give up any hope of people looking beyond their own interests. That is where both Rawls and Habermas differ from, say, the communitarians, for whom all criteria for public argument have to come out of shared community value and norms.

Chapter 7

1. An electronic search of *Sage Public Administration Abstracts* at the end of 2003 turns up only eight references, with only two of those from periodicals that might be called public administration journals (Vanderheiden 2001; Hunold 2001).

Chapter 8

1. Habermas observes, "thanks to their rhetorical content, texts combed against the grain contradict what they state . . ." (1987b, 189). This problem is of particular importance to critical theorists, as the employment of dialectics that underlies their social and economic critique might be characterized as mere rhetoric. But dialectics in critical theory is regarded as "the discourse of instruction and merely a prolegomenon to rigorous analysis" (Habermas 1973a, 79). Critical theorists are not interested in "standing the primacy of logic over rhetoric, canonized since Aristotle, on its head" as Habermas claims Jacques Derrida wishes to do (Habermas 1987b, 1998, 187). Derrida's deconstructionist project would leave little of the infrastructure of science and philosophy intact. Habermas accepts the impossibility of so specializing the languages of philosophy and science that they are cleansed of everything metaphorical and rhetorical (ibid., 189–190). In the effort to do so, the distinction between sophism and rhetoric, so valued by Socrates, would be irretrievably lost. As a result, there would be no firm ground remaining on which one could assert a claim of expertise in any public debate. Neither could there be any set of criteria on the basis of which competing validity claims could be judged in Habermas's ideal speech situation. In short, deliberative democracy, as conceived by Habermas, would become impossible.

Chapter 10

1. Brulle defines an Astroturf organization as looking like a grassroots organization, but it "is a nonrepresentative organization that could not pass the legal criteria of a representative one. . . . It is based on economic or political sponsorship and/or mass mailings" (Brulle 2000, 91).

Chapter 11

1. All quotations of Bacon are from the "Great Books" editions (Chicago: Encyclopedia Britannica, 1952).

2. Such abstractions are of limited scope and their purpose is methodological rather than substantive. The conflicts implicit in pluralist society require that philosophical conceptions be presented in such abstract form. Those same conflicts prevent such philosophical conceptions from taking on the general and unqualified character of comprehensive doctrines (Rawls 1993, 154–155).

References

Abraham, David. 1994. "Persistent Facts and Compelling Norms: Liberal Capitalism, Democratic Socialism, and the Law." *Law and Society Review* 28: 939–946.

Ackerman, Bruce, and James S. Fishkin. 2004. *Deliberation Day.* New Haven: Yale University Press.

Alario, Margarita. 1994. "Environmental Destruction and the Public Sphere: On Habermas's Discursive Model and Political Ecology." *Social Theory and Practice* 20: 327–341.

Alford, C. Fred. 1985. *Science and the Revenge of Nature.* Gainesville: University of Florida Press.

Allison, Graham T. 1971. *The Essence of Decision.* Boston: Little, Brown.

Anderson, Benedict R. 1983. *Imagined Communities: Reflections on the Origin and Spread of Nationalism.* London: Verso Press.

Andresen, Steinar. 2002. "The International Whaling Commission (IWC): More Failure than Success?" In *Environmental Regime Effectiveness: Confronting Theory with Evidence,* Edward L. Miles et al., 379–403. Cambridge, Mass.: The MIT Press.

Aron, Joan B. 1980. "Citizens' Participation at Government Expense." In *Comparative Policy and Citizen Participation,* ed. Charles R. Foster, 54–69. New York: Pergamon.

Arrow, Kenneth J. 1968. "Mathematical Models in the Social Sciences." In *Readings in the Philosophy of the Social Sciences,* ed. May Brodbeck, 635–667. New York: Macmillan.

Austen-Smith, David. 1992. "Strategic Models of Talk in Political Decision Making." *International Political Science Review* 13: 45–58.

Avio, Kenneth L. 1999. "Habermasian Ethics and Institutional Law and Economics." *Kyklos* 52: 511–535.

Axelrod, Regina S. 2005. "Democracy and Nuclear Power in the Czech Republic." In *The Global Environment: Institutions, Law, and Policy,* ed. Regina S. Axelrod, David Leonard Downie, and Norman J. Vig, 261–283. Washington, D.C.: CQ Press.

Axelrod, Regina S., Norman J. Vig, and Miranda A. Schreurs. 2005. "The European Union as an Environmental Governance System." In *The Global Environment: Institutions, Law, and Policy,* ed. Regina S. Axelrod, David Leonard Downie, and Norman J. Vig, 200–224. Washington, D.C.: CQ Press.

Baber, Walter F. 1983. *Managing the Future: Matrix Models for the Postindustrial Polity.* University: University of Alabama Press.

Baber, Walter F. 1988. Impact Assessment and Democratic Politics. *Policy Studies Review* 8: 172–178.

Baber, Walter F. 2004. "Ecology and Democratic Governance: Toward a Deliberative Model of Environmental Politics." *Social Science Journal* 41: 331–346.

Baber, Walter F., and Robert V. Bartlett. 1989. "Bureaucracy or Analysis: Implications of Impact Assessment for Public Administration." In *Policy through Impact Assessment: Institutionalized Analysis as a Policy Strategy,* ed. Robert V. Bartlett, 143–153. Westport, Conn.: Greenwood Press.

Baber, Walter F., and Robert V. Bartlett. 2001. "Toward Environmental Democracy: Rationality, Reason, and Deliberation." *Kansas Journal of Law and Public Policy* 11: 35–64.

Bachrach, Peter. 1975. "Interest, Participation, and Democratic Theory." In *Participation in Politics,* ed. J. Roland Pennock and John W. Chapman, 39–55. New York: Lieber-Atherton.

Bacon, Francis. 1952 (1620). *Novum Organum.* Chicago: Encyclopedia Britannica.

Barber, Benjamin R. 1984. *Strong Democracy: Participatory Politics for a New Age.* Berkeley: University of California Press.

Barnes, Parker. 1999. "The Administrative Requirements of the Coastal Zone Management Program: Ogburn-Matthews v. Loblolly Partners." *South Carolina Environmental Law Journal* 8: 123–129.

Barry, Brian. 1989. *Theories of Justice.* Berkeley: University of California Press.

Barry, John, and Marcel Wissenburg. 2001. *Sustaining Liberal Democracy: Ecological Challenges and Opportunities.* New York: Palgrave.

Bartlett, Robert V. 1986. "Ecological Rationality: Reason and Environmental Policy." *Environmental Ethics* 8: 221–239.

Bartlett, Robert V., ed. 1989. *Policy Through Impact Assessment: Institutionalized Analysis as a Policy Strategy.* Westport, Conn.: Greenwood Press.

Bartlett, Robert V. 1994. "Evaluating Environmental Policy Success and Failure," in *Environmental Policy in the 1990s: Toward a New Agenda,* ed. Norman J. Vig and Michael E. Kraft, 167–187. Washington, D.C.: CQ Press.

Bartlett, Robert V. 1998. "Rationality and the Logic of the National Environmental Policy Act." In *Debating the Earth: The Environmental Politics Reader,* ed. John Dryzek and David Schlosberg, 85–95. New York: Oxford University Press.

Bartlett, Robert V. 2005. "Ecological Reason in Administration: Environmental Impact Assessment and Green Politics." In *Managing Leviathan: Environmental*

Politics and the Administrative State, second ed., ed. R. Paehlke and D. Torgerson. Peterborough, Ontario: Broadview Press.

Bartlett, Robert V., and Walter F. Baber. 1999. "From Rationality to Reasonableness in Environmental Administration: Moving beyond Proverbs." *Journal of Managment History* 5: 55–67.

Bartlett, Robert V., Walter F. Baber, and Carolyn D. Baber. 2005. "Innovation in State Environmental Policy: A View from the West." In *Environmental Politics and Policy in the West,* second ed., ed. John Freemuth and Zachary Smith. Boulder: University Press of Colorado.

Bartlett, Robert V., and Priya A. Kurian. 1999. "The Theory of Environmental Impact Assessment: Implicit Models of Policy Making," *Policy and Politics* 27: 415–433.

Baumgartner, Frank, and Beth Leech. 1998. *Basic Interests: The Importance of Groups in Politics and in Political Science.* Princeton: Princeton University Press.

Beck, Ulrich. 1992. *Risk Society: Towards a New Modernity.* London: Sage.

Beck, Ulrich. 1995. *Ecological Enlightenment: Essays on the Politics of the Risk Society.* Atlantic Highlands, N.J.: Humanities Press.

Beck, Ulrich. 1999. *World Risk Society.* Cambridge: Polity Press.

Beckerman, Wilfred. 1999. "Sustainable Development and Our Obligations to Future Generations." In *Fairness and Futurity: Essays on Environmental Sustainability and Social Justice,* ed. Andrew Dobson, 71–92. Oxford: Oxford University Press.

Beehler, Rodger. 1978. *Moral Life.* Oxford: Basil Blackwell.

Beierle, Thomas C., and Jerry Cayford. 2002. *Democracy in Practice: Public Participation in Environmental Decisions.* Washington, D.C.: Resources for the Future.

Bell, Derek. 2002. "How Can Political Liberals Be Environmentalists?" *Political Studies* 50: 703–724.

Bellone, C. 1980. *Organization Theory and the New Public Administration.* Boston: Allyn and Bacon.

Benhabib, Seyla. 1990. "Communicative Ethics and Current Controversies in Practical Philosophy." In *The Communicative Ethics Controversy,* ed. Seyla Benhabib and Fred Dallmayr, 330–369. Cambridge, Mass.: The MIT Press.

Benhabib, Seyla. 1996. "Toward a Deliberative Model of Democratic Legitimacy." In *Democracy and Difference: Contesting the Boundaries of the Political,* ed. Seyla Benhabib, 67–94. Princeton: Princeton University Press.

Benhabib, Seyla, and Fred Dallmayr, eds. 1990. *The Communicative Ethics Controversy.* Cambridge, Mass.: MIT Press.

Bennett, Jane. 1987. *Unthinking Faith and Enlightenment: Nature and the State in a Post-Hegelian Era.* New York: New York University Press.

Bennett, Jane. 1994. *Thoreau's Nature: Ethics, Politics, and the Wild.* Thousand Oaks, Calif.: Sage.

Bennett, Jane. 1995. "The Wild Thoreau." *Canadian Review of American Studies* 25: 127–137.

Bennett, Jane. 1997. "The Enchanted World of Modernity." *Cultural Values* 1: 1–28.

Bennett, Jane. 2001. *The Enchantment of Modern Life.* Princeton: Princeton University Press.

Benton, Ted. 1999. "Sustainability and Accumulation of Capital: Reconciling the Irreconcilable?" In *Fairness and Futurity, Essays on Environmental Sustainability and Social Justice,* ed. Andrew Dobson, 199–229. Oxford: Oxford University Press.

Bernstein, Richard J., ed. 1985. *Habermas and Modernity.* Cambridge, Mass.: The MIT Press.

Berry, Jeffrey M. 1997. *The Interest Group Society,* third ed. New York: Longman.

Bessette, Joseph M. 1980. "Deliberative Democracy: The Majority Principle in Republican Government." In *How Democratic Is the Constitution?* ed. Robert A. Goldwin and William A. Schambra, 102–116. Washington, D.C.: American Enterprise Institute.

Bessette, Joseph M. 1994. *The Mild Voice of Reason: Deliberative Democracy and American National Government.* Chicago: University of Chicago Press.

Birnie, Patricia W. 1985. *International Regulation of Whaling: From Conservation of Whaling to Conservation of Whales and Recognition of Whale Watching.* New York: Oceana.

Blatter, Joachim, and Helen Ingram, eds. 2001. *Reflections on Water: New Approaches to Transboundary Conflicts and Cooperation.* Cambridge, Mass.: The MIT Press.

Boggs, James P. 1993. "Procedural vs. Substantive in NEPA Law: Cutting the Gordian Knot." *Environmental Professional* 15: 25–34.

Bohman, James. 1994. "Complexity, Pluralism, and the Constitutional State: On Habermas's *Faktizität und Geltung.*" *Law and Society Review* 28: 897–930.

Bohman, James. 1995. "Public Reason and Cultural Pluralism." *Political Theory* 23: 253–290.

Bohman, James. 1996. *Public Deliberation: Pluralism, Complexity, and Democracy.* Cambridge, Mass.: The MIT Press.

Bohman, James. 1998. The Coming of Age of Deliberative Democracy. *Journal of Political Philosophy* 6: 399–423.

Bohman, James. 2000. "The Division of Labor in Democratic Discourse: Media, Experts, and Deliberative Democracy." In *Deliberation, Democracy, and the Media,* ed. Simone Chambers and Anne Costain, 47–64. Lanham, Md.: Rowman and Littlefield.

Bookchin, Murray. 1981. "The Concept of Social Ecology." *CoEvolution Quarterly,* no. 32 (winter): 15–22.

Bookchin, Murray. 1982. *The Ecology of Freedom: The Emergence and Dissolution of Hierarchy.* Palo Alto, Calif.: Cheshire Publishing.

Bookchin, Murray. 1999. "The Concept of Social Ecology." In *Ecology,* ed. Carolyn Merchant, 152–162. Atlantic Highlands, N.J.: Humanities Press.

Bosso, Christopher. 1991. "Adaptation and Change in the Environmental Movement." In *Interest Group Politics,* third ed., ed. Allan J. Cigler and Burdett A. Loomis, 151–176. Washington, D.C.: CQ Press.

Bosso, Christopher J. 2000. "Environmental Groups and the New Political Landscape." In *Environmental Policy: New Directions for the Twenty-First Century,* fourth ed., ed. Norman J. Vig and Michael E. Kraft, 55–76. Washington, D.C.: CQ Press.

Bosso, Christopher J., and Deborah Lynn Guber. 2003. "The Boundaries and Contours of American Environmental Activism." In *Environmental Policy: New Directions for the Twenty-First Century,* ed. Norman J. Vig and Michael E. Kraft, 79–101. Washington, D.C.: CQ Press.

Brandeis, Louis D. 1932. *Other People's Money: And How the Bankers Use It.* New York: Frederick A. Stokes.

Brandl, John E. 1998. *Money and Good Intentions Are Not Enough.* Washington, D.C.: Brookings.

Brazil, Wayne. 1986. "Special Masters in Complex Cases: Extending the Judiciary or Reshaping Adjudication?" *University of Chicago Law Review* 53: 394–423.

Brewer, Richard. 2003. *Conservancy: The Land Trust in America.* Hanover, N.H.: University Press of New England.

Brooks, Harvey. 1984. "The Resolution of Technically Intensive Public Policy Disputes." *Science, Technology, and Human Values* 9: 48.

Brown, Lester. 2001. *Building an Economy for the Earth.* London: Earthscan and Earth Policy Institute.

Brown, William P. 1998. *Groups, Interests, and U.S. Public Policy.* Washington, D.C.: Georgetown University Press.

Brulle, Robert J. 2000. *Agency, Democracy, and Nature: The U.S. Environmental Movement from a Critical Theory Perspective.* Cambridge, Mass.: The MIT Press.

Brulle, Robert J. 2002. "Habermas and Green Political Thought: Two Roads Converging." *Environmental Politics* 11: 1–20.

Bryant, Bunyan. 1995. *Environmental Justice: Issues, Policies, and Solutions.* Washington, D.C.: Island Press.

Bryner, Gary C. 2001. *Gaia's Wager: Environmental Movements and the Challenge of Sustainability.* Lanham, Md.: Rowman and Littlefield.

Bullard, Robert. 1993. *Confronting Environmental Racism: Voices from the Grassroots.* Boston: South End Press.

Bullard, Robert. 1994. *Unequal Protection: Environmental Justice and Communities of Color.* San Francisco: Sierra Club Books.

Bullard, Robert. 1999. "Environmental Racism and the Environmental Justice Movement." In *Ecology*, ed. Carolyn Merchant, 254–265. Atlantic Highlands, N.J.: Humanities Press.

Buthe, Tim. 2002. "Taking Temporality Seriously: Modeling History and the Use of Narratives as Evidence." *American Political Science Review* 96: 481–494.

Caldecott, Leonie, and Stephanie Leland, eds. 1983. *Reclaim the Earth: Women Speak Out for Life on Earth*. London: Women's Press.

Caldwell, Lynton K. 1982. *Science and the National Environmental Policy Act: Redirecting Policy through Procedural Reform*. University: University of Alabama Press.

Caldwell, Lynton K. 1996. *International Environmental Policy*, third ed. Durham, N.C.: Duke University Press.

Caldwell, Lynton K. 1998. *The National Environmental Policy Act: An Agenda for the Future*. Bloomington: Indiana University Press.

Calhoun, Craig, ed. 1992. *Habermas and the Public Sphere*. Cambridge, Mass.: The MIT Press.

Camacho, David, ed. 1998. *Environmental Injustices, Political Struggles: Race, Class, and the Environment*. Durham, N.C.: Duke University Press.

Camilleri, Joseph, Kamal Malhota, and Majed Tehranian. 2000. *Reimagining the Future: Towards Global Governance*. Victoria, Australia: Global Governance Reform Project.

Carstens, Ann-Marie. 2002. "Lurking in the Shadows of Judicial Process: Special Masters in the Supreme Court's Original Jurisdiction Cases." *Minnesota Law Review* 86: 625–716.

Carter, Neil. 2001. *The Politics of the Environment: Ideas, Activism, Policy*. Cambridge: Cambridge University Press.

Cawley, R. McGreggor, and William Chaloupka. 1997. "American Governmentality: Michel Foucault and Public Administration." *American Behavioral Scientist* 41: 28–42.

Chaloupka, William. 1999. *Everybody Knows: Cynicism in America*. Minneapolis: University of Minnesota Press.

Chambers, Simone. 1996. *Reasonable Democracy: Jürgen Habermas and the Politics of Discourse*. Ithaca, N.Y.: Cornell University Press.

Clark, Jo. 1997. *Watershed Partnerships: A Strategic Guide for Local Conservation Efforts in the West*. Denver: Western Governors' Association.

Cohen, Jean-Louis. 1982. *Class and Civil Society: The Limits of Marxian Critical Theory*. Amherst: University of Massachusetts Press.

Cohen, Joshua. 1989. "Deliberation and Democratic Legitimacy." In *The Good Polity: Normative Analysis of the State*, ed. Alan Hamlin and Philip Pettit, 17–34. Oxford: Basil Blackwell.

Cohen, Joshua. 1996. "Procedure and Substance in Deliberative Democracy." In *Democracy and Difference: Contesting the Boundaries of the Political,* ed. Seyla Benhabib, 95–119. Princeton: Princeton University Press.

Cohen, Joshua. 1997. "Deliberation and Democratic Legitimacy." In *Deliberative Democracy: Essays on Reason and Politics,* ed. James Bohman and William Rehg. Cambridge, Mass.: The MIT Press.

Cohen, Joshua, and Rogers, Joel. 1992. "Secondary Associations and Democratic Governance." *Politics and Society* 20: 393–472.

Cohen, Joshua, and Rogers, Joel. 2003. "Power and Reason." In *Deepening Democracy: Institutional Innovations in Empowered Participatory Governance,* ed. Archon Fung and Erik Olin Wright, 237–255. New York: Verso.

Cohen, Joshua, and Charles Sabel. 1997. "Directly-Deliberative Polyarchy." *European Law Journal* 3: 313–342.

Collard, Andre. 1988. *Rape of the Wild.* London: Women's Press.

Council on Environmental Quality. 1993. *Environmental Quality: 23rd Annual Report of the Council on Environmental Quality.* Washington, D.C.: CEQ, 1993.

Cronin, Ciaran. 2003. "Democracy and Collective Identity: In Defense of Constitutional Patriotism." *European Journal of Philosophy* 11 (no. 1): 1–29.

Darier, Eric. 1999. Discourses of the Environment. London: Blackwell.

Davion, Victoria, and Clark Wolf, eds. 2000. *The Idea of a Political Liberalism: Essays on Rawls.* Lanham, Md.: Rowman and Littlefield.

Davis, Kenneth Culp. 1942. "An Approach to Problems of Evidence in the Administrative Process." *Harvard Law Review* 55: 364–425.

Davis, Kenneth Clup. 1969a. *Discretionary Justice: A Preliminary Inquiry.* Baton Rouge: Louisiana State University Press.

Davis, Kenneth Culp. 1969b. "Judicial Notice." *Arizona State Law Journal* 69: 513–532.

Davis, Stanley. 1988. "A Fresh Look at Hypothetical Questions and Ultimate Answers: The Kansas Experience." *University of Kansas Law Review* 36: 311–355.

d'Eaubonne, Francoise. 1999. "The Time for Ecofeminism." In *Ecology,* ed. Carolyn Merchant, 174–196. Atlantic Highlands, N.J.: Humanities Press.

deLeon, Peter. 1997. *Democracy and the Policy Sciences.* Albany: State University of New York Press.

DeLuca, Kevin Michael. 2001. "Rethinking Critical Theory: Instrumental Reason, Judgment, and the Environmental Crisis." *Environmental Ethics* 23: 307–326.

de-Shalit, Avner. 2000. *The Environment: Between Theory and Practice.* Oxford: Oxford University Press.

De Tocqueville, Alexis. 1961. *Democracy in America.* New York: Schocken Books.

Devall, William, and George Sessions. 1985. *Deep Ecology: Living as if Nature Mattered.* Salt Lake City: Gibbs, Smith.

Diesing, Paul. 1962. *Reason in Society: Five Types of Decision and Their Social Conditions.* Urbana: University of Illinois Press.

Dietz, Thomas M., and Robert W. Rycroft. 1987. *The Risk Professionals.* New York: Russell Sage Foundation.

Dizard, Jan. 1993. "Going Wild: The Contested Terrain of Nature." In *In the Nature of Things: Language, Politics, and the Environment,* ed. Jane Bennett and William Chaloupka, 111–137. Minneapolis: University of Minnesota Press.

Dobson, Andrew. 1996. "Democratizing Green Theory: Preconditions and Principles." In *Democracy and Green Political Thought: Sustainability, Rights and Citizenship,* ed. Brian Doherty and Marius de Geus, 132–148. London: Routledge.

Dobson, Andrew. 1998. *Justice and the Environment: Conceptions of Environmental Sustainability and Theories of Distributive Justice.* Oxford: Oxford University Press.

Dobson, Andrew, ed. 1999. *Fairness and Futurity: Essays on Environmental Sustainability and Social Justice.* Oxford: Oxford University Press.

Dobson, Andrew. 2000. *Green Political Thought,* third ed. London: Routledge.

Dobson, Andrew. 2003. *Citizenship and the Environment.* Oxford: Oxford University Press.

Doherty, Brian, and Marius de Geus, eds. 1996. *Democracy and Green Political Thought: Sustainability, Rights, and Citizenship.* London: Routledge.

Donahue, John. 1997. *Disunited States: What's at Stake as Washington Fades and the States Take the Lead.* New York: Basic Books.

Dorf, Michael, and Charles Sabel. 1998. "A Constitution of Democratic Experimentalism." *Columbia Law Review* 98: 267–473.

Dowie, Mark. 1995. *Losing Ground: American Environmentalism at the Close of the Twentieth Century.* Cambridge, Mass.: The MIT Press.

Downs, Anthony. 1972. "Up and Down with Ecology—The 'Issue-Attention Cycle.'" *Public Interest* 28: 38–50.

Doyal, Len, and Ian Gough. 1999. "Human Needs and Social Change." In *Ecology,* ed. Carolyn Merchant, 107–111. Atlantic Highlands, N.J.: Humanities Press.

Dror, Yehezkel. 1968. *Public Policy Making Reconsidered.* Scranton, Penn.: Chandler.

Dryzek, John S. 1983. "Ecological Rationality." *International Journal of Environmental Studies* 21: 5–10.

Dryzek, John S. 1987. *Rational Ecology: Environment and Political Economy.* Oxford: Basil Blackwell.

Dryzek, John S. 1990a. "Green Reason: Communication Ethics for the Biosphere." *Environmental Ethics* 12: 195–210.

Dryzek, John S. 1990b. *Discursive Democracy: Politics, Policy, and Political Science.* New York: Cambridge University Press.

Dryzek, John S. 1996. *Democracy in Capitalist Times*. New York: Oxford University Press.

Dryzek, John S. 1997. *The Politics of the Earth: Environmental Discourses*. Oxford: Oxford University Press.

Dryzek, John S. 2000. *Deliberative Democracy and Beyond: Liberals, Critics, Contestations*. Oxford: Oxford University Press.

Dryzek, John S., and Christian List. 2003. "Social Choice Theory and Deliberative Democracy: A Reconciliation." *British Journal of Political Science* 33: 1–28.

Dryzek, John S., David Downes, Christian Hunold, and David Schlosberg. 2003. *Green States and Social Movements: Environmentalism in the United States, United Kingdom, Germany, and Norway*. Oxford: Oxford University Press.

Duff, John. 2001. "The Coastal Zone Management Act: Reverse Pre-emption or Contractual Federalism?" *Ocean and Coastal Law Journal* 6: 109–118.

Duffy, Robert J. 2003. *The Green Agenda in American Politics: New Strategies for the Twenty-First Century*. Lawrence: University Press of Kansas.

Dunlap, Riley. 1991. "Public Opinion in the 1980s: Clear Consensus, Ambiguous Commitment." *Environment* 33 (no. 8): 10–15, 32–37.

Dunlap, Riley. 1995. "Public Opinion and the Environment." In *Conservation and Environmentalism: An Encyclopedia*, ed. Robert Paehlke, 535–537. New York: Garland.

Duverger, Maurice. 1954. *Political Parties: Their Organization and Activity in the Modern State*. New York: Wiley.

Dworkin, Ronald. 2000. *Sovereign Virtue: The Theory and Practice of Equality*. Cambridge, Mass.: Harvard University Press.

Eckersley, Robyn. 1992. *Environmentalism and Political Theory: Toward an Ecocentric Approach*. Albany: State University of New York Press.

Eckersley, Robyn. 1996. "Greening Liberal Democracy: The Rights Discourse Revisited." In *Democracy and Green Political Thought: Sustainability, Rights and Citizenship*, ed. Brian Doherty and Marius De Geus, 212–236. London: Routledge.

Eckersley, Robyn. 1999a. "The Failed Promise of Critical Theory." In *Ecology*, ed. Carolyn Merchant, 65–76. Atlantic Highlands, N.J.: Humanities Press.

Eckersley, Robyn. 1999b. "The Discourse Ethic and the Problem of Representing Nature." *Environmental Politics* 8: 24–49.

Eckersley, Robyn. 2000. "Deliberative Democracy, Ecological Representation and Risk: Towards a Democracy of the Affected." In *Democratic Innovation: Deliberation, Representation, and Association*, ed. Michael Saward, 117–132. London: Routledge.

Ehrlich, Paul R., and Anne H. Ehrlich. 1996. *Betrayal of Science and Reason: How Anti-Environmental Rhetoric Threatens Our Future*. Washington, D.C.: Island Books.

Elliot, Charles. 1994. "Towards Moral Communication and Consensus." *Cambridge Journal of Education* 24: 393–398.

Ellul, Jacques. 1964. *The Technological Society.* New York: Alfred A. Knopf.

Elster, Jon. 1984. *Ulysses and the Sirens: Studies in Rationality and Irrationality.* Cambridge: Cambridge University Press.

Epstein, Richard. 1992. "A New Regime for Expert Witnesses." *Valpariso University Law Review* 26: 757–764.

Erickson, Robert. 1993. *State-House Democracy: Public Opinion and Policy in the American States.* New York: Cambridge University Press.

Estlund, David. 1997. "Beyond Fairness and Deliberation: The Epistemic Dimension of Democratic Authority." In *Deliberative Democracy: Essays on Reason and Politics,* ed. James Bohman and William Rehg, 173–204. Cambridge, Mass.: The MIT Press.

Evans, Judy. 1995. "Ecofeminism and the Politics of the Gendered Self." In *The Politics of Nature,* ed. Andrew Dobson and Paul Lucardie, 177–189. New York: Routledge.

Evans, Mark. 1999. "Is Public Justification Central to Liberalism?" *Journal of Political Ideologies* 4: 117–127.

Faber, Daniel, ed. 1998. *The Struggle for Ecological Democracy: Environmental Justice Movements in the United States.* New York: Guilford.

Fairfax, Sally K., Lauren Gwin, Mary Ann King, Leigh Raymond, Laura A. Watt. 2005. *Beyond Bucks and Acres: The Limits of Land Acquisition as a Conservation Policy in the United States, 1785–2002.* Cambridge, Mass.: The MIT Press.

Fairfield, Paul. 1999. "Deliberative Democracy." *Review of Politics* 61: 541–543.

Ferrara, Alessaandro. 2001. "Of Boats and Principles: Reflections on Habermas's Constitutional Democracy." *Political Theory* 29 (no. 6): 782–791.

Fishkin, James S. 1991. *Democracy and Deliberation: New Directions for Democratic Reform.* New Haven: Yale University Press.

Fishkin, James S. 1995. *The Voice of the People: Public Opinion and Democracy.* New Haven: Yale University Press.

Fishkin, James S. 1999. "Toward Deliberative Democracy: Experimenting with an Ideal." In *Citizen Competence and Democratic Institutions,* ed. Stephen L. Elkin and Karol Edward Soltan. University Park: Pennsylvania State University Press.

Fishkin, James S., and Robert Luskin. 1999. "Bringing Deliberation to Democratic Dialogue." In *A Poll with a Human Face: The National Issues Convention Experiment in Political Communication,* ed. Maxwell McCombs and Amy Reynolds. Mahwah, N.J.: Lawrence Erlbaum.

Fisk, Milton. 1989. *The State and Justice: An Essay in Political Theory.* New York: Cambridge University Press.

Flynn, Jeffrey. 2003. "Habermas on Human Rights: Law, Morality, and Intercultural Dialogue." *Social Theory and Practice* 29 (no. 3): 431–458.

Foreman, Christopher. 2002. "The Civic Sustainability of Reform." In *Environmental Governance,* ed. Donald Kettle, 146–176. Washington: Brookings Institute Press.

Forsyth, Tim. 2003. *Critical Political Ecology: The Politics of Environmental Science*. New York: Routledge.

Fraser, Nancy. 1992. Rethinking the Public Sphere: A Contribution to the Critique of Actually Existing Democracy. In *Habermas and the Public Sphere*, ed. Craig Calhoun, 109–142. Cambridge, Mass.: The MIT Press.

Freeman, Samuel. 1990. "Reason and Agreement in Social Contract Views." *Philosophy and Public Affairs* 19: 122–57.

Friedman, Richard B. 1973. "On the Concept of Authority in Political Philosophy." In *Concepts in Social and Political Philosophy*, ed. Richard E. Flathman, 121–146. New York: Macmillan.

Friedman, Thomas. 2002. *Longitudes and Attitudes: Exploring the World after September 11*. New York: Farrar, Straus, and Giroux.

Fung, Archon. 2003. "Recipes for Public Spheres: Eight Intitutional Design Choices and Their Consequences." *Journal of Political Philosophy* 11: 338–367.

Fung, Archon, and Erik Olin Wright. 2003. "Thinking about Empowered Participatory Governance." In *Deepening Democracy: Institutional Innovations in Empowered Participatory Governance*, ed. Archon Fung and Erik Olin Wright, 3–42. New York: Verso.

Gabardi, Wayne. 2001. "Contemporary Models of Democracy." *Polity* 33: 547–568.

Galanter, Marc. 1974. "Why the 'Haves' Come Out Ahead: Speculations on the Limits of Legal Change." *Law and Society* 9: 95–160.

Garner, Robert. 2003. "Animals, Politics, and Justice: Rawlsian Liberalism and the Plight of Non-humans." *Environmental Politics* 12: 2–22.

Gastil, John. 2000. *Back by Popular Demand: Revitalizing Representative Democracy through Deliberative Elections*. Berkeley: University of California Press.

Gaus, Gerald. 1997. "Reason, Justification, and Consensus: Why Democracy Can't Have It All." In *Deliberative Democracy: Essays on Reason and Politics*, ed. James Bohman and William Rehg, 205–242. Cambridge, Mass.: The MIT Press.

Gerth, H. H., and C. W. Mills, eds. 1946. *From Max Weber: Essays in Sociology*. New York: Oxford University Press.

Giddens, Anthony. 1985. "Reason without Revolution? Habermas's *Theorie des kommunikativen Handelns*. " In *Habermas and Modernity*, ed. Richard J. Bernstein, 95–121. Cambridge, Mass.: The MIT Press.

Gibbard, Allan. 1991. "Constructing Justice." *Philosophy and Public Affairs* 20: 264–279.

Gifford, Daniel. 1997. "Federal Administrative Law Judges: The Relevance of Past Choices to Future Directions." *Administrative Law Review* 49: 1–41.

Gismondi, Michael, and Richardson, Mary. 1994. "Discourse and Power in Environmental Politics." In *Is Capitalism Sustainable? Political Economy and the Politics of Ecology*, ed. Martin O'Connor, 232–252. New York: Guilford Press.

Glaberson, William. 1988. "Coping in the Age of 'NIMBY.'" *New York Times,* June 19, 1988, sect. 3, p. 1.

Goodin, Robert E. 1992. *Green Political Theory.* Cambridge, Mass.: Polity.

Goodin, Robert E. 1996. "Enfranchising the Earth, and Its Alternatives." *Political Studies* 44: 835–849.

Gormley, William T. 1987. "Intergovernmental Conflict on Environmental Policy: The Attitudinal Connection." *Western Political Quarterly* 40: 285–303.

Gottlieb, Robert. 1993. *Forcing the Spring: The Transformation of the American Environmental Movement.* Washington, D.C.: Island Press.

Graham, Frank. 1990. *The Audubon Ark: A History of the National Audubon Society.* New York: Knopf.

Gregg, Benjamin. 1997. "Democracy in Normatively Fragmented Societies." *Review of Politics* 59: 927–930.

Grofman, B. 1993. Public Choice, Civic Republicanism, and American Politics: Perspectives of a Reasonable Choice Modeler. *Texas Law Review* 71: 1541–1587.

Guber, Deborah Lynn. 2003. *The Grassroots of a Green Revolution: Polling America on the Environment.* Cambridge, Mass.: The MIT Press.

Gundersen, Adolph G. 1995. *The Environmental Promise of Democratic Deliberation.* Madison: University of Wisconsin Press.

Gundersen, Adolph G. 2000. *The Socratic Citizen: A Theory of Deliberative Democracy.* Lanham, Md.: Lexington Books.

Gutmann, Amy. 1999. *Democratic Education.* Princeton: Princeton University Press.

Gutmann, Amy. 2003. *Identity in Democracy.* Princeton: Princeton University Press.

Gutmann, Amy, and Dennis Thompson. 1996. *Democracy and Disagreement.* Cambridge, Mass.: Belknap Press of Harvard University.

Gutmann, Amy, and Dennis Thompson. 2004. *Why Deliberative Democracy?* Princeton: Princeton University Press.

Habermas, Jürgen. 1970. *Toward a Rational Society.* Boston: Beacon Press.

Habermas, Jürgen. 1971. *Knowledge and Human Interests.* Boston: Beacon Press.

Habermas, Jürgen. 1973a. *Theory and Practice.* Boston: Beacon Press.

Habermas, Jürgen. 1973b. "A Postscript to *Knowledge and Human Interests.*" *Philosophy of the Social Sciences* 3: 157–189.

Habermas, Jürgen. 1974. "The Public Sphere." *New German Critique* 1 (no. 3): 49–55.

Habermas, Jürgen. 1976. *Legitimation Crisis.* London: Heinemann.

Habermas, Jürgen. 1979. *Commmunication and the Evolution of Society.* Boston: Beacon Press.

Habermas, Jürgen. 1987a. *The Theory of Communicative Action,* vol. 2: *Lifeworld and System.* Boston: Beacon Press.

Habermas, Jürgen. 1987b. *The Philosophical Discourse of Modernity.* Cambridge, Mass.: The MIT Press.

Habermas, Jürgen. 1990. *Moral Consciousness and Communicative Action.* Cambridge, Mass.: Polity.

Habermas, Jürgen. 1992. *Postmetaphysical Thinking: Philosophical Essays.* Cambridge, Mass.: The MIT Press.

Habermas, Jürgen. 1995. "Reconciliation through the Public Use of Reason: Remarks on John Rawls's *Political Liberalism.*" *Journal of Philosophy* 92: 109–131.

Habermas, Jürgen. 1996. *Between Facts and Norms: Contributions to a Discourse Theory of Law and Democracy.* Cambridge, Mass.: The MIT Press.

Habermas, Jürgen. 1997. "Popular Sovereignty as Procedure." In *Deliberative Democracy: Essays on Reason and Politics,* ed. James Bohman and William Rehg, 35–65. Cambridge, Mass.: The MIT Press.

Habermas, Jürgen. 1998a. *The Inclusion of the Other.* Cambridge, Mass.: The MIT Press.

Habermas, Jürgen. 1998b. *The Structural Transformation of the Public Sphere.* Cambridge, Mass.: The MIT Press.

Habermas, Jürgen. 2001a. *On the Pragmatics of Social Interaction.* Cambridge, Mass.: The MIT Press.

Habermas, Jürgen. 2001b. "Constitutional Democracy: A Paradoxical Union of Contradictory Principles." *Political Theory* 29: 766–781.

Habermas, Jürgen. 2002. *Religion and Rationality.* Cambridge, Mass.: The MIT Press.

Hajer, Maarten. 1995. *The Politics of Environmental Discourse: Ecological Modernization and the Policy Process.* New York: Oxford University Press.

Hand, Learned. 1901. "Historical and Practical Considerations Regarding Expert Testimony." *Harvard Law Review* 15: 40–80.

Hardin, Garrett. 1968. "The Tragedy of the Commons." *Science* 162: 1243–1248.

Hardin, Garrett. 1974. "Lifeboat Ethics: The Case against Helping the Poor." *Psychology Today* (September): 38–43, 123–126.

Hardin, Russell. 2003. "Street-Level Epistemology and Democratic Participation." In *Debating Deliberative Democracy,* ed. James Fishkin and Peter Laslett, 163–181. Malden, Mass.: Blackwell.

Hargrove, Eugene. 1989. "Beginning the Next Decade: Taking Stock." *Environmental Ethics* 11: 3–4.

Hargrove, Eugene. 1994. "Overcoming Environmental Newspeak." *Environmental Ethics* 16: 115–116.

Hargrove, Eugene. 2000. "The Next Century and Beyond." *Environmental Ethics* 22: 3.

Hauptmann, Emily. 2001. "Can Less Be More? Leftist Deliberative Democrats' Critique of Deliberative Democracy." *Polity* 33: 397–421.

Hayim, Gila J. 1992. "Naturalism and the Crisis of Rationalism in Habermas." *Social Theory and Practice* 18: 187–209.

Hayward, Bronwyn M. 1995a. "Beyond Liberalism? Environmental Management and Deliberative Democracy." Paper presented at the annual meeting of the American Political Science Association, Chicago, August 31–September 3.

Hayward, Bronwyn M. 1995b. "The Greening of Participatory Democracy: A Reconsideration of Theory." *Environmental Politics* 4: 215–236.

Hayward, Tim. 1998. *Political Theory and Ecological Values.* New York: St. Martin's Press.

Healey, Patsy. 1993. "Planning through Debate: The Communicative Turn in Planning Theory." In *The Argumentative Turn in Policy Analysis and Planning,* ed. Frank Fischer and John Forester, 233–253. Durham, N.C.: Duke University Press.

Heilbroner, Robert L. 1996. *Inquiry into the Human Prospect, Updated and Reconsidered for the Nineteen Nineties,* second rev. ed. New York: W. W. Norton.

Henderson, A. M., and Talcott Parsons, eds. 1947. *Max Weber: The Theory of Social and Economic Organization.* New York: Oxford University Press.

Hill, Ronald. 2001. "Global Consumption and Distributive Justice: A Rawlsian Perspective." *Human Rights Quarterly* 23: 171–189.

Hirst, Paul Q. 1994. *Associative Democracy: New Forms of Economic and Social Governance.* Amherst: University of Massachusetts Press.

Holub, Robert. 1991. *Jürgen Habermas: Critic in the Public Sphere.* London: Routledge.

Horkheimer, Max. 1974. *Eclipse of Reason.* New York: Seabury Press.

Horkheimer, Max, and Theodore Adorno. 1972. *The Dialectic of Enlightenment.* New York: Seabury Press.

Huber, Peter. 1991. *Galileo's Revenge: Junk Science in the Courtroom.* New York: Basic Books.

Huckfeldt, Robert, Paul Johnson, and John Sprague. 2002. "Political Environments, Political Dynamics, and the Survival of Disagreement." *Journal of Politics* 64: 1–21.

Hunold, Christian. 2001. "Corporatism, Pluralism, and Democracy: Toward a Deliberative Theory of Bureaucratic Accountability." *Governance: An International Journal of Policy and Administration* 14: 151–167.

Ingram, David. 1993. "The Limits and Possibilities of Communicative Ethics for Democratic Theory." *Political Theory* 21: 294–321.

Janicke, Martin. 1996. "Democracy as a Condition for Environmental Policy Success: The Importance of Non-Institutional Factors." In *Democracy and the Environment: Problems and Prospects,* ed. William M. Lafferty and James Meadowcroft, 71–85. Chaltenham: Edward Elgar.

Jay, Martin. 1973. *The Dialectical Imagination: A History of the Frankfurt School and the Institute of Social Research, 1923–1970.* Boston: Little, Brown.

Jennings, Cheri, and Jennings, Bruce. 1993. "Green Fields/Brown Skin: Postings as a Sign of Recognition." In *In the Nature of Things: Language, Politics, and the Environment*, ed. Jane Bennett and William Chaloupka, 173–194. Minneapolis: University of Minnesota Press.

John, DeWitt. 1994. *Civic Environmentalism: Alternatives to Regulation in States and Communities*. Washington, D.C.: CQ Press.

Johnson, Phillip. 1987. "Fecund Mysteries: The Dark and Muddy Ground of the Estuary." *Wilderness* 50 (no. 177): 37–44, 53–56.

Kale, Steven. 2002. "Women, the Public Sphere, and the Persistence of Salons." *Historical Studies* 25 (no. 1): 115–149.

Karkkainen, Bradley C. 2003. "Toward Ecologically Sustainable Democracy?" In *Deepening Democracy: Institutional Innovations in Empowered Participatory Governance*, ed. Archon Fung and Erik Olin Wright, 208–224. New York: Verso.

Katz, Elihu, and Paul Lazarsfeld. 1955. *Personal Influence*. Glencoe, Ill.: Free Press.

Kaufman, Arnold S. 1968. *The Radical Liberal: New Man in American Politics*. New York: Atherton Press.

Kaufman, Arnold S. 1969. "Human Nature and Participatory Democracy." In *Bias of Pluralism*, ed. William E. Connolly, 178–200. New York: Atherton.

Kelber, Mim. 1994. "The Women's Environment and Development Organization." *Environment* 36 (no. 8): 43–45.

Kelch, Thomas. 1999. "The Role of the Rational and the Emotive in a Theory of Animal Rights." *Environmental Affairs Law Review* 27: 1–49.

Kelly, Erin. 1997. "Environmentalists Finding Nontraditional Allies." *Gannett News Service*, October 11, 1997.

Kelly, Marisa, and Steven Maynard-Moody. 1993. "Policy Analysis in the Post-Positivist Era: Engaging Stakeholders in Evaluating the Economic Development Districts Program." *Public Administration Review* 53: 135–142.

Kirkman, Robert. 2002. *Skeptical Environmentalism: The Limits of Philosophy and Science*. Bloomington: Indiana University Press.

Knight, Jack. 1999. "Constitutionalism and Deliberative Discourse." In *Deliberative Politics: Essays on Democracy and Disagreement*, ed. Stephen Macedo, 159–169. New York: Oxford University Press.

Knight, Jack, and James Johnson. 1994. "Aggregation and Deliberation: On the Possibility of Democratic Legitimacy." *Political Theory* 22: 277–296.

Knight, Jack, and James Johnson. 1997. "What Sort of Equality Does Deliberative Democracy Require?" In *Deliberative Democracy: Essays on Reason and Politics*, ed. James Bohman and William Rehg, 279–319. Cambridge, Mass.: The MIT Press.

Kriz, Margaret. 1994. "Super Fight." *National Journal* (January 29): 224–229.

Kriz, Margaret. 1995. "The Greening of a Conservative." *National Journal* (June 6): 1419.

Kuntz, Phil. 1990. "Coastal Management Measure Gives States More Control." *Congressional Quarterly Weekly Report* 48: 3595.

Kurian, Priya A. 2000. *Engendering the Environment? Gender in the World Bank's Environmental Policies.* Burlington, Vermont: Ashgate.

Kurian, Priya A., and Robert V. Bartlett. 2003. "Ethics and Justice Needs for Sustainable Development." In *Institutional Issues Involving Ethics and Justice,* ed. Robert Charles Elliot. In *Encyclopedia of Life Support Systems,* developed under the auspices of UNESCO. Oxford: EOLSS Publishers.

LaDuke, Winona. 1999. "From Resistance to Regeneration." In *Ecology,* ed. Carolyn Merchant, 266–271. Atlantic Highlands, N.J.: Humanities Press.

Lafferty, William M., and James Meadowcroft, eds. 1996. *Democracy and the Environment: Problems and Prospects.* Bookfield, Vermont: Edward Elgar.

LaLonde, Martin. 1993. "Allocating the Burden of Proof to Effectuate the Preservation and Federalism Goals of the Coastal Zone Management Act." *Michigan Law Review* 93: 438–477.

Laslett, Peter. 2003. "Environmental Ethics and the Obsolescence of Existing Political Institutions." In *Debating Deliberative Democracy,* ed. James Fishkin and Peter Laslett, 212–224. Malden, Mass.: Blackwell.

Lee, Kai. 1993. *Compass and Gyroscope: Integrating Science and Politics for the Environment.* Washington, D.C.: Island Press.

Leib, Ethan J. 2004. *Deliberative Democracy in America: A Proposal for a Popular Branch of Government.* University Park: Pennsylvania State University Press.

Leiss, William. 1972. *The Domination of Nature.* New York: George Braziller.

Lester, James, David Allen, and Kelly Hill, eds. 2001. *Environmental Injustice in the United States.* Boulder: Westview.

Levine, Peter. 2000. *The New Progressive Era: Toward a Fair and Deliberative Democracy.* Lanham, Md.: Rowman and Littlefield.

Lindblom, Charles. 1977. *Politics and Markets.* New York: Basic Books.

Lindstrom, Matthew J., and Zachary A. Smith. 2001. *The National Environmental Policy Act: Judicial Misconstruction, Legislative Indifference, and Executive Neglect.* College Station: Texas A&M University Press.

Lippmann, Walter. 1922. *Public Opinion.* New York: Harcourt, Brace.

Lipschutz, Ronnie D. 1996. *Global Civil Society and Global Environmental Governance.* Albany: State University of New York Press.

Lipschutz, Ronnie D. 2004. *Global Environmental Politics: Power, Perspectives, and Practice.* Washington, D.C.: CQ Press.

Lovelock, J. E. 1979. *Gaia: A New Look at Life on Earth.* New York: Oxford University Press.

Lowi, Theodore. 1964. "American Business, Public Policy, Case Studies, and Political Theory." *World Politics* 16: 677–715.

Lowi, Theordore. 1967. "The Public Philosophy: Interest Group Liberalism." *American Political Science Review* 61: 5–24.

Lowi, Theodore. 1979. *The End of Liberalism: The Second Republic of the United States,* second ed. New York: W. W. Norton.

Lowry, William. 1992. *The Dimensions of Federalism: State Governments and Pollution Control Policies.* Durham, N.C.: Duke University Press.

Luke, Timothy W. 1997. *Ecocritique: Contesting the Politics of Nature, Economy, and Culture.* Minneapolis: University of Minnesota Press.

Lunney, Leslie. 1994. "Protecting Juries from Themselves: Restricting the Admission of Expert Testimony in Toxic Tort Cases." *Southern Methodist University Law Review* 48: 103–185.

MacIntyre, Alasdair C. 1984. *After Virtue: A Study in Moral Theory,* second ed. South Bend, Ind.: University of Notre Dame Press.

MacIntyre, Alasdair. 1988. *Whose Justice? Which Rationality?* South Bend, Ind.: University of Notre Dame Press.

Mackie, Gerry. 1998. "All Men Are Liars: Is Deliberation Meaningless?" In *Deliberative Democracy,* ed. Jon Elster, 69–96. New York: Cambridge University Press.

MacRae, Duncan, and Dale Whittington. 1997. *Expert Advice for Policy Choice.* Washington, D.C.: Georgetown University Press.

Majone, Giandomenico. 1989. *Evidence, Argument, and Persuasion in the Policy Process.* New Haven: Yale University Press.

Mannheim, Karl. 1948. *Man and Society in an Age of Reconstruction: Studies in Modern Social Structure.* New York: Harcourt Brace.

Manning, Russ. 1981. "Environmental Ethics and Rawls' Theory of Justice." *Environmental Ethics* 3: 155–165.

Mansbridge, Jane. 1983. *Beyond Adversarial Democracy.* Chicago: University of Chicago Press.

Marcuse, Herbert. 1964. *One-Dimensional Man.* London: Routledge and Kegan Paul.

Marcuse, Herbert. 1972. *Counterrevolution and Revolt.* London: Allen Lane.

Mason, Michael. 1999. *Environmental Democracy.* New York: St. Martin's Press.

Mathews, Freya. 1991. Democracy and the Ecological Crisis. *Legal Services Bulletin* 16 (no. 4): 157–159.

Mathews, Freya, ed. 1996. *Ecology and Democracy.* London: Frank Cass.

McCarthy, Thomas. 1978. *The Critical Theory of Jürgen Habermas.* Cambridge, Mass.: Polity.

McCarthy, Thomas. 1997. "Practical Discourse: On the Relation of Morality to Politics." In *Habermas and the Public Sphere,* ed. Craig Calhoun, 51–72. Cambridge, Mass.: The MIT Press.

McCloskey, Michael. 1993. "Twenty Years of Change in the Environmental Movement: An Insider's View." In *American Environmentalism: The U.S. Environmental Movement, 1970–1990,* ed. Riley E. Dunlap and Angela G. Mertig, 77–88. Philadelphia: Taylor and Francis.

McSpadden, Lettie. 1995. "The Courts and Environmental Policy." In *Environmental Politics and Policy: Theories and Evidence,* second ed., ed. James P. Lester, 242–274. Durham, N.C.: Duke University Press.

McWilliams, Wilson Carey. 1973. *The Idea of Fraternity in America.* Berkeley: University of California Press.

Menand, Louis. 2001. *The Metaphysical Club.* New York: Farrar, Straus, and Giroux.

Merchant, Carolyn. 1989. *Ecological Revolutions.* Chapel Hill: University of North Carolina Press.

Merchant, Carolyn. 1996. *Earthcare: Women and the Environment.* New York: Routledge.

Merton, Robert K. 1957. *Social Theory and Social Structure.* Glencoe, Ill.: Free Press.

Metzenbaum, Shelly H. 2002. "Measurement that Matters: Cleaning up the Charles River." In *Environmental governance,* ed. Donald Kettle, 58–117. Washington, D.C.: Brookings Institute Press.

Michelman, Frank I. 1997. "How Can the People Ever Make the Laws? A Critique of Deliberative Democracy." In *Deliberative Democracy: Essays on Reason and Politics,* ed. James Bohman and William Rehg, 145–171. Cambridge, Mass.: The MIT Press.

Milbrath, Lester W. 1963. *The Washington Lobbyist.* Chicago: Rand McNally.

Miles, Edward L. 2002. "Sea Dumping of Low-Level Radioactive Waste, 1964 to 1982." In *Environmental Regime Effectiveness: Confronting Theory with Evidence,* ed. Edward L. Miles, Arild Underdal, Steinar Andresen, Jørgen Wettestad, Jon Birger Skjærseth, and Elaine M. Carlin, 87–116. Cambridge, Mass.: The MIT Press.

Millemann, Beth. 1991. "Coastal Legislation: Acts of Spigotry." *Sierra* 104 (no. 13): 22.

Miller, David. 1995. *On Nationality.* Oxford: Clarendon Press.

Miller, David. 1999. "Social Justice and Environmental Goods." In *Fairness and Futurity: Essays on Environmental Sustainability and Social Justice,* ed. Andrew Dobson, 151–172. Oxford: Oxford University Press.

Minteer, Ben A., and Bob Pepperman Taylor, eds. 2002. *Democracy and the Claims of Nature: Critical Perspectives for a New Century.* Lanham, Md.: Rowman and Littlefield.

Morone, James. 1990. *The Democratic Wish.* New York: Basic Books.

Mouffe, Chantal. 1996. "Democracy, Power, and the Political." In *Democracy and Difference: Contesting the Boundaries of the Political,* ed. Seyla Benhabib, 245–256. Princeton: University Press.

Mouffe, Chantal. 1999. "Deliberative Democracy or Agonistic Pluralism." *Social Research* 66: 745–758.

Mumford, Lewis. 1970. *The Myth of the Machine: The Pentagon of Power.* New York: Harcourt Brace Jovanovich.

Munger, Michael. 2000. *Analyzing Policy: Choices, Conflicts, and Practices.* New York: W. W. Norton.

Murphy, Raymond. 1994. *Rationality and Nature: A Sociological Inquiry into a Changing Relationship.* Boulder: Westview.

Natural Resources Law Center. 1995. *The Watershed Source-Book: Watershed-Based Solutions to Natural Resource Problems.* Boulder: University of Colorado.

Negt, Oskar, and Alexander Kluge. 1993. *The Public Sphere and Experience.* Minneapolis: University of Minnesota Press.

Niebuhr, Reinhold. 1944. *The Children of Light and the Children of Darkness.* New York: Charles Scribner's Sons.

Norton, Bryan. 1989. "Intergenerational Equity and Environmental Decisions: Using Rawls' Veil of Ignorance." *Ecological Economics* 1: 137–159.

Norton, Bryan. 1999. "Ecology and Opportunity: Intergenerational Equity and Sustainable Options." In *Fairness and Futurity: Essays on Environmental Sustainability and Social Justice,* ed. Andrew Dobson, 118–150. Oxford: Oxford University Press.

Nussbaum, Martha C. 1995. "Emotions and Women's Capabilities." In *Women, Culture, and Development,* ed. Martha C. Nussbaum and Jonathan Glover, 360–395. Oxford: Oxford University Press.

O'Connor, James. 1999. "Socialism and Ecology." In *Ecology,* ed. Carolyn Merchant, 163–172. Atlantic Highlands, N.J.: Humanities Press.

Offe, Claus. 1985. "New Social Movements: Challenging the Boundaries of Institutional Politics." *Social Research* 52: 817–868.

Offe, Claus. 1990. "Reflections on the Institutional Self-Transformation of Movement Politics: A Tentative Stage Model." In *Challenging the Political Order: New Social Movements in Western Democracies,* ed. Russell J. Dalton and Manfred Kuechler, 232–250. New York: Oxford University Press.

Offe, Claus. 1997. "Micro Aspects of Democratic Theory: What Makes for the Deliberative Competence of Citizens? In *Democracy's Victory and Crisis,* ed. Axel Hadenius, 81–104. Cambridge: Cambridge University Press.

O'Leary, Rosemary. 2003. "Environmental Policy in the Courts." In *Environmental Policy: New Directions for the Twenty-First Century,* ed. Norman J. Vig and Michael E. Kraft, 151–173. Washington, D.C.: CQ Press.

Olson, Mancur. 1965. *The Logic of Collective Action.* Cambridge, Mass.: Harvard University Press.

O'Neil, John. 1998. "Rhetoric, Science, and Philosophy." *Philosophy of the Social Sciences* 28: 205–225.

Ophuls, William. 1977. *Ecology and the Politics of Scarcity: Prologue to a Political Theory of the Steady State.* San Francisco: W. H. Freeman.

Ophuls, William. 1997. *Requiem for Modern Politics: The Tragedy of the Enlightenment and the Challenge of the New Millennium.* Boulder: Westview Press.

Ophuls, William, and A. Stephen Boyan, Jr. 1992. *Ecology and the Politics of Scarcity Revisited.* New York: W. H. Freeman.

Osborne, John. 1990. "Judicial/Technical Assessment of Novel Scientific Evidence." *University of Illinois Law Review* (1990): 497–546.

Outhwaite, William. 1994. *Habermas: A Critical Introduction.* Stanford: Stanford University Press.

Paden, Roger. 1997. "Rawls's Just Savings Principle and the Sense of Justice." *Social Theory and Practice* 23: 27–52.

Paehlke, Robert C. 1989. *Environmentalism and the Future of Progressive Politics.* New Haven: Yale University Press.

Paehlke, Robert C. 1996. "Environmental Challenges to Democratic Practice." In *Democracy and the Environment,* ed. William M. Lafferty and James Meadowcroft, 18–38. Cheltenham: Edward Elgar.

Paehlke, Robert C. 2003. *Democracy's Dilemma: Environment, Social Equity, and the Global Economy.* Cambridge, Mass.: The MIT Press.

Parkinson, John. 2003. "Legitimacy Problems in Deliberative Democracy." *Political Studies* 51: 180–196.

Pateman, Carole. 1970. *Participation and Democratic Theory.* Cambridge: Cambridge University Press.

Pepper, David. 1996. *Modern Environmentalism: An Introduction.* London: Routledge.

Pitkin, Hanna. 1967. *The Concept of Representation.* Berkeley: University of California Press.

Plant, Judith, ed. 1989. *Healing the Wounds: The Promise of Ecofeminism.* London: Green Print.

Platt, Rutherford H. 1985. "Congress and the Coast." *Environment* 27 (no. 7): 12–17, 34–40.

Plevin, Arlene. 1997. "Green Guilt: An Effective Rhetoric or Rhetoric in Transition?" *Technical Communication Quarterly* 6: 125–139.

Plumwood, Val. 1993. *Feminism and the Mastery of Nature.* London: Routledge.

Plumwood, Val. 1998. "Inequality, Ecojustice, and Ecological Rationality." In *Debating the Earth: The Environmental Politics Reader,* ed. John S. Dryzek and David Schlosberg, 559–583. New York: Oxford University Press.

Plumwood, Val. 2002. *Environmental Culture: The Ecological Crisis of Reason.* New York: Routledge.

Pogge, Thomas W. 1992. "Cosmopolitan Sovereignty." *Ethics* 103: 48–75.

PollingReport.Com. 2003. "Problems and Priorities: CBS News Poll, 10–12 November." Accessed December 8, 2003. See http://www.pollingreport.com/prioriti.htm.

Polanyi, Michael. 1964. *Science, Faith, and Society.* Chicago: University of Chicago Press.

Ponting, Clive. 1991. *A Green History of the World.* New York: Penguin.

Porter, Gareth, Janet Welsh Brown, and Pamela S. Chasek. 2000. *Global Environmental Politics,* third ed. Boulder: Westview Press.

Postema, Gerald. 1995. "Public Practical Reason: Political Practice." In *Nomos XXXVII: Theory and Practice,* ed. Ian Shapiro and Judith DeGrew, 345–385. New York: New York University Press.

Pritchard, Michael S., and Wade L. Robison. 1981. "Justice and the Treatment of Animals: A Critique of Rawls." *Environmental Ethics* 3: 55–61.

Putnam, Robert D. 2001. *Bowling Alone.* New York: Touchstone.

Rabe, Barry G. 1999a. "Federalism and Entrepreneurship: Explaining American and Canadian Innovation in Pollution Prevention and Regulatory Integration." *Policy Studies Journal* 27: 288–306.

Rabe, Barry G. 1999b. "Sustainability in a Regional Context: The Case of the Great Lakes Basin." In *Toward Sustainable Communities: Transition and Transformations in Environmental Policy,* ed. Daniel A. Mazmanian and Michael E. Kraft, 247–282. Cambridge, Mass.: The MIT Press.

Rabe, Barry G. 2003. "Power to the States: The Promise and Pitfalls of Decentralization. In *Environmental Policy: New Directions for the Twenty-First Century,* ed. Norman J. Vig and Michael E. Kraft, 33–56. Washington, D.C.: CQ Press.

Rawls, John. 1971. *A Theory of Justice.* Cambridge, Mass.: Harvard University Press.

Rawls, John. 1993. *Political Liberalism.* New York: Columbia University Press.

Rawls, John. 1995. "Reply to Habermas." *Journal of Philosophy* 92 (no. 3): 132–180.

Rawls, John. 1999a. *A Theory of Justice,* rev. ed. Cambridge, Mass.: Harvard University Press.

Rawls, John. 1999b. *The Law of Peoples.* Cambridge, Mass.: Harvard University Press.

Rawls, John. 1999c. *Collected Papers.* Ed. Samuel Freeman. Cambridge, Mass.: Harvard University Press.

Rawls, John. 2001. *Justice as Fairness: A Restatement.* Cambridge, Mass.: Belknap Press of Harvard University Press.

Raymond, Leigh. 2004. "Habitat Conservation Plans: Bigger and Better Than Ever?" Paper presented at the Western Political Science Association Annual Meeting, Portland, Oregon, March 2004.

Raymond, Leigh, and Sally K. Fairfax. 2002. "The 'Shift to Privatization' in Land Conservation: A Cautionary Essay." *Natural Resources Journal* 42: 599–639.

Rehg, William. 1997. "Reason and Rhetoric in Habermas's Theory of Argumentation." In *Rhetoric and Hermeneutics in Our Time: A Reader,* ed. Walter Jost and Michael J. Hyde, 358–377. New Haven: Yale University Press.

Remer, Gary. 1999. "Political Oratory and Conversation: Cicero versus Deliberative Democracy." *Political Theory* 27: 39–64.

Renner, Rebecca. 1995. "Global Control of Persistent Organic Pollutants Advocated." *Environmental Science and Technology* 29: 357.

Rice, Tom W., and Alexander F. Sumberg. 1997. "Civic Culture and Governmental Performance in the American States." *Publius: The Journal of Federalism* 27: 99–114.

Rorty, Amélie Oksenberg. 1985. "Varieties of Rationality, Varieties of Emotion." *Social Science Information* 24: 343–353.

Rosenbaum, Walter A. 2002. *Environmental Politics and Policy,* fifth ed. Washington, D.C.: CQ Press.

Rothenberg, Lawrence. 2002. *Environmental Choices: Policy Responses to Green Demands.* Washington, D.C.: CQ Press.

Rucht, Dieter. 1990. "The Strategies and Action Repertoires of New Movements." In *Challenging the Political Order: New Social and Political Movements in Western Democracies,* ed. Russell J. Dalton and Manfred Kuechler, 156–175. New York: Oxford University Press.

Rustin, Charles. 1999. "Habermas, Discourse Ethics, and International Justice." *Alternatives: Social Transformation and Human Governance* 24: 167–192.

Sagoff, Mark. 1988. *The Economy of the Earth.* New York: Cambridge University Press, 1988.

Sagoff, Mark. 1999. "The View from Quincy Library: Civic Engagement in Environmental Problem Solving." In *Civil Society, Democracy, and Civic Renewal,* ed. Robert K. Fullinwider, 151–183. Lanham, Md.: Rowman and Littlefield.

Satchell, Michael. 1992. "A Whiff of Discrimination." *U.S. News and World Report* 112 (May 4): 34–35.

Sandel, Michael J. 1996. *Democracy's Discontent.* Cambridge, Mass.: Belknap Press of Harvard University Press.

Sanders, Lynn. 1997. "Against Deliberation." *Political Theory* 25: 347–376.

Saward, Michael. 1993. "Green Democracy?" In *The Politics of Nature: Explorations in Green Political Theory,* ed. Andrew Dobson and Paul Lucardie, 63–80. London: Routledge.

Schattschneider, E. E. 1960. *The Semi-Sovereign People.* New York: Holt, Rinehart, and Winston.

Scheuerman, William E. 1999. "Between Radicalism and Resignation: Democratic Theory in Habermas's *Between Facts and Norms.*" In *Habermas: A Critical Reader,* ed. Peter Dews, 153–177. Oxford: Basil Blackwell.

Schlosberg, David. 1998. "Resurrecting the Pluralist Universe." *Political Research Quarterly* 51: 583–615.

Schlosberg, David. 1999. *Environmental Justice and the New Pluralism: The Challenge of Difference for Environmentalism.* Oxford: Oxford University Press.

Schmandt, Jurgen, and James Everett Katz. 1986. "The Scientific State: A Theory with Hypotheses." *Science, Technology, and Human Values* 11: 40–52.

Schneider, Anne Larason, and Helen Ingram. 1997. *Policy Design for Democracy.* Lawrence: University Press of Kansas.

Shabani, Omid. 2003. "Critical Theory and the Seducement of the 'Art of the Possible.'" *Canadian Journal of Political Science* 36 (no. 2): 270–299.

Shapiro, Ian. 2003. "Optimal Deliberation." In *Debating Deliberative Democracy,* ed. James Fishkin and Peter Laslett, 121–137. Malden, Mass.: Blackwell.

Shutkin, William A. 2000. *The Land That Could Be: Environmentalism and Democracy in the Twenty-First Century.* Cambridge, Mass.: The MIT Press.

Simon, Herbert A. 1964. "Rationality." In *A Dictionary of the Social Sciences,* ed. J. Gold and W. L. Kolb, 573–574. New York: Free Press of Glencoe.

Simon, Herbert A. 1976a. *Administrative Behavior,* third ed. New York: Free Press.

Simon, Herbert A. 1976b. "From Substantive to Procedural Rationality." In *Method and Appraisal in Economics,* ed. Spiro J. Latsis, 129–148. New York: Cambridge University Press.

Simon, Herbert A. 1978. "Rationality as Process and as Product of Thought." *American Economic Review* 68 (no. 2): 1–16.

Simon, Herbert A. 1981. *Sciences of the Artificial,* second ed. Cambridge, Mass.: The MIT Press.

Simon, Jonathan. 1994. "Between Power and Knowledge: Habermas, Foucoult, and the Future of Legal Studies." *Law and Society Review* 28: 947–961.

Singer, Brent. 1988. "A Extension of Rawls's Theory of Justice to Environmental Ethics." *Environmental Ethics* 10: 217–231.

Smith, Graham. 2001."Taking Deliberation Seriously: Institutional Design and Green Politics." *Environmental Politics* 10: 72–93.

Smith, Graham. 2003. *Deliberative Democracy and the Environment.* New York: Routledge.

Smith, Graham. 2004. "Liberal Democracy and the 'Shaping' of Environmentally Enlightened Citizens." In *Liberal Democracy and Environmentalism: The End of Environmentalism,* ed. Marcel Wissenburg and Yoram Levy, 139–151. London: Routledge.

Snidal, Duncan, and Alexander Thompson. 2003. "International Commitments and Domestic Politics: Institutions and Actors at Two Levels." In *Locating the Proper Authorities: The Interaction of Domestic and International Institutions,* ed. Daniel Drezner, 197–230. Ann Arbor: University of Michigan Press.

Soroos, Marvin S. 1993. "From Stockholm to Rio: The Evolution of Global Environmental Governance." In *Environmental Policy in the 1900s: Toward a New Agenda*, second ed., ed. Norman J. Vig and Michael E. Kraft, 299–321. Washington, D.C.: CQ Press.

Spragens, Thomas A. Jr. 1990. *Reason and Democracy.* Durham, N.C.: Duke University Press.

Stavrianos, L. F. 1976. *The Promise of the Coming Dark Age.* San Francisco: W. H. Freeman.

Stone, Deborah. 2002. *Policy Paradox: The Art of Political Decision Making,* rev. ed. New York: W. W. Norton.

Sunstein, Cass. 1985. "Interest Groups in American Public Law." *Stanford Law Review* 38: 29–87.

Sunstein, Cass R. 1999. "Agreement without Theory." In *Deliberative Politics: Essays on Democracy and Disagreement,* ed. Stephen Macedo, 123–150. New York: Oxford University Press.

Sunstein, Cass. 2003. "The Law of Group Polarization." In *Debating Deliberative Democracy,* ed. James Fishkin and Peter Laslett, 80–101. Malden, Mass.: Blackwell.

Susskind, Lawrence E. 1994. *Environmental Diplomacy: Negotiating More Effective Global Agreements.* New York: Oxford University Press.

Switzer, Jacqueline, and Gary Bryner. 1998. *Environmental Politics: Domestic and Global Dimensions,* second ed. New York: St. Martin's Press.

Tam, Henry. 1998. *Communitarianism: A New Agenda for Politics and Citizenship.* New York: New York University Press.

Tatalovich, Raymond, and Mark Wattier. 1999. "Opinion Leadership: Elections, Campaigns, Agenda Setting, and Environmentalism." In *The Environmental Presidency,* ed. Dennis L. Soden, 147–187. Albany: State University of New York Press.

Taylor, Bob Pepperman. 1992. *Our Limits Transgressed: Environmental Political Thought in America.* Lawrence: University of Kansas Press.

Taylor, Roger. 1993. "The Environmental Implications of Liberalism." *Critical Review* 6: 265–283.

Taylor, Serge. 1984. *Making Bureaucracies Think.* Stanford: Stanford University Press.

Theunissen, Michael. 1999. "Society and History: A Critique of Critical Theory." In *Habermas: A Critical Reader,* ed. Peter Dews, 241–271. Malden, Mass.: Blackwell.

Thomas, Caroline. 1992. *The Environment in International Relations.* London: Royal Institute of International Affairs.

Thomas, Craig. 2003. "Habitat Conservation Planning." In *Deepening Democracy: Institutional Innovations in Empowered Participatory Governance,* ed. Archon Fung and Erik Olin Wright, 144–172. New York: Verso.

Tokar, Brian. 1999. "Creating a Green Future." In *Ecology*, ed. Carolyn Merchant, 112–118. Atlantic Highlands, N.J.: Humanities Press.

Torgerson, Douglas. 1999. *The Promise of Green Politics: Environmentalism and the Public Sphere*. Durham, N.C.: Duke University Press.

Turner, Dennis. 1983. "Judicial Notice and Federal Rule of Evidence 201—A Rule Ready for Change." *University of Pittsburgh Law Review* 45: 181–207.

Valadez, Jorge M. 2001. *Deliberative Democracy, Political Legitimacy, and Self-Determination in Multicultural Societies*. Boulder: Westview Press.

Vanderheiden, Steve. 2001. "Habitat Conservation Plans and the Promise of Deliberative Democracy." *Public Integrity* 3: 205–220.

Voegelin, Eric. 1969. *The New Science of Politics*. Chicago: University of Chicago Press.

Voegelin, Eric. 1975. *From Enlightenment to Revolution*, ed. John Hollowell. Durham, N.C.: Duke University Press.

Vogler, John. 2000. *The Global Commons: Environmental and Technological Governance*, second ed. New York: John Wiley.

Wainright, Hilary. 1994. *Arguments for a New Left: Answering the Free Market Right*. Oxford: Basil Blackwell.

Walker, Jack L. 1966. "A Critique of the Elitist Theory of Democracy." *American Political Science Review* 60: 285–296.

Walzer, Michael. 1991. "Constitutional Rights and the Shape of Civil Society." In *The Constitution of the People: Reflections on Citizens and Civil Society*, ed. Robert E. Calvert, 113–126. Lawrence: University Press of Kansas.

Walzer, Michael. 1994. "Multiculturalism and Individualism." *Dissent* 41: 185–191.

Walzer, Michael. 1999. "Deliberation, and What Else?" In *Deliberative Politics: Essays on Democracy and Disagreement*, ed. Stephen Macedo, 58–69. New York: Oxford University Press.

Wapner, Paul. 1996. *Environmental Activism and World Civic Politics*. Albany: State University of New York Press.

Warren, Karen, ed. 1994. *Ecological Feminism*. London: Routledge.

Weale, Albert. 1992. *The New Politics of Pollution*. Manchester: Manchester University Press.

Weber, Edward. 2003. *Bringing Society Back In: Grassroots Ecosystem Management, Accountability, and Sustainable Communities*. Cambridge, Mass.: The MIT Press.

Weber, Edward and Christina Herzog. 2003. "Connecting the Dots: United States Grassroots Ecosystem Management and Sustainable Communities." In *Two Paths toward Sustainable Forests: Public Values in Canada and the United States*, ed. Bruce A. Shindler, Thomas M. Beckley, and Mary Carmel Findley, 170–193. Corvallis: Oregon State University Press.

Weber, Max. 1978. *Economy and Society: An Outline of Interpretive Sociology.* Ed. G. Roth and C. Wittich. Berkeley: University of California Press.

Weidner, Helmut, and Martin Janicke. 2002. *Capacity Building in National Environmental Policy: A Comparative Study of 17 Countries.* New York: Springer-Verlag.

Weiss, Edith. 1999. "The Emerging Structure of International Environmental Law." In *The Global Environment,* ed. Norman J. Vig and Regina Axelrod, 98–115. Washington, D.C.: CQ Press.

Wellmer, Albrecht. 1985. "Reason, Utopia, and the Dialectic of Enlightenment." In *Habermas and Modernity,* ed. Richard J. Bernstein, 35–66. Cambridge, Mass.: The MIT Press.

Wenz, Peter. 1988. *Environmental Justice.* Albany: State University of New York Press.

White, Harvey. 1998. "Race, Class, and Environmental Hazards." In *Race, Class, and the Environment,* ed. David Camacho, 61–81. Durham, N.C.: Duke University Press.

White, Stephen. 1988. *The Recent Work of Jürgen Habermas: Reason, Justice, and Modernity.* Cambridge: Cambridge University Press.

Whitebook, Joel. 1985. "Reason and Happiness: Some Psychoanalytic Themes in Critical Theory." In *Habermas and Modernity,* ed. Richard J. Bernstein, 140–160. Cambridge, Mass.: The MIT Press.

Williams, David. 1999. "Dialogical Theories of Justice." *Telos* 114: 109–131.

Wilson, James Q. 1980. *The Politics of Regulation.* New York: Basic Books.

Wissenburg, Marcel L. J. 1998. *Green Liberalism: The Free and the Green Society.* London: UCL Press.

Wolin, Shedon S. 2004. *Politics and Vision.* Princeton: Princeton University Press.

Wolf, Hazel. 1994. "The Founding Mothers of Environmentalism." *Earth Island Journal* 9 (no. 1): 36–37.

Wood, Diane. 1997. "Generalist Judges in a Specialized World." *Southern Methodist University Law Review* 50: 1755–1768.

Wrong, Dennis H. 1994. *The Problem of Order: What Unites and Divides Society.* New York: Free Press.

Young, Iris. 1989. "Polity and Group Difference: A Critique of the Idea of Universal Citizenship." *Ethics* 99: 250–274.

Young, Iris. 1990a. *Justice and the Politics of Difference.* Princeton: Princeton University Press.

Young, Iris. 1990b. "The Idea of Community and the Politics of Difference." In *Feminism/Post-Modernism,* ed. L. J. Nicholson, 300–323. London: Routledge.

Young, Iris. 1996. "Communication and the Other: Beyond Deliberative Democracy." In *Democracy and Difference: Contesting the Boundaries of the Political,* ed. Seyla Benhabib, 120–135. Princeton: Princeton University Press.

Young, Iris. 1999. "Justice, Inclusion, and Deliberative Democracy." In *Deliberative Politics: Essays on Democracy and Disagreement,* ed. Stephen Macedo, 151–158. NewYork: Oxford University Press.

Young, Iris. 2000. *Inclusion and Democracy.* New York: Oxford University Press.

Zemans, Frances. 1983. "Legal Mobilization: The Neglected Role in the Political System." *American Political Science Review* 77: 690–703.

Zeitler, Amy A. 2000. "Environmental Democracy: An Analysis of Brownfields Policymaking." Ph.D. dissertation, Purdue University, West Lafayette, Ind.

Zoeteman, K. 1991. *Gaiasophy: The Wisdom of the Living Earth.* Hudson, N.Y.: Lindesfarne Press.

Zolo, Danilo. 1997. *Cosmopolis: Prospects for World Governance.* Cambridge: Polity Press.

Zwart, Ivan. 2003. "A Greener Alternative? Deliberative Democracy Meets Local Government." *Environmental Politics* 12: 23–48.

Index